Here in This Year

Here in This Year

Seventeenth-Century Nahuatl Annals of the Tlaxcala-Puebla Valley

Edited and translated

by

Camilla Townsend

with an essay by

James Lockhart

Stanford University Press
Stanford, California

Stanford University Press
Stanford, California

This book has been published with the assistance of the Rutgers University Department of History.

Maps of the Tlaxcala-Puebla Region and the City of Puebla de Los Angeles, 1691 were prepared by Jeffrey Ward.

Library of Congress Cataloging-in-Publication Data

Here in this year : seventeenth-century Nahuatl annals of the Tlaxcala-Puebla Valley / edited and translated by Camilla Townsend ; with an essay by James Lockhart.
    p.   cm.
  Includes bibliographical references and index.
  ISBN 978-0-8047-6379-0 (casebound : alk. paper)
  1. Manuscripts, Nahuatl—Mexico—Puebla de Zaragoza Region. 2. Manuscripts, Nahuatl—Mexico—Tlaxcala de Xicohténcatl Region. 3. Indians of Mexico—Mexico—Puebla de Zaragoza Region—History—17th century—Sources. 4. Indians of Mexico—Mexico—Tlaxcala de Xicohténcatl Region—History—17th century—Sources. 5. Puebla de Zaragoza Region (Mexico)—History—17th century—Sources. 6. Tlaxcala de Xicohténcatl Region (Mexico)—History—17th century—Sources. I. Townsend, Camilla, 1965–
  F1219.54.A98H47 2010
  972'.47—dc22

2009034487

Contents

Maps, Tables, and Figures

Preface

I HAD BEEN HARD AT WORK for some time on a study of the seventeenth-century Tlaxcalan annalist don Juan Buenaventura Zapata y Mendoza when Jim Lockhart handed
on to me a file of papers which he said would provide valuable context. In it I found
photocopies of the documents presented in this volume—two sets of annals from the
Tlaxcala-Puebla valley which were roughly contemporary to Zapata's. Jim had made the
copies in the 1970s in the Biblioteca Nacional de Antropología e Historia in Mexico City
while on a research trip. Since then, he had studied them in relation to his own work and
had also shared them at one point with one of his graduate students, Frances Krug, and
also with Arthur Anderson, thinking that perhaps one or all of them would one day
publish an edition. All three of their lives in fact took different directions, but in the file I
found their transcriptions, notes, and partial translations, silent testimony to the work that
they had once poured into the project. That was in 2003. Several more years would go by
before I felt myself deeply enough immersed in the annalistic genre to be able to do
effectively what had not yet been done—that is, bring the project to completion. Our
field's knowledge of Nahuatl had deepened considerably in the more than twenty years
since the project was last officially on the table, especially as concerns the relationships
between clauses and certain vocabulary of the everyday language of postcontact times;
thus I found I needed to begin the translation all over, as it were, even as I listened
attentively to what the three of them were in a sense whispering over my shoulder.

My own study of Nahuatl had begun in 1998, in a Yale Summer Language School
course taught by Jonathan Amith. After that I had plugged away on my own, thanking the
fates for a talent with languages I certainly had done nothing to deserve. Then in early
2002 I learned to my joy that Michel Launey and James Lockhart would be teaching a
follow-up seminar for those of Amith's former students who were interested. Both men
gave generously of their time and energy that summer, making it possible for me to
move forward by leaps and bounds in a way otherwise impossible. Jim went further to
answer a continuous stream of questions from me in the months and years that followed.

I was already interested in the Nahuas' cultural productions, doing some work with
cantares (songs) but more with annals, especially don Juan Zapata. I was fortunate
enough to receive grants from the National Endowment for the Humanities and the
American Philosophical Society which enabled me to devote significant time to my new
interest. As I proceeded I accrued many intellectual debts beyond those to my Nahuatl
teachers, but three people in particular emerged as central—Frances Krug, Susan
Schroeder, and Luis Reyes. Frances had worked with Jim on a doctoral dissertation
which reached an advanced stage but for health reasons unfortunately never was completed. She gathered an almost exhaustive compendium of the entries in nearly all the
extant annals from the region of Puebla and Tlaxcala; her work has been a central
reference for me for years now. If in one set of annals the entry for the year 1576 does not
make sense, one will often on consulting Krug's work find five or six other entries for
that year laid out side by side, with their commonalities and subtle differences pointed
out. (Some of the important conclusions she was able to draw from this extraordinarily

painstaking work will be discussed in the introduction that follows.) Sue Schroeder sent me the copy of Zapata's work that inspired me in my study of annals in the first place, but she did much more than that. She has been a beacon of a kind, for she alone in our field as it exists in this country has worked actively and constantly to keep the Nahuatl annals in full view; her untiring efforts have helped to bring the works of Chimalpahin, the premier annalist, within reach of the English-speaking world. Finally, it was the late Luis Reyes García, an extremely talented translator and historian/anthropologist and a speaker of Nahuatl from childhood, who brought the annals of the Tlaxcala-Puebla valley into the arena of modern scholarship. In 2003, when I was in Tlaxcala to do archival research on don Juan Zapata, he spoke to me on the phone and was kindness itself. He was already very sick with the illness that would later prove mortal, and could not see me in person, but he nevertheless opened doors for me while I was there. He himself, along with Andrea Martínez Baracs, published a transcription and translation of Zapata's lengthy work. (Indeed, Andrea Martínez recently published *Un gobierno de indios: Tlaxcala, 1519–1750*, an excellent work partially based on Zapata which I was unable to obtain until preparation of this book was in its final stages, and thus unfortunately could not incorporate into my commentary.) Many of Reyes' students worked on other annals from the area, always producing quality editions. Not least in importance (from my point of view) is the *Anales del Barrio de San Juan del Río*, edited by Lidia Gómez García, Celia Salazar Exaire, and María Elena Stefanón López, a set of annals closely related to the Annals of Puebla in this volume.

As I continued to work with the sets presented here, I came to the conclusion that some elements were so mysterious as to require further primary research. I sought background in published Spanish chronicles and cabildo records found in the collections of the New York Public Library, and I consulted the manuscript holdings of the John Carter Brown Library as they pertained to don Manuel de los Santos Salazar, a vital force behind the surviving annals of the Tlaxcalan region, as the introduction will demonstrate. When I was at the Bibliothèque Nationale in Paris to look at Zapata's original manuscript, I surveyed other related materials from the Tlaxcala-Puebla valley.[1] I ended by traveling to Mexico to consult the original manuscripts, as the photocopies I had were not always adequate. The Annals of Tlaxcala are indeed still there; I found that only the first page as it existed in the 1970s was missing, and so I left a photocopy of that page with the original. The Annals of Puebla have been declared a national treasure, as they mention Juan Diego's purported sighting of the Virgin of Guadalupe, and thus are in a vault away from public view. Fortunately, digital images are available in the library.

In the latter stages, as I was working on the introduction, it occurred to me that the person who should really write an analysis of the texts in relation to postconquest language evolution was not I, but Jim. I could do it in some fashion, but the texts deserved

---

[1]In this book, rather than referring to Zapata's original folios, I consistently cite the excellent edition by Reyes and Martínez so that readers can easily consult the passages and see the larger context for themselves. However, when quoting Zapata directly, I use my own transcriptions, which vary somewhat from the published version, in that I do not resolve overbars, standardize spellings, alter punctuation, etc., as the edition does.

more than the segment I would produce. I could look at the Annals of Puebla and recognize certain Stage 3 phenomena, but Jim with his decades of experience could review the same material and see its place in the overall Nahuatl corpus and the general evolution of the language. I asked him if he would write a separate chapter to be included within the covers of the book itself, and he kindly agreed. Though a bit unorthodox, the arrangement is, I believe, highly suitable.

My debts to individuals and in many cases their associated institutions are perhaps too numerous to name, but I will do my best. At Rutgers, my chairman, Paul Clemens, helped me to obtain much-needed funding from the Department of History. My inspiring colleagues, Indrani Chatterjee and Julie Livingston, brought me into the fold of their seminar on Vernacular Epistemologies, where the participants gave me invaluable advice. My fellow board members of the *Colonial Latin American Review* have always been for me a model of scholarship; on this occasion I particularly wish to thank Raquel Chang-Rodríguez for inviting me to present on the annals at CUNY's graduate center, where I also received helpful comments. Richard Green, director of Medieval and Renaissance Studies at Ohio State University, invited me to present the annals to a wide array of responsive scholars. Certain archivists and librarians went beyond any notion of duty: Sandra Francis and Beatrice Dey at the New York Public Library, Ken Ward at the John Carter Brown, and Genaro Díaz, José Francisco Tovar Ruiz, and el ingeniero Miguel Angel Gasca at the BNAH. At Stanford University Press, Norris Pope and his entire staff have been unfailingly helpful. Mapmaker Jeffrey Ward did marvelously painstaking work.[2]

Noble David Cook kindly helped me untangle my confusion regarding some of the epidemics in the texts. Bradley Scopyk, who came to stay for a few days in the summer of 2007 in order that I might help him with Nahuatl, actually ended up being the one to help me in several regards, forcing me to rethink certain elements of grammar that I had taken for granted, and pointing out several works on Tlaxcala previously unknown to me. Within the community of students of Nahuatl, many have offered the warmth of their regard and much scholarly help. Stafford Poole patiently read both the Nahuatl and my translations for certain church-related segments I found confusing and offered me his perspectives. Doris Namala and Stephanie Wood have both generously shared with me their own ongoing work in relevant areas. Matthew Restall has offered trenchant insight and practical help on numerous occasions. And Caterina Pizzigoni has caused me to

---

[2]Reconfiguring a city's streets and landmarks as they were more than three hundred years ago is no mean feat. To create the map of Puebla, we had at our disposal a 1698 "Plano de la Ciudad de los Angeles," signed by Cristóbal de Guadalajara and housed at the Archivo General de Indias (Seville), which was published in the 1961 edition of López de Villaseñor. This, in combination with the careful scholarship of Manuel Toussaint on the history of Puebla's churches and the extraordinary study by Hugo Leicht of Puebla's colonial streets, allowed us to envision the city as it then was, as well as locate all the features which played a significant role in the life of the writer of this volume's annals. Of course, not all elements were included. Had the writer of the annals been a Cholulan living in the barrio of Santiago, for example, his references and thus the choices we made would have been somewhat different. Finally, even the general map of the geographic area required some research, as some small settlements now have different names or have shifted in other ways. A 1681 parish census published by Peter Gerhard was immensely helpful.

rethink several issues with her innate good sense and wisdom. In a different arena, my husband, John Nolan, has been a true partner in parenting, a point that is not at all irrelevant, for it is that which has made it possible for me to find the time to do the work that appears in this book.

But there is one person more than any other whom I particularly wish to thank in these pages, and that is, of course, Jim. Not only did he inspire the project in the first place, but he also literally read every word more than once, finding many mistakes and making crucial suggestions. I cannot convey my gratitude for all that I have learned from him since that summer of 2002. Teachers have been important to me since I was quite small, and there are many to whom I owe a great deal. But none has ever taught me as much as he. Sometimes as I work with the annals of the Tlaxcala-Puebla valley, seeing how the authors borrowed from each other, taught each other, worked to pass on what had come down to them from the ancients, hoped that young people would pick up their work and carry it on, I also think of the community of scholars who have studied the Nahuas over the intervening centuries. I am profoundly grateful to be a part of that chain, grateful that Jim reached out his hand to me.

C. T.
Highland Park, New Jersey
June, 2009

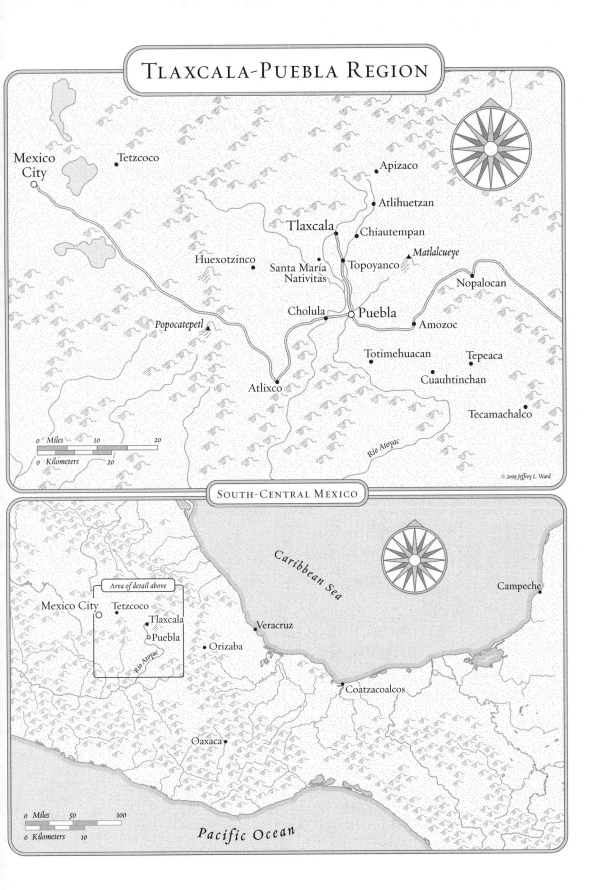

TLAXCALA-PUEBLA REGION

Mexico City

Tetzcoco

Apizaco

Atlihuetzan

Tlaxcala

Chiautempan

Huexotzinco

Santa María Nativitas

Topoyanco

Matlalcueye

Nopalocan

Cholula

Puebla

Amozoc

Popocatepetl

Totimehuacan

Tepeaca

Cuauhtinchan

Tecamachalco

Atlixco

Río Atoyac

0 Miles 10 20

0 Kilometers 20

© 2009 Jeffrey L. Ward

SOUTH-CENTRAL MEXICO

Caribbean Sea

Campeche

Area of detail above

Mexico City

Tetzcoco

Tlaxcala

Puebla

Veracruz

Orizaba

Río Atoyac

Coatzacoalcos

Oaxaca

0 Miles 50 100

0 Kilometers 10

Pacific Ocean

THE CITY OF PUEBLA DE LOS ANGELES, 1691

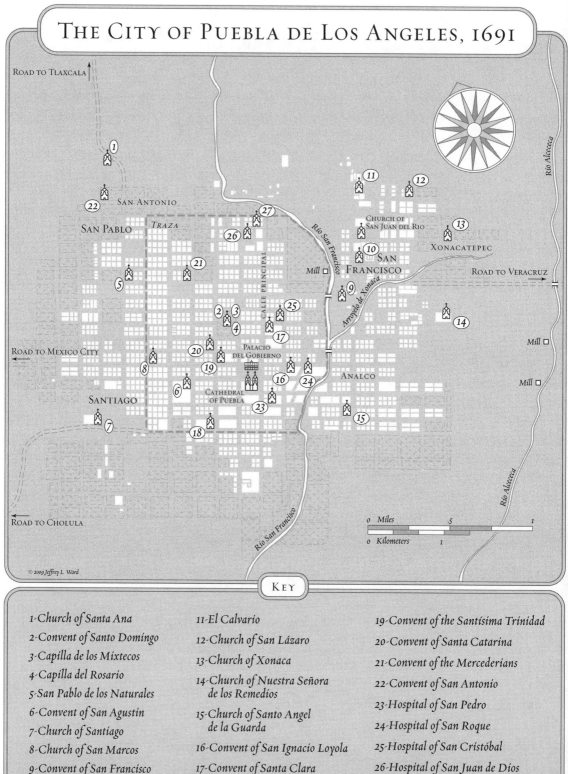

ROAD TO TLAXCALA

SAN ANTONIO

SAN PABLO

SAN PABLO · TRAZA

Río San Francisco

CHURCH OF
SAN JUAN DEL RIO

XONACATEPEC

CALLE PRINCIPAL

Mill

SAN
FRANCISCO

ROAD TO VERACRUZ

Arroyo de Xonaca

ROAD TO MEXICO CITY

PALACIO
DEL GOBIERNO

Mill

ANALCO

Mill

SANTIAGO

CATHEDRAL
OF PUEBLA

ROAD TO CHOLULA

Río San Francisco

Río Alceca

Río Alceca

Miles   0   .5   1
Kilometers   0   1

© 2009 Jeffrey L. Ward

KEY

1-Church of Santa Ana

2-Convent of Santo Domingo

3-Capilla de los Mixtecos

4-Capilla del Rosario

5-San Pablo de los Naturales

6-Convent of San Agustín

7-Church of Santiago

8-Church of San Marcos

9-Convent of San Francisco

10-Church of Santa Cruz

11-El Calvario

12-Church of San Lázaro

13-Church of Xonaca

14-Church of Nuestra Señora
de los Remedios

15-Church of Santo Angel
de la Guarda

16-Convent of San Ignacio Loyola

17-Convent of Santa Clara

18-Convent of Santa Inés

19-Convent of the Santísima Trinidad

20-Convent of Santa Catarina

21-Convent of the Mercederians

22-Convent of San Antonio

23-Hospital of San Pedro

24-Hospital of San Roque

25-Hospital of San Cristóbal

26-Hospital of San Juan de Dios

27-Church of San José

Introduction

The Spanish law officials summoned the indigenous people and told them that they were going to take bread-making from them. They set a penalty on them, giving them a deadline of a day not to make bread. . . . On Monday, the 21st day of the month of September, right on the feast day of San Mateo, on Monday and Tuesday, there was already hunger. No more did either wheat bread or tortillas appear in either marketplace or shop. When anyone secretly made half a carrying frame full and took it to the marketplace, even if it was tortillas, the Spaniards just fought over it. . . . Only weeping prevailed. And then everyone got worked up, priests, Spaniards and indigenous alike, so that everyone took the side of the indigenous people.

Annals of Puebla for 1682

ON THE MORNING of September 23, 1682, the brightly colored tiles of the buildings on Puebla's town square must have been glinting in the sun, but nothing else was as usual. The previous week, a group of Spaniards had secured from the alcalde mayor (the highest local magistrate) monopoly rights over all bread-making in the city: they were to control not only the making of wheat bread, but even of tortillas. It had seemed to these men a lucrative scheme indeed, but within two days they had proven themselves unequal to the task. Apparently it had not been evident to them just how many mouths the city's indigenous people customarily fed. Now the town's indigenous community, normally peaceful, poured into the streets in protest. They shouted, "Bread, bread, bread, lord captain! We will starve! We will starve!"[1] Their leader presented a letter to the alcalde mayor. It said that if the Spaniards wanted to usurp indigenous roles, then so be it, but in that case, they could also perform labor service and meet the tribute requirements. "Let the Spaniards do whatever service there is and pay the tribute," they wrote bluntly. It seemed to the indigenous that their argument was effective. The native reporter on these events commented: "When he heard that, the alcalde mayor quickly ordered that a decree be issued, so that a proclamation was hastily made that the indigenous people would make bread." Then he added somewhat smugly, "And he ordered that the Spaniards be imprisoned."

Historians interested in indigenous experiences are accustomed either to reading be-tween the lines in European narratives or to collecting native sources in dozens of bits and pieces until together, they take on meaning. It is rare indeed that a historian of early Latin America can read a first-person account of public events and find that it unmis-takably offers a perspective that only a native person would have had. The historical annals of colonial Mexico, written in Nahuatl, are immensely valuable in that they do just that; they deserve far more attention than they have so far received.

The indigenous narrator who tells us of Puebla's 1682 bread riot has the power to open a door for us leading rather directly into the world he once inhabited. His was a

---

[1]Entry for 1682, Annals of Puebla (this volume). For more on the previous regulation of wheat bread making and selling, see Loyde Cruz 1999 and López Gonzaga 1999.

complex universe, and although in September of that year he felt very angry with the Spaniards, there were of course many days when he felt that he held far more in common with them than not. Eight months later, when English and Dutch pirates attacked the relatively nearby city of Veracruz, his heart bled for his Spanish and black neighbors who had to go and fight the marauding savages. He even spared some sympathy for their tearful women and the many well-to-do families whose horses were commandeered. "They even took the poor little donkeys," he sighed.[1] Yet two years later, his disgust with interfering legislative authorities surfaced again with a vengeance. Indigenous residents of Puebla, who were legally constrained to live in certain barrios in order to ease the collection of tribute, had for generations flouted such restrictions; now the alcalde mayor took it upon himself to order them to collect in their own barrios, under pain of public whipping. He promised he would distribute lands where the refugees would be allowed to reside, but he did nothing about it; chaos reigned in the beleaguered barrios. Finally the city's indigenous governor was able to convince him to desist, ironically on grounds that it would be impossible under the circumstances to orchestrate the usual tribute collection. The governor had reason to be pleased with the end of the story: once again, indigenous people had come out on top, and plotters and planners had come to grief. He himself oversaw the writing of the set of historical annals which recorded the events in such detail.[2] We know of his experience and his thinking today only because of the document he produced. The Spaniards in such situations would report only that there had been a change of policy, but not allude to all the causes, some of which did not reflect well on either their own judgment or their degree of control over the populace. And this is only one of the myriad insights which such a set of indigenous annals may provide.

In recent years, scholars have made excellent use of the abundant Nahuatl sources preserved in Mexico and elsewhere. The nearly exclusive attention traditionally paid to formal texts prepared in cooperation with Franciscans and other religious has been complemented by work with more unself-consciously produced mundane documents — wills, land transfers, petitions, etc.[3] Relatively little studied have been the historical annals.[4] These were produced by Nahuas for Nahuas, without any regard for the Spanish world as an audience or any supervision by Spaniards in either the clerical or legal branches. Yet we have not turned to them with any frequency, partly because they are few and far between compared to the rich lodes of mundane sources, but also because the genre is not well understood. A reader who turns to a set of annals without any preparation is likely to find them dry, terse, even confusing. It has for some time been understood that the sixteenth- and early seventeenth-century annals which treat pre-conquest subjects should not be tossed aside as inscrutable or be taken literally as

---

[1] Entry for 1683, Annals of Puebla (this volume).

[2] For a study of the authorship of the annals, see the fifth section of this introduction, "Tlaxcaltecapan in Cuitlaxcohuapan: the world of don Miguel" (pp. 29–40).

[3] For an introduction to the work that has been done, students are advised to consult "A Historian and the Disciplines" in Lockhart 1999, especially pp. 350–67. For a current overview of the nature of the varying projects that have been undertaken, see the introduction to Lockhart, Sousa and Wood 2007.

[4] For an early analytical synthesis of the genre see Lockhart 1992, pp. 376–92.

transparent presentations of fact, but rather analyzed as to what they reveal regarding patterns of religious or political belief, the perspectives of individual communities, negotiations for power, etc.[5] Now it is time that we recognize as well all that the colonial annals which treat their own times may offer us, not only in terms of indigenous *mentalité* but also in terms of "hard" information on indigenous lives, the very element which seems more doubtful in the material treating bygone centuries. The annals are perhaps as close as we are ever going to come to an indigenous diary or set of letters. If we become more familiar with the ways in which the genre channels the expression of the writer, we will be able to decode much more of what such a writer has to tell us.

Furthermore, studying the indigenous annals, beyond enhancing our understanding of indigenous experience, may help us as scholars at some point to shed our own parochialism, to understand the ways in which the figures we study are both the same as and different from other peoples in somewhat comparable situations—where agriculture has fully taken hold but well defined nation-states have not yet emerged. The annals genre as it existed in early medieval Europe, for example, and the pre-colonial Marathi texts of India, are in some ways breathtakingly similar to the tradition that seems to have existed in Mexico. In the east Frankish kingdom, for the year 838, an anonymous writer of annals recorded an earthquake, the building of some ships, the passing of the kingship, the celebration of a great religious festival, disputes between two royal brothers, and the appearance of a comet; he could almost have traded places with one of his Nahuatl-speaking peers of later centuries.[6] The Nahuas become more interesting, not less so, when they take their place on the stage of the world's peoples.

But they themselves and their own version of an annals genre must be more fully understood before any such forays into comparative history or literature can be effectively undertaken. There is a solid basis for doing this in work that has already been undertaken on the annals produced in the vicinity of Mexico City in the sixteenth century. We have usable editions available to us of the Annals of Tlatelolco, the "Annals of Juan Bautista," the Codex Aubin, and many other more truncated sets, culminating in the seventeenth century in the extensive works of don Domingo de San Antón Muñón Chimalpahin Quauhtlehuanitzin, now called just Chimalpahin, the premier Nahuatl annalist who produced a large annalistic corpus.[7] In his generation, the historical works of don Fernando Alvarado Tezozomoc, don Fernando de Alva Ixtlilxochitl, and Cristóbal del Castillo are also of interest, though they directed themselves mainly to a Spanish audience. To the east, a few important sets of Nahuatl annals came into being in the

---

[5]Examples of studies which take this approach are Gillespie 1989 and Schroeder 1991.

[6]Annals of Fulda, in Reuter 1992. Reuter comments, "The seemingly disinterested objectivity of the genre, found over long stretches even of the Annals of Fulda, whose authors were by no means dispassionate observers of events, can be very deceptive" (p.2). Hayden White (1987) wrote revealingly about medieval annals in his now classic work. A number of illustrative sets are available in print and even in translation. On the Marathi *bakhar* and its relationship to other kinds of literature see Guha 2004.

[7]Chimalpahin is the obvious exception to the general truth that the annals have been relatively little studied. See especially Schroeder 1991, Chimalpahin 1997 (Anderson and Schroeder), 2001 (Tena), and 2006 (Lockhart, Schroeder, and Namala).

sixteenth century, among them the works now known as the Historia Tolteca-Chichimeca (part of which could be called the Annals of Cuauhtinchan), the various pictorial annals covered with alphabetic writing which are also from Cuauhtinchan, and the Annals of Tecamachalco. Generally, however, the central valley dominated in the early production of Nahuatl alphabetic annals, and in that area, the tradition reached its apogee with the work of Chimalpahin. After him, future generations became more removed from the styles and forms their forebears had once used to keep track of history; eventually their earnest efforts to recount their history came to be marked more by ignorance of the past than by any deep familiarity with it.

The annals genre, however, did not decline as precipitously in the Tlaxcala-Puebla valley to the east, where the second half of the seventeenth century saw a remarkable florescence of the annals-keeping tradition. The Tlaxcalans' role in the conquest as an ally of the Spaniards guaranteed them certain privileges afterward, privileges which, as we will see, helped them to isolate themselves somewhat from Spanish culture. Then, too, in the course of the seventeenth century, Puebla, Mexico's second city, attained a sort of golden age, becoming known for its churches, craftsmanship, music, and wealth; the indigenous community would undoubtedly have been affected by the pride and energy that were part and parcel of the era. Thus in this region, on the one hand the retention of some knowledge of the old forms, and on the other the deep acculturation born of generations of contact leading to relatively widespread literacy and cultural enthusiasm, apparently led to the production and preservation of a remarkable number of interesting annalistic documents. Twenty-four survive, eight as original documents and the remainder as copied-out fragments. And in-text references indicate that these twenty-four were merely points of production in a wider network.[1]

This book brings two of these sets of annals into print for the first time, one from Puebla and one from Tlaxcala, both manuscripts in the keeping of the Biblioteca Nacional de Antropología e Historia in Mexico City.[2] To render them as intelligible as possible, I offer an introduction in five parts: 1) a political history of the Tlaxcala-Puebla valley from the indigenous perspective; 2) background on the Mexican annals genre in general; 3) background on the Tlaxcala-Puebla family of annals; and 4) and 5) studies of the probable authors of these two particular texts and the worlds in which they lived. Armed with this information, readers should be able to make direct use of the documents for a multiplicity of purposes.

The political history of the Tlaxcala-Puebla Valley

THE NAHUAS, like most people around the world before the formation of nation-states, spent a good deal of their time forging alliances and deciding when to break them. When a group of people had been together long enough, they constituted in their own minds

---

[1] For a nearly complete list, see Gibson and Glass 1975. Only one is thus far known to have escaped their attention, in the Archive of the Cathedral of Puebla, Volume 6 of the Colección de Papeles Varios. A facsimile has been published: see Gómez García et al. 2000.

[2] BNAH, Archivo Histórico, Gómez Orozco 184 (Annals of Puebla) and Colección Antigua 872 (Annals of Tlaxcala). The former has recently been removed from the accessible collection and placed in a vault, but digital images are available on site.

what we might call an "ethnic group." The predominant organizational form, the *altepetl* or small state, consisted of subgroups, but its people saw themselves as having more in common with each other than with anyone else in the world and generally (though not always) remained unified. For at least two centuries before the arrival of the Europeans, the complex altepetl of Tlaxcala constituted a variation on this theme: the four sub-altepetl of Ocotelolco, Tizatla,[3] Quiyahuiztlan and Tepeticpac governed themselves independently, each having a separate *tlatoani* (king, literally "speaker"), but they nevertheless remained invested in an overarching identity as people of Tlaxcala and faithfully rotated duties among themselves in a fixed order. At any one time the ruler of one of the four subaltepetl presided over the whole. They shared a meaningful history, having migrated together from the north in relatively recent times, vanquishing various foes along the way, most notably the Otomi, whose lands they now held, and many of whom remained in the area as a tribute-paying population. Still, they had already experienced significant internal splintering, and their shared history and common in-terests might not have been enough to ensure that the complex altepetl held together. The concomitant rise to power of the Mexica in nearby Tenochtitlan probably helped them to continue to conceive of themselves as one. In their numbers lay some strength. Unlike most of the altepetl that surrounded them, they were never conquered by the Mexica.[4]

When the Spaniards arrived in 1519, the Tlaxcalans, having protected their inde-pendence for many years, were at first determined not to let these well armed strangers dictate to them. After sending the Otomi in first, they themselves attacked, still hoping to repel the invaders. The battle was a draw; both sides withdrew to nurse their wounded—and the Tlaxcalans to bury their dead. A few days later, just before dawn, the people of a number of villages near the Spanish camp woke to unexpected violence: mounted and armored lancers had approached stealthily, and now galloped through town, skewering people and setting homes ablaze with impunity. Day after day, the newcomers did this in different places. Mounted behind one of them rode a young woman, "one of us people here," as the Tlaxcalans described her, meaning that she was not one of the foreigners from across the sea. She spoke Nahuatl, and shouted repeatedly that the strangers wanted to make peace, that they would willingly ally with them in their ongoing struggles against the Mexica.[5]

Thus it was that the Tlaxcalans made their famous bargain with the Spaniards.[6] They held to it in the succeeding years—though not without some inner turmoil the next year, in 1520, when the deadly pox broke out, and the supposedly invulnerable strangers were driven ignominiously from Tenochtitlan. Their eventual decision not to waver brought its rewards. With their help, the Spaniards defeated the Mexica in 1521, and then the

---

[3]Many scholars represent the word as "Tizatlan." In the sources, it appears with and without the *n*. The expectable construction would be *tiça(tl)* + *tlah*, "place of abundance of chalk." Thus I have used "Tizatla" (with *z* instead of the *ç* of early texts because the word is well known).

[4]For more on what can be deduced about the preconquest history of Tlaxcala, see Gibson 1967, pp. 1–15, and Lockhart 1992, pp. 20–23.

[5]See Townsend 2006.

[6]For a study of the motivations of indigenous allies of the Spaniards in this period, including the Tlaxcalans, see Oudijk and Restall 2007.

Tlaxcalans accompanied the conquerors to surrounding territories, convincing them all to put up their arms and join the new polity. Hernando Cortés has not become known to posterity as a man who paid all his debts, but he and his successors paid this one, at least to some extent. Tlaxcala was not given out in encomienda to pay tribute and perform labor for a particular conqueror, or worse yet, divided up by subaltepetl to be given to several different conquerors; rather they paid their taxes directly to the king. A Spanish magistrate/administrator and his staff came to live in their midst, but few others did; no Spanish city was established in their territory. (Instead, as we will see, the important city of Puebla, which normally would have been in the center of the Tlaxcalan territory, was established on their southern border, leaving the Tlaxcalans far less inundated than they would have been.)

The people continued to govern their internal affairs much as they always had in the decade after the Spanish victory, but they found that one important change had occurred. The tlatoani of Ocotelolco, the most powerful of the four subaltepetl at that time, was treated by the foreigners as though he had sole control over all the people of Tlaxcala, which bred significant resentment, as all tasks, including the paramount rulership, had always rotated in a fixed order. In the 1530s, when the Spaniards introduced a form of the cabildo (municipal council) through which they wished the indigenous sector to be governed, they ignored the traditional rotation, regularly giving Ocotelolco the governorship and other key positions. The dissatisfaction of the other three subaltepetl gradually grew to a crisis point, and by the mid-1540s a Spanish review committee had to be brought in to resolve the problem. In the new model, a rotating governor (himself Tlaxcalan) would serve with regidores (councilmen) and alcaldes (judges) from all the constituent altepetl.[1] It was agreed that the indigenous noblemen would elect a governor from among themselves for a period of two years. Ocotelolco, having had too much power of late, would pass to the rear of the line, and then the usual order of rotation would pick up where it had left off. The first governor would thus be from Tizatla, the next from Quiyahuiztlan, the next from Tepeticpac, the next from Ocotelolco again. Each subaltepetl would elect three regidores and one alcalde annually. The four tlatoque (plural of tlatoani) would sit on the council as regidores for life; thus although they would not actually govern the cabildo, they would remain highly influential. In keeping with Tlaxcalan traditions, the governing council would thus be a relatively large group; twenty-one men (governor, four alcaldes, twelve regular regidores, four tlatoque) would serve at any one time, out of a population of about 220 electors, noblemen who were particularly prominent in their communities, probably mostly the heads of lordly houses (teccalli).[2] Because the positions were rotating and elected, virtually all prominent men could thus assume that they would take part in governing their people during the course of their lifetimes—if not actually on the cabildo then by filling a host of lesser offices—and all noblemen of any stripe understood that they would be closely related to someone who

[1]In a Spanish cabildo, the regidores were generally of higher social rank and served longer terms than the alcaldes. The indigenous, however, interpreted the alcaldes as being of greater importance because there were fewer of them in any given roster.

[2]See TA, pp. 5–6.

was thus participating. When those who usually held office were not serving, they used a word to describe themselves which comes close to meaning "resting."[3]

The indigenous nobility had a long history of intertwined power and responsibility. Each tlatoani (king) was in reality a particularly powerful *teuctli*, or dynastic lord of a particular lineage; the remaining *teteuctin* (plural of teuctli) in the conglomeration were still powerful as well, with independent bases; they were the tlatoani's advisers and supporters—and in times of strife, his greatest threats. In Tlaxcala all the *pipiltin* (the nobility, plural of *pilli*) were relatives of a teuctli and were members of a teccalli or lordly house headed by him. Their vassals, the commoners, were called *macehualtin* (plural of *macehualli*). A teuctli held land on behalf of his people, distributing it to all those in the teccalli who used it, macehualtin and pipiltin, and in some cases to *te-ixhuihuan*, or higher-level dependents. Often people passed those plots on to their children, but sometimes the teuctli had to intervene to reassign land. In the colonial period, it was debatable how much power the teteuctin and their family members had or should have. In the whole eastern region they often traditionally wielded more power than in the central valley, where they were more fully understood to be integrated into the altepetl. Still, their greater power was far from universally acknowledged. There was ongoing controversy in the courts, the macehualtin often arguing that their teuctli was essentially just an officer of their subunit, who should have little power over them, as they all belonged to a constituent unit of the altepetl, and the teuctli trying to obscure the difference between the teccalli and the larger unit. Yet even though the people may have resented the ability of the teteuctin to grow rich by collecting tribute from them, the lords did in fact often employ their growing knowledge of the Spanish language and customs to defend them.[4]

Indeed, the Tlaxcalan nobility's volubility probably saved the people from having Mexico's second largest Spanish city founded in their midst. The Spaniards needed a major population center between Mexico City and the port of Veracruz, for this pathway (the trunk line) was to be at the heart of the country for some time to come. Tlaxcala was the obvious choice, but the administration wanted it to be a place where Spaniards would not be as dependent on indigenous labor as they generally seemed to be, and where wheat (rather than maize) would be grown in abundance. They selected a former no-man's land called Cuitlaxcohuapan (originally Cuetlaxcohuapan, a word of disputed and unclear etymology) between Tlaxcala, Tepeaca, and Cholula, directly south of Tlaxcala along the Atoyac River. Though the people of Totimehuacan had once laid claim to the area, since their military devastation in the preceding century, no one actually lived there; the people of nearby Cholula now held a theoretical claim to the territory. It was to be a Spanish-only settlement, and the citizens could not expect to receive encomiendas, only extensive lands. But this did not mean that they actually envisioned starting up a new city without any aid at all from indigenous people. The crown informed Tlaxcala that rather than paying their annual tribute in goods, they would have to send a certain number of able-

---

[3]We learn this from the most prolific of the Tlaxcalan annalists, Zapata (passim, p. 334 et alia).

[4]On the role of the teuctli among the eastern Nahuas and its evolution in the colonial era, see Lockhart 1992, pp. 102–113, and Reyes García 1977.

bodied men to the new settlement every week for a few years. In the spring and summer
of 1531, at least seven thousand men came.

They began to build the city of "Puebla de los Angeles," serving as carpenters, ma-
sons, woodchoppers, water carriers, domestic servants, fine artisans, musicians, scribes,
and translators. For the next two hundred years the indigenous persisted in calling the
place Cuitlaxcohuapan, though the Franciscan friars who accompanied them (and then
the other Spanish settlers) spoke only of Puebla or the Ciudad de los Angeles. In the fall
of 1532, torrential rains caused flooding which destroyed the initial clay buildings. Major
labor drafts were needed once again, of course. In the hour of Spanish need, the Tlaxcalans actually petitioned to raise their quota in exchange for being allowed permanent
exemption from certain other burdens—such as the crown's request that they create and
staff food-selling businesses along the road from Veracruz to the capital. By participating
so eagerly, the Tlaxcalans succeeded in gaining another end as well: they kept the Spanish population within their own altepetl to a minimum. The bishopric had originally been
set up in their city, as was to be expected, but the bishop of Tlaxcala soon complained
that Tlaxcala was a poor place from which to head an archdiocese, and before long the
episcopal seat was also moved to Puebla.[1]

Perhaps in the rebuilding the Spaniards consulted indigenous craftsmen who were
experienced in the region. In any case, they selected a better spot, along the banks of a
rivulet called the San Francisco which drained into the Atoyac a few miles to the west.
The place was further removed from the most fertile farmlands, but higher and drier. This
time, the site took. For many years, there were more indigenous people than Spaniards in
the town, though they were not at first permanent residents. They came from Tlaxcala,
Cholula, Tepeaca, and elsewhere in the region. For over a decade the crown continued to
renew the demand that the indigenous provide what they called temporary *ayuda* (aid,
succor, support). But then, in the early 1540s, at the time of the passage of the reforming
New Laws, the royal government at last ended the arrangement, much to the Spanish
Pueblans' chagrin. Indigenous people were now to be allowed to settle in the city; they
would be free of tribute demands, except that they would be responsible for certain public
works (drainage systems, public festivals, etc.) and would have to be willing to hire their
labor out to Spaniards. The city was already becoming known for its obrajes (shops,
works, proto-factories), where textiles and ceramics were produced. Over the remaining
years of the sixteenth century, numerous extended families responded to this offer, pulled
up stakes in their homelands and moved to the city of Puebla de los Angeles.[2]

The new city was truly a collective effort, dependent on the contributions of a variety
of corporate entities. The *traza*, or planned central section of the city, was just to the west
of the rivulet that cut through town. The Franciscans' convent looked down on it from
a hill on the east bank. Almost all of the Tlaxcalans lived in the area immediately

---

[1]See Hirschberg 1979. The bishop claimed that he wished to protect Tlaxcala as a purely indigenous community from the influence of the Spaniards, but that explanation would seem to be an
example of giving the king the reasons he wished to hear.

[2]Some of their motives may be deduced by studying the problems they faced in the surrounding
countryside. See Prem 1988.

surrounding the fathers, known as the barrio of San Francisco. Not long after, a second indigenous barrio of Santiago Apóstol was constructed on the far west side of the city, and there settled most of the Cholulteca and their cousins the people of Tepeaca and Huexotzinco. They came in large numbers, due to the proximity of their home cities. The Augustinians were their spiritual shepherds. A third, much smaller indigenous barrio, San Pablo de los Naturales, was founded just to the north, somewhat nearer to the central Spanish part of the city. Some of its residents apparently came from Tlatelolco and Tetzcoco, people who had been part of the "Aztec" Triple Alliance and who now provided some of the most acculturated artisans in the country. The Dominicans, not to be outdone by the other friars, took responsibility for them and allowed some of them to live near their own church so they could reside near to where they worked and sold their goods. The sector under the protection of the Dominicans included another community of Tlaxcalans as well, people who had come in the first wave of migrants and settled on a substantial territory—which they apparently owned—just north of the city on the road to Tlaxcala. Sometimes their barrio was called Santa Ana—or increasingly San Antonio, after the local monastery— but when the name was mentioned at all in official documents it was paired with San Pablo de los Naturales, under which it was politically subsumed.[3]

Each indigenous community largely governed itself, and thus in time each came to envision itself as an altepetl, divided into varying ethnic neighborhoods or barrios (the Nahuatl word *tlaxilacalli*, the usual term for subdivisions of an altepetl, does not surface in the annals included in this volume). Each group acquired its own *alguacil* (constable), who, as time went on and the population increased, was asked to take on more and more responsibility.[4] The alcaldes and regidores normal for an altepetl were apparently still lacking. The *fiscal* (indigenous church steward) also spoke for the altepetl on certain public occasions, we learn from the annals.[5] Sometimes there were problems between the

---

[3]Marín Tamayo 1989 (pp. 66–72) has studied the origins of the original barrios, based on Puebla's early cabildo records, housed in the Archivo del Ayuntamiento de Puebla. He could find no official mention of the indigenous settlers of San Pablo being from Mexico City, which was asserted by early chroniclers, but there are archival references (see Altman 2000, p. 213, and López de Villaseñor 1961, p. 444). On the question of the Dominicans allowing them to lodge nearby, see Zerón Zapata, pp. 84–85, and Marín Tamayo 1989, p. 62. The Tlaxcalan community called Santa Ana had an interesting history; the Franciscans originally established a tiny chapel dedicated to the saint next to their convent, but in 1550 it was moved to the northern neighborhood, and lands were granted to the Tlaxcalans who were to live there. Don Juan Bautista, who would later serve as first indigenous governor, owned an orchard in the vicinity. See Leicht 1967, p. 363; López de Villaseñor 1961, pp. 147, 438, 446; Marín Tamayo 1989, p. 67; Toussaint 1954, p. 210. For a budding study on Cholula's relationship with the satellite community of migrants who moved to Puebla, see Gutiérrez 2008.

The study of the whole topic of the internal organization of the indigenous sector in Puebla and its evolution is still in gestation. It is likely that some of the facts I have reported above, making my best judgments from the existing literature, will be challenged or appear in a different light as future research continues to get closer to the sources.

[4]On the early mentions of these *alguaciles de barrio*, see Marín Tamayo 1989, pp. 72–75. Through the ambiguities of the word *barrio* one cannot ascertain whether there was an alguacil for each smaller barrio or only one for each of the larger proto-altepetl.

[5]Annals of Puebla, entry for 1565; the term *altepetl* is already used.

various groups relating to communication issues and the need to find a way to divide public service tasks equitably. In the 1590s, the Spaniards began to refer to one don Juan Bautista as the *gobernador* of the whole indigenous community. He seems to have been from Tizatla and to have had connections with the altepetl of San Pablo de los Naturales.[1] Apparently, the other indigenous neighborhoods would accept his authority only if a traditional indigenous-style rotation of office was established, for in the earliest years of the seventeenth century, just such an arrangement was formalized. Together, the three neighborhoods established a cabildo of their own, with all the usual offices, through which power and responsibility for assigned tasks would be shared and rotated in perfect Nahua tradition. In 1601, the first official regidores and alcaldes were installed as cabildo members, and in 1610, a grand public ceremony was held to mark the occasion of the formal recognition of the three constituent groups as altepetl and their political unification as one greater altepetl.[2] Thus a miscellaneous group of indigenous immigrants operating inside a major Spanish city had over time reconstituted the typical Nahua organizational form of a complex altepetl, much the same as Tlaxcala, only with three subaltepetl instead of the canonical four.

The formation of a well organized and fully legitimated indigenous conglomerate to ensure fairness and order must have delighted no one more than the people of the barrio known as "San Juan del Río," the oldest part of San Francisco. In Nahuatl the quarter was called Tlaxcaltecapan ("the place where the Tlaxcalans are").[3] It sat perched on the banks of a rivulet called Almoloyan which ran down to the Río San Francisco. Many of the people worked in textile mills powered by the surrounding waters. They maintained a very old chapel and a newer church, both dedicated to San Juan Bautista (John the

---

[1] Spanish documents of the 1590s mentioning don Juan Bautista as indigenous alcalde are noted in Leicht 1967, p.178. Since an entry for 1601 in the present Annals of Puebla gives that year as the date of the first appointment of three alcaldes, one for each altepetl, he may have first been alcalde for the whole community and then formally or informally attained the status of governor. The present annals, so punctilious in naming the governors and their order, cannot help us here, because the years 1580 to 1600 are missing in all related sets. (Apparently some borrower of the original pages never returned them.) Although otherwise no one repeated in the office in the time recorded by the text, it seems extremely likely that in the time before traditions jelled, don Juan Bautista the first governor was the same person as the third governor of the same name who is mentioned in the entry for 1610. If so, he was from Tizatla in Tlaxcala. He owned land in Puebla located between San Pablo and Santa Ana (López de Villaseñor 1961, p. 147), which was the only other barrio where Tlaxcalans lived in any numbers at that time (see above.) Later, a large population of Tlaxcalans would make Analco its home, but in the year 1600, Analco was considered little more than an offshoot of Tlaxcaltecapan.

[2] Entries for 1601 and 1610, Annals of Puebla (this volume). It is possible that the need for an arrangement that would satisfy the entire indigenous community was heightened by the fact that in this period the Spanish authorities were demanding major *congregaciones* in the region, forcing natives scattered in small hamlets to settle in larger population centers so that tribute might be more easily collected. Certain Mixteca migrants were being resettled in Puebla, and other uprooted individuals may have landed there as well. See Hoekstra 1993, pp. 108–18. It was also a period when the obrajes were expanding considerably, with the attendant labor requirements. See Altman 2000.

[3] In the Annals of Puebla it seems that Tlaxcaltecapan at times means San Juan del Río specifically and sometimes the larger entity of San Francisco. See n. 2, p. 32.

Baptist). On the street running from the church down to the Almoloyan, the people had built a public washhouse channeling the flow of three gushing springs, and they took good care of the structure.[4] The author of our present Annals of Puebla, who lived in the community, proudly records the formation of the tripartite indigenous cabildo: "The cabildo session was held in the *sala real* (royal chamber, central feature of Puebla's main governmental building)." It was before his time, but the detail suggests that a prede-cessor, possibly even a relative, was actually present and perhaps first wrote the entry. The keeper of the annals (or one of his predecessors) evinced a particular interest in Tizatla, perhaps indicating that he understood his forebears to have migrated from that part of Tlaxcala. The connection was very much alive in his mind. In some ways, of course, the experiences of those who had remained behind in Tlaxcala diverged sharply from their kin who had taken an alternate path and settled in Cuitlaxcohuapan. After all, in the former they lived in relative isolation, and in the latter they lived side by side with people of different languages and cultures, not only Spaniards, but also Africans and indigenous people from a variety of other places. In some ways, however, the world views of the two groups, those who stayed at home and those who left, remained very much of a piece. An exploration of the histories they each kept elucidates both aspects of their reality.

The Nahuatl Annals Genre

IN THE ANCIENT TRADITION of the *xiuhpohualli*[5] (year-count, or yearly account), as far as we understand it, a timeline was marked out, each segment labeled according to the ancient Mesoamerican calendar with standard year signs (One Reed, Two Flint-knife, Three House, Four Rabbit, etc). Next to the line unfolded a set of glyphs, designed to elicit from trained readers an impressive oral performance narrating the events of that year that were important to the altepetl as a whole.[6] Sometimes the year-count was intended to reify a relationship between two or more entities, and different glyphs telling their somewhat different stories might appear on either side of the line or in areas of the document designated by distinct place-name glyphs. Circumstantial evidence indicates that in performances, more than one xiuhpohualli would often be presented in quick succession, representing the different elements of the corporate political entity being celebrated. These year counts might be short and report the events of a single tlatoani's reign, or they might be long, extending for centuries, with certain time periods stylis-tically foreshortened for practicality's sake. We cannot know with absolute certainty how

---

[4]For a study of the streets as they were mentioned in contemporary documents, see Leicht 1967, pp. 12–13. On the churches and chapels in the barrio, see Toussaint 1954.

[5]This was the term most often used, but in fact there existed a range of conceptions of the form, and thus different designations. We sometimes see *xiuhtlacuilolli* (year painting, or year writing) or *xiuhamatl* (year paper) or even *altepetlacuilolli* (altepetl painting or writing). See Lockhart 1992, p. 376.

[6]The best entrée into the literature on the surviving pictorials is Boone 2000. We need a great deal more work on what can be deduced from the alphabetic annals about the verbal performances. As a step in that direction, see Townsend 2009. There I study a 1550s courtroom drama that relied on traditional usages of the xiuhpohualli, and I give careful consideration to what the more verbose sixteenth-century annals may demonstrate to us.

much latitude the performers or reciters were allowed –whether they adhered strictly to a pre-set script, or were encouraged to take some initiative and develop themes of interest to their audiences. The latter seems far more likely, however, as will be seen. No pre-conquest pictographic annals survive. The images that art historians have studied all date from the mid-sixteenth century or later, and though some scholars have proven very successful in gleaning from them a sense of how the Nahuas understood history, they cannot bring us any closer to an understanding of the actual oral performances. For that, our only clues must come from the alphabetic annals that were produced well after the conquest.

Almost as soon as they arrived, the Spanish friars began to take indigenous students, teaching them not only the Christian faith but also the Roman alphabet, in order that they might be more effectively instructed. In this regard, it stood the indigenous in good stead that, having a long tradition of living as sedentary agriculturalists, a class of noblemen had attempted to organize society and bolster their authority by keeping and interpreting a rich painted tradition—for they immediately saw the utility of an alphabetic system.[1] In the 1540s and 1550s, the Roman alphabet spread throughout central Mexico; numerous men became literate in every sense of the word.[2] They wrote what their Spanish teachers asked them to write; but they also wrote what they wanted to write themselves. They recorded legends and songs. They turned the tradition of making a statement as one lay dying into the tradition of leaving a will. They wrote down property settlements. They went to court with petitions when they disagreed about what had been decided.

Some also did their best to transfer the surviving xiuhpohualli into alphabetic texts. This was easier conceived of than accomplished, however, in that they had to find a way to recreate both the oral performance and the painted record, and relatively few of them were experts in either skill. The earliest extant set of annals dates from the 1540s; it is, not surprisingly, the Annals of Tlatelolco, where the Franciscans' Colegio de Santa Cruz, the first school for indigenous youth, was located. It is a purely alphabetic text; any visual artifact the speaker had referred to as he performed has disappeared beyond recall. Little by little, certain talented men learned to blend the two traditions, and we find sets of annals that consist of some traditional glyphs alongside alphabetic renderings of what the glyphs are meant to convey and hint at. Soon it became more difficult for young men to make head or tail of the old pictorials. In the 1560s, one frustrated student of his people's traditions who lived in the Tlaxcala-Puebla valley simply wrote about the year 1442 "and

---

[1]Precontact Nahuatl writing, though highly pictorial, had the capacity to indicate sounds in terms of syllables. When necessary any proper name could be expressed syllabically. In principle anything in human speech could have been represented. The system as it existed in central Mexico at contact, however, did not reproduce speeches, songs, or any actual utterances, tasks for which the Roman alphabet was well adapted.

[2]There is ongoing discussion concerning the question of whether or not Native American forms of expression constituted true literacy. See Boone and Mignolo 1994. I would like to bypass this debate, as it seems to me clear that the indigenous in the precontact era were indeed communicating with each other using writing, but that at the same time, they stood in danger of losing their ability to communicate in the traditional fashion as long as the glyphs remained the domain of a select few and were largely restricted to conveying names, dates, quantities, details of costume and ritual, bare events such as death or accession to the throne, etc., and much was left to oral narration.

in that year a great many things happened."[3] He, like numerous others, did not even try to illustrate his own set of annals.

Nahuatl annals have been known for their terseness, but this is probably only because we are often looking at materials dating from this era of confusion, when the writers were well aware they should put down more, but did not know what exactly to put. The surviving early alphabetic annals give every indication that performers had traditionally included relatively lengthy or dramatic speeches: at moments of conflict, where we find dialog, and at moments of ceremonial resolution, where we find grave pronouncements. Examples are literally everywhere, beginning with the earliest set, the Annals of Tlatelolco. In the beginning of that text, the people leave the Seven Caves and wander for thirteen years, eating snakes and rabbits, prickly pear and cactus. The leader makes proclamations regularly. ("I will guide you"; "Daughter, go with this man," etc.)

When the people attempt to settle in the lands of the Culhuaque, social conflict reaches a fevered pitch—and the dialog becomes extensive. The Culhua ruler sets the Mexica to do virtually impossible tasks, which they manage to perform anyway. At each stage there is verbal exchange. After each event, the astounded and impressed Culhuaque ask questions reminiscent of other accounts, essentially asking each other in various ways, "Who *are* these Mexica, anyway?" Finally a resolution is reached—at least temporarily—through a great dialog. The Mexica ask the Culhuaque for some land to build their houses, and request that the ruler give one of his sons to become their own ruler, to establish their own royal line. "Yes," says the king's mother. "Give them my precious pearl, my quetzal feather, my grandchild." The ruler comes to see their new town once the houses are constructed. And he says, "O Mexica, you have attained great merit [have earned land]." He faces the thought of leaving his son with them as an independent king. And he weeps, in typical Nahua ceremonial style. Then follows a long period of years in which there is relatively little conflict, and relatively little dialog. The Mexica continue to march forward through time, their power ever increasing. (The great battle between the Tenochca and Tlatelolca that occurred in 1472 is passed over with as little comment as possible, of course, as their defeat was an embarrassment to the Tlatelolca.) Then the Spaniards arrive. Conflict ensues. And with the conflict once again comes dialog. The story of the years 1519 through 1521 is told in great though intermittent detail, the action propelled forward through verbal exchanges. This same phenomenon occurs in every one of the known sixteenth-century alphabetic annals: periods of quiet, usually recorded in relatively terse language, are interrupted by periods of crisis, represented in vivid dialog.[4]

The pattern was not restricted merely to the Central Valley, for we see it in the best-developed eastern text of the era as well, the Historia Tolteca-Chichimeca, in effect the Annals of Cuauhtinchan. In the beginning we find the lists of people who have departed from the Seven Caves and are on the move through the landscape. The ones whose story the audience is following arrive in the region of Tollan, and the newcomers experience conflict with those who are already settled there, and hence with each other. Speech erupts almost immediately. When a king demands a certain wife, warfare breaks out that

[3]The Annals of Tecamachalco in Celestino Solís and Reyes García 1992, p. 20.

[4]The Annals of Tlatelolco in Barlow 1948, pp. 37–47.

involves several kings and their peoples. "Said Icxicohuatl, said Quetzaltehueyac, 'Why is there fighting? Why are the Toltecs being destroyed? Did I start it? Did I demand the woman for whom we are now confronting each other, for whom we are making war?'" Most such rhetorical questions were meant to be answered with a resounding "No!" Certainly the leader was underscoring the fact that this disaster was not his fault. He finished grandly: "Let Huemac die, who made us fight!"[1]

Eventually, having traveled quite far to the east, and having endured bad treatment for long enough, the leaders of the people hold a great meeting and decide to fight back. They make a grand statement, having come to this resolution, and they cry: "'Will it eat us? Or will it eat them, the arrow and shield of the Olmeca-Xicalanca?' Then they wept, Icxicohuatl, Quetzaltehueyac." Unfortunately, their ritual weeping is in vain. This does not turn out to be the all-important moment of settlement after all. The people experience some military success, but are forced to move on not long after. Eventually, they give up their wandering life of sleeping in fields and caves and make a permanent home. A great proclamation is made—several times, in fact. Years pass without great conflict, and without speech incidents, until the people attempt to reject a Tlatelolcan-born prince who is being foisted on them. "When they found out who would be king, then a Chimalpaneca woman named Nanotzin got angry. She said, 'Will he be our king? Is [our king] not Ayapancatl? It will not be.'"[2] Dialog continues after the Tlatelolca meet their own nemesis in the persons of the Tenochca, and Axayacatl (king of the victorious Tenochca) begins to send his minions to the region to arrange affairs in Cuauhtinchan as he pleases. The constant verbal accusations and negotiations effectively end only when the Spaniards come and replace the Tenochca ruling government.

Interestingly, the extant early annals offer evidence that kernels of important speech exchanges were memorized verbatim, but that performers also amplified as they chose. In the Codex Aubin, for example, a set of annals from San Juan Moyotlan—one of four subaltepetl in Mexico City—dating from the 1560s and 70s, elements of particular speeches appear that are much expanded in material copied out by Chimalpahin forty years later. In the days when the Mexica are still weak, the leader Huitzilihuitl is defeated in battle by the Tepaneca and the Culhuaque. He and his daughter are brought before Coxcoxtli, king of Culhuacan. "Huitzilihuitl felt great compassion for his daughter, since not even a little [clothing] was on her. He said to the king, 'Grant some little thing to my daughter, O King.' And [the king] said to him. 'I do not consent. She will stay as she is.'"[3] The same story appears in Chimalpahin's work in much fuller form. Yet in the midst of the more detailed account, almost exactly the same speeches are uttered.[4]

---

[1] Historia Tolteca Chichimeca in Kirchoff et al. 1976, p. 155.

[2] Ibid., p. 219.

[3] The Codex Aubin in Dibble 1963, pp. 31–32. "Yn uitzilliuitl yn iychpoch cenca quitlaocolti yn atle ma ytla ytech uetzia quilhui yn tlahtouani Ma ytlatzin xictlaocolli y nochpochtzin tlatouanie auh niman quilhui camo niçia çan iuh yaz."

[4] Chimalpahin 1997, 2: 76. "Auh in yehuatl yn huehue huitzillihuitl ynic quinhuicaque yn ich-poch cenca quitlaocoltia yn atle ma ytlatzin ytech huetzia quilhuitacic yn tlahtohuani coxcoxtli yn huitzillihuitl tlahtohuanie ma ytlahtzin xicmotlaocollili y nochpochtzin auh niman quinanquilli quilhui camo nicia çan iuh yaz."

Whether Chimalpahin was copying a narration that had originally been taken down from a fuller performance or perhaps himself felt that it was his right to elaborate, or whether the author of the Codex Aubin (or his informant) could only remember the most important speeches of a fuller story he had once heard and he found it acceptable to repeat only part, almost does not matter. In any of these cases, we are witnessing the phenomenon of Nahuas perceiving the xiuhpohualli as a somewhat flexible organism in which certain kernels remained the same but were subject to additions and deletions. It is thus evident how the tradition could endure in its essentials, and yet become terse in certain circumstances—as when the glyphs were no longer readable, or the reciters could no longer remember everything—although it originally was not, and most people understood that it was not. The most likely primary source of the frequent postcontact terseness is that writers of alphabetic versions were basing themselves on pictographic manuscripts of which the oral component had been lost. In the colonial period, the terse entries handed down from the somewhat beclouded past would often give way to more voluble discourse when the writer got to the period he knew more about, his own lifetime; few annalists hesitated to elaborate on what they witnessed themselves.

The very flexibility of the genre also presumably allowed for another subtlety which may be lost on us as modern readers if we do not take care; although on one level each and every set of annals simply celebrates the ongoing existence of the altepetl and records a history that is of interest to everyone who lives there, on another level, a particular faction within the altepetl may be presenting (indeed, usually is presenting) a certain perspective on events. The Annals of Tlatelolco, for example, not only recount the steady rise of a great power; they also ultimately rehearse the arguments that took place within the altepetl in the year 1521 about whether they should or should not stand by the Tenochca; this teller, having lived to see the outcome, seems to view the results of that debate as a mark of foolishness more than of courageous loyalty. If we did not know that there were two schools of thought on responsible leadership, and did not know that there had been a vigorous debate followed by a terrible military loss, it would be difficult to understand why, for example, the annalist has Malintzin demand, just before the Tlatelolca decide to side with the Tenochca, "Is Quauhtemoc still such a small child [so irresponsible]? He has no pity on the children and women; the old men have already perished. Here are the rulers of Tlaxcala, Huexotzinco, Cholula, Chalco, Acolhuacan, Cuernavaca, Xochimilco, Mizquic, Cuitlahuac, and Culhuacan [who have come to join the Spaniards]." At the same time, other speakers remind the audience of former Tenochca abuses of the Tlatelolca.[5] These are hardly simple reminders of Tlatelolcan wisdom and greatness; rather, this segment at least is the composition of a Tlatelolcan who on some level wished that another course had been taken. Similarly, as other scholars have noted, in the early eastern text of the Historia Tolteca-Chichimeca, a long-standing land-related wrangle between various subaltepetl makes its way into the discourse that we find in the text, for when the project was being carried out, an actual

---

[5]For the best translation of the conquest-period segment of the Annals of Tlatelolco, see Lockhart 1993 (this passage is on p. 265). For more on differences of opinion regarding responsible rulership, see Townsend 2006, pp. 104–06.

court battle was underway.[1] In short, recognizing that we must seek to understand all the factional tensions that underlie the surviving documents will likewise render the annals of the Tlaxcala-Puebla valley more illuminating than they would otherwise be.

The Tlaxcala-Puebla family of annals

ONE OF WHAT WE might call the mid-way documents, containing both glyphs and text, apparently made its way from Tlaxcala to Puebla during the sixteenth-century migration. It is no longer extant. We can only surmise that such a document existed because all but one of the historical annals of the sixteenth century that do survive in Puebla include verbatim quotations of the same set of material, and that material is also found in several of the surviving Tlaxcalan manuscripts: readers of the two sets of annals in this book will see that the Puebla set shares material from the Tlaxcalan set in early entries.[2] The identical material ends in 1538, but it is highly likely that the piece migrated significantly later than that, when alphabetic literacy was more widespread and permanent indigenous settlement in Puebla a feature of life; the entries later than the 1530s would not have been replicated, not because they weren't there, but because the annalists in Cuitlaxcohuapan would at that point have turned to recording the new city's foundation and history.

The document that served as inspiration for Puebla's annalists clearly contained some glyphs stemming from the old tradition. Nearly all of the extant documents from there include a bar running down the left hand margin divided into years named with glyphs according to the Mesoamerican calendar right next to the year as given in the Christian tradition. All the text entries in the documents that contain this bar begin with the suggestive phrase "Here in this year" (*nican ipan xihuitl*), not generally found in annals, as if someone were pointing to a painted document and explaining what he saw in each place. The word "nican" can in certain circumstances have a temporal or sequential meaning ("here at this point") as opposed to its more usual spatial one ("here in this place"), but the spatial connotation is telling and has precedent in the Nahuatl documentary corpus.[3] I have taken the phrase for the title of the book because it demonstrates the crucial nature of the year as the organizer and framework of all Nahuatl annals, and yet is also a sort of signature of a particular subgroup of annals. The Tlaxcalan set does not use the phrase, but it does not need to, as the full year in indigenous style is written out in words which are incorporated into the body of each entry, as well as being indicated with a pictorial glyph in the margin. The glyphs are in straight rows running down the left margin, just where the bar runs in the Puebla corpus.

---

[1]Discussions of what was occurring in Cuauhtinchan in this era are the unifying thread in a remarkable collection of scholarly opinion on the Mapa de Cuauhtinchan No. 2, Carrasco and Sessions 2007.

[2]Recognition of this fact may at first be difficult because the Tlaxcalan set misdates a string of preconquest events as occurring twenty years earlier than they actually did. Compare the entries in the two texts for 1505 and 1525, or 1510 and 1530.

[3]In the earliest large-scale Nahuatl documentary production, the early censuses of the Cuernavaca region, each separate fact is introduced by *iz catqui*, "here is," in apparent literal reference to a pictorial manuscript in front of the writer/speaker (Cline 1993, throughout). Traces of the same *iz catqui* turn up in Nahuatl testaments in various places in the following decades and centuries.

That there was probably one major root text is further suggested by the fact that at least three of the documents in the Puebla corpus have their major passages accompanied by almost exactly the same set of illustrations, suggestive of the content of the paragraphs. They use a skull to mark passages about epidemics or death in war, a mitre to commemorate the accession or death of a bishop, a sun or a comet to mark meteorological phenomena, a crown or a lion to note the accession or death of a king, and a picture of the structure itself to record the building of a church, cathedral, fountain, etc. All of these topics, and even the symbols used, are somewhat reminiscent of the most traditional Nahuatl annals. And yet none of these symbols are actually precontact in form; the old Nahuas would have employed a man on a reed mat and special seat, for example, to denote a new king, or a bundled corpse to denote death. (Only in one place do I find what appears to be a preconquest glyph: the sign for water, a bit above the mention of the people of the altepetl building a public water supply.)[4] It seems that the traditional glyphs had been visually translated or transformed into symbols that made more sense to people educated in the European tradition; indeed, the writers probably no longer had the training needed to do them in the old style. Certainly the main responsibility for announcing basic topics has been moved from the once-complex glyphs, now drastically simplified, to the alphabetic text.

That a traveler made his way from Tlaxcala to Puebla with an annalistic document carefully stowed among his most precious things, and that he then shared his material with numerous others, makes perfect sense in the context of annals-writing in the Tlaxcala-Puebla valley and beyond. Frances Krug has already proven that all the extant annals in the valley belong to what may be called a single "family."[5] So much sharing and mutual copying occurred that they are literally all "genetically related." There is no set of annals that does not share at least some of its material, verbatim, with at least one other set. At first glance, there are enough discrepancies that one might argue that the commonalities are essentially a coincidental result of the fact that the annalists were all interested in the same phenomena: natural disasters, changes in rulership, etc. That is, if three of them happen to refer to the same events in the same year, but in slightly different ways, it may only prove that they shared interests common to all Nahua annalists. However, there is more to the story; if strings of language are truly genetically related, actually copied one from the other, then there will be evidence of genetic mutations having been passed on. Indeed, it turns out that when we look for errors, inaccurate dates and strange turns of phrase—sentences that two or three different people would be entirely unlikely to come up with on their own—we find ample proof that all the documents are to some degree related.

It was not just that there happened to be a particularly active group of friends who

---

[4]Even this case is doubtful. In the entry for 1636, the text reports the completion of a municipal water project. In the Puebla cathedral annals, a glyph appears just above, with the 1635 entry, which could be a European-style crown, but is distinctly different from other crowns in the manuscript in that it contains the preconquest water symbol. Possibly one of the copyists misunderstood what he was seeing and thus rendered the water in the shape of a crown.

[5]Frances Krug, "The Nahuatl Annals of the Tlaxcala-Puebla Region," unfinished PhD dissertation, Department of History, UCLA. For a summary, see Krug and Townsend 2007.

shared an interest in history and established a lasting pattern in the region. It was that the act of keeping a set of annals, by definition, included seeking out the work of predecessors, including statements of prominent men representing different segments of the political entity whose history the annals claimed to record. And it was a closed circle. No other sources would do. The longest manuscript in the region, over 200 folios, written by a member of the Tlaxcalan cabildo in the second half of the seventeenth century, drew on a wide variety of documents. The author, don Juan Buenaventura Zapata y Mendoza, is a known figure whose life we can research. He could read Spanish and would have had access to Spanish books. He was a community leader and had easy access to governmental records kept in Nahuatl. But the text itself indicates that he used none of these, seeking out instead statements of the tlatoque, as he called his fellow officeholders. In his mind, it was their combined experience which constituted the altepetl.[1]

Thus the two sets of annals presented in this book share substantial material with other annals from the region. Very few original manuscripts survive, but in the early nineteenth century, the scholar, antiquarian enthusiast and patron of the Nahua world Faustino Galicia Chimalpopoca copied and translated as many xiuhpohualli as he could find, and José Fernando Ramírez, director of Mexico's Museo Nacional, later compiled them and many others—sometimes copying them over himself—into a collection which he labeled "Anales antiguos de México y sus contornos." That collection is now in the Biblioteca Nacional de Antropología e Historia in Mexico, and though its usefulness is reduced by its consisting as it does of copies (and sometimes copies of copies) containing transcription errors and some introduced interpretations, it provides a valuable context for the few surviving original manuscripts.[2]

Looking at the corpus as a whole reveals at least one significant difference between the work produced in Tlaxcala and that ultimately generated in Puebla. A real understanding of the native calendar was lost. Originally, the four year signs (Reed, Flint-knife, House, Rabbit) were cyclically aligned with thirteen years (1 Reed, 2 Flint-knife, 3 House, 4 Rabbit, 5 Reed, 6 Flint-knife, 7 House, 8 Rabbit, 9 Reed, 10 Flint-knife, 11 House, 12 Rabbit, 13 Reed, beginning over 1 Flint-knife, 2 House, etc.).[3] After four thirteen-year series, or 52 years, the cycle would begin again. It was, in our terms, as if a new century were beginning. In each 52-year unit, of course, a particular year ("9 Reed," for example) would occur only once. For someone deeply familiar with the system, specifying that an event occurred in the year 9 Reed in a particular 52-year bundle was as clear as saying that the event happened in 1610. But for those fully immersed in the

---

[1]For a full transcription and translation into Spanish of his work, see Zapata 1995. For more on the subject of this paragraph, see Townsend 2010.

[2]The collection, housed in the BNAH, will henceforth be referred to as the AAMC. The set of annals closest to the Annals of Tlaxcala in this volume is the one labeled Anales de Puebla y Tlaxcala, no. 1, pt. 3 [1519–1691], p. 765. The one closest to this volume's Annals of Puebla is entitled Anales de Puebla y Tlaxcala, no. 2 [1524–1674], p. 802.

[3]Scholarship on indigenous calendrical matters is voluminous but often very technical. A very down-to-earth treatment of the Nahua calendar and the way it was manipulated by political authorities to serve their own ends is Hassig 2001. A highly accessible explanation of the math involved in the Mesoamerican calendars in general is found in Byland 1993.

Christians' Gregorian calendar, having lost track of the significance of 13 or 52 years, it was not clear at all, and the Christian dates were sorely needed. For long-term dating, the Nahua system had always suffered from the fact that it made no overt distinction between 52-year cycles. However, keepers of annals were deeply invested in the maintenance of tradition, and so even in circles most divorced from real knowledge of the traditional calendar, the years with their Christian dates were also usually labeled with the name of "Reed," "Flint-knife," "House," or "Rabbit." The Puebla annals are of that kind, though the original sixteenth-century document brought from Tlaxcala must have been based on the thirteen-year cycle, since it survives in some form in nearly all the Tlaxcalan texts we have, including the one reproduced in this book. Here, the full indigenous name of the year ("8 Reed") is written out in words in every entry to the very end, and a glyph representing the native word is also always present. Furthermore, the ending of the 52-year bundles is regularly marked, though beginning at a non-native year-zero, that is, the arrival of Cortés in 1519. Still, it is not safe to assume that all or even most literate indigenous in Tlaxcala necessarily were equally comfortable with the ancient calendar at the end of the seventeenth century. We may possibly simply be seeing the insistent traditionalism of a particular individual, as even don Juan Zapata, the most discursive and highly educated Tlaxcalan annalist, himself dropped most indigenous year labels in the period in which he was composing his own entries, though he understood them well enough to have included them in the earlier work he copied out.[4]

Still, if the Pueblan annalists at least had been reduced to a somewhat fuzzy understanding of the traditional calendar and were clinging to its cyclical and cellular nature without retaining any of the mathematical details, we must nevertheless avoid falling into the trap of being at all condescending toward them as actual historians or at least record-keepers. It is important that we as readers divest ourselves of any assumptions we may harbor about indigenous patterns of historical thought being non-linear, circular, dominated by omens or free from concerns about "accuracy." The two xiuhpohualli presented here were none of these things; their writers produced linear histories of the real world in which they lived, and they seem to have been quite concerned about "accuracy." I say this because most of what they recorded can be confirmed in Spanish records; when they said a bell was hung on a certain date in June, for example, the Spanish documents often say the same.

When the dates do not align with what the Spaniards recorded, there is generally a single explanation. At first, the indigenous would of course have been keeping the calendar by the old style. The Christian calendar was then overlaid by finding a dated event in Spanish records that seemed to match a dated event in the indigenous records and establishing a correlation. ("Ah, they say the bishop came in 1545. So we will place '1545' next to the year '3 Reed' which mentions the bishop and proceed from there.") But if in fact the Spanish records were not referring to the same visit (or the same

---

[4]In fact, where the traditional year signs, either in pictoglyphs or in words, have been inserted in the latter half of Zapata's text, they are in the hand of don Manuel de los Santos Salazar, who was one of the forces behind the Annals of Tlaxcala, this volume. See the fourth section of this introduction, "Topoyanco in Tlaxcala: the world of don Manuel" (pp. 21–28).

bishop), then a whole series of events was misdated. It is thus typical to find strings of errors in which the dates are all off by the same number of years. One clear example of this phenomenon occurs in the set of Tlaxcalan annals presented here, where someone made the assumption that Cortés arrived in what the Europeans called "1501" (rather than 1519) and thus dated the following series of events nineteen years earlier than they actually occurred.

For similar reasons, annals within the same family may regularly be off in relation to each other—not only in relation to the Spanish calendar—by a fixed number of years. The Annals of Tlaxcala in this volume, for example, and the annals of don Juan Zapata report many of the same events one year off for about a twenty-year period. I am convinced that the calendars of all the different local communities were not fully correlated with each other.[1] They were in theory, but it was not possible in reality for thousands of settlements across a vast space to have begun keeping count at the same point and then to have maintained records without gaps. Even if tribute collection under the Triple Alliance did push them to align themselves more perfectly ("We will all agree that it is now the year 9 House—your priests were wrong if they thought differently"), it was still possible for keepers of annals to introduce discrepancies. If one settlement, for example, put an earthquake that was known to have occurred when the writer's grandfather was ten years old in the year 2 Reed, but the next remembered it in connection with the drought that began in the year 3 Flint-knife and put it there, the two calendars might have a whole string of events off from each other by a year. Add to this an observable tendency to date any important past event 1 Reed, where the 52-year cycle strictly begins. Together these phenomena explain why the year 1519 in different closely-related sets of annals has been correlated with the years 1 Reed, 2 Flint-knife, 12 House, and 3 House. A related kind of error could continue even into the writers' own lives if one of them remembered the year of a certain vivid event wrongly, and then tried to calculate when other events must have occurred based on that; probably this is what explains the discrepancy between the annals of this volume and don Juan Zapata's.

Each set of annals in this volume also passes over one particular period twice. In the case of the Tlaxcalan annals, they are the years following the conquest, and in the case of the annals of Puebla, they are the years following the royal decision to allow the indigenous to settle there. This type of repeating often happens in sixteenth-century Nahuatl annals. Historians have tended to interpret it as a form of disorderliness that was perfectly acceptable within the genre. In a recent study of my own, however, I have argued that there is ample evidence that the Nahuas did this intentionally whenever they were covering a particularly important period in their history: at such times, it seemed to be desirable to include the statements of two or four of the subunits that together made up the greater political entity, or perhaps simply different elements of community experience that needed to be represented. In the preconquest era, these histories would have been presented in performance, where it would have been clear to the audience, as one speaker followed another, what was occurring. In the alphabetic texts, however, we are simply

----

[1]There is longstanding scholarly debate on this point. I am convinced by the arguments in Kirchoff 1976 and Hassig 2001.

left with unapologetic backtracking to an earlier date, followed by coverage of the same period from a slightly different perspective. Despite the adoption of alphabetic literacy, the keepers of annals were still very much working within a traditional—very orderly—frame of reference. Of course, all of this may have been lost on the late seventeenth-century writers represented in this volume, who probably simply copied what others had left for them from years before; they were most likely replicating a fossilized form.[2]

It is not merely in these various details but in their essential nature that that both the Pueblan and Tlaxcalan annals presented here conform to the traditional model of the xiuhpohualli. Both treat the genre's most typical topics as they existed before the conquest: changes of high governmental officials, rotation of duties between constituent units, religious ceremonies, building projects, epidemics, wars, and memorable meteorological phenomena. The specifics are different (a governor is elected rather than a king, pirates attack rather than the Mexica, a cathedral is built rather than a pyramid temple) but the underlying themes remain the same. Still, despite their commonalities, the two deserve individualized study if we are to gain insight into the families, subaltepetls and perspectives which motivated their production.

Topoyanco in Tlaxcala: the World of don Manuel

IN THEORY, the xiuhpohualli were anonymous productions celebrating the life of an entire altepetl or corporate sociopolitical entity. In fact, however, they were created by individuals who belonged to particular extended families and subaltepetls and who necessarily held certain special perspectives on events. All Nahua readers would have been aware of this. To some extent, they apparently expected a writer of annals to give himself away, for the majority did so to some degree or other. Certainly in the old days, before the arrival of the Spaniards, it would have been clear enough in a public performance which extended family or subaltepetl had the floor. In the alphabetic annals, we find writers who occasionally use the first person or sign their names, and others who would not dream of doing so but cannot help mentioning it when their own children are born or prevent themselves from roundly condemning the actions of political rivals. The annals of the Tlaxcala-Puebla valley are no different. Don Juan Buenaventura Zapata y Mendoza included his most ornate signature, graphically reported the robbery of his house, and lambasted his enemies. The writer of the sixteenth-century annals of Tecamachalco, very near Puebla, remained officially anonymous, but when speaking of one don Mateo Sánchez, he happened to mention his marriage, the birth of his children, the death of his wife, his second marriage (and even the location of the wedding), and finally the deaths of a beloved nephew and of his daughter. No one else's life story was alluded to in such detail.[3]

If we approach the texts with the idea that there must have been a particular provenance, we can often find it. In the case of the annals of Tlaxcala, it is apparent that the writer was keenly interested in the affairs of Topoyanco. Topoyanco was on one level simply a settlement within the subaltepetl of Ocotelolco, but its history was more com-

---

[2]Townsend 2009.
[3]Annals of Tecamachalco in Celestino Solís and Reyes García 1992.

plicated than first appears. What the Spaniards called the city of Tlaxcala was in fact merely the ever more densely populated point where the four quadrants intersected. Each altepetl also had a major settlement located in its heartland, where, probably, a major tlatoani had once had his seat. For Ocotelolco, this provincial center was Topoyanco. By the 1550s these provincial quasi-capitals each had deputies (*tenientes*) assigned by the central cabildo, presumably to maintain order and see to the carrying out of altepetl tasks. Then by the 1590s if not before, Topoyanco, like each of the other three provincial centers, had its own local provincial alcalde, of cabildo rank but apparently functioning primarily in Topoyanco itself. This figure is sometimes mentioned in the present Annals of Tlaxcala, more than the general alcalde for Ocotelolco who sat on the cabildo in Tlaxcala city. For at least some of the town's residents, there would thus have been a sense of patriotic attachment to Topoyanco rather than to Ocotelolco as a whole.[1]

Simply identifying a likely place of origin, however, may not tell us enough of what we would like to know concerning our set of annals. Who might have written it, and under what circumstances? Here it becomes necessary to know the context, in the form of other related documents, in order to look for clues. The lengthy manuscript of don Juan Zapata helps lead us to a likely family, whose central figure at that time was named don Manuel de los Santos Salazar. In his work Zapata often referred to a close friend, don Bernabé Salazar, a nobleman who lived on his lands in Topoyanco, though he officially belonged to Zapata's own subaltepetl, Quiyahuiztlan.[2] He was descended from one Tececepotzin of Quiyahuiztlan, who, in the 1550s, changed his name to Hernando de Salazar, and, when elected governor of the cabildo, was able to take the title "don."[3] The family claimed, probably with truth, that this august ancestor was himself related to the tlatoani of Quiyahuiztlan at the time of the conquest.[4] Though don Bernabé was attached to his home in Topoyanco, he himself gave Quiyahuiztlan as his affiliation.[5] He was active on the cabildo, even becoming governor, and lived to see his son, don Manuel de los Santos Salazar, do two things few indigenous men ever did. First, in 1675, he was accepted by the Franciscan order as a novice in the convent of Puebla; the friars chose

---

[1]See TA, pp. 14, 34, 125–26; Lockhart 1992, pp. 21–23; and Gibson 1967, p. 111, n. 64. Zapata begins to mention the provincial alcaldes in 1590; especially a passage on pp. 198–99 makes it clear that they were actually based in the four centers. A passage in the Annals of Tlaxcala for 1577 refers to the establishment, apparently in Topoyanco, of an "ofiço yaxca cabirdo," an "office belonging to the cabildo," which is mysterious enough, but very likely it refers to a physical facility that could have been used by the deputies who had long been there.

[2]In Zapata's text, don Bernabé is several times named in connection with Topoyanco; Zapata even says (p. 638) that he is buried there. However, he is also consistently mentioned as formally belonging to Quiyahuiztlan ("puhqui quiahuiztlan"). In his application to become a novice of the Franciscan order, don Bernabé's son also said that he was from Topoyanco, but was descended from the highest nobility of Quiyahuiztlan. His witnesses were all long-time residents of Topoyanco. See John Carter Brown Library, Providence, Rhode Island. Puebla de los Angeles Papers, Libro de Informaciones de Novicios IV, Manuel Salazar, May 27, 1675.

[3]See TA, p. 138.

[4]See Libro de Informaciones de Novicios (note 2 above).

[5]Within Zapata's entry for 1683, we find: "niscripano de cabildo D. Ber.[ue] Antonio de salasar puhqui quiahuiztlan," "I the notary of the cabildo don Bernabé Antonio de Salazar, belonging to Quiyahuiztlan" (p. 600).

merely to leave out *limpieza*, or purity of blood lines, in their usual list of qualifications.[6]
He then, for reasons unknown to us, left the Franciscans and became a secular priest; in
1685 he was ordained and said mass for the first time. He became the *cura beneficiado*
first of San Lorenzo Quauhpiaztlan, and later of Santa Cruz.[7] To acquire such a position
was to attain the highest level among the lower clergy; he was a respected parish priest.[8]
After the death of the Salazars' old family friend, don Juan Zapata, don Manuel took his
manuscript from his children. He gave it an ornate title page, annotated it in the margins
with Spanish commentary, and in certain places squeezed in some highly unusual calendrical symbols, particularly some rabbits that are seen nowhere else.[9] Nowhere else, that
is, except in the set of annals presented here.

The annals of this volume thus not only derive from Topoyanco, but also bear the
rabbit year signs known to have been a favorite of the highly educated don Manuel de los
Santos Salazar. I would not argue, though, that the annals are actually his work, but rather
a product of his family. Someone started to keep them long before don Manuel's adulthood. The entries become slightly more detailed in the 1630s, as if the narrator were suddenly speaking from his own experience; in 1639, he mentions the time of day that an
event occurred for the first time, and afterward he does so frequently. There are also
stylistic changes: the viceroy, for example, is no longer the *virrey* or *visorrey*, as he has
been, but rather, simply the *rey* (literally king).[10] Perhaps the person who originally wrote
these words was don Manuel's father, don Bernabé, or his grandfather, or some other
older relative. It seems likely that it was so, for we know that don Juan Zapata in his work
consulted with his friend don Bernabé; substantial material from the present set of annals
appears appended to Zapata's work in the form of marginal additions in Zapata's own
handwriting, and first person statements in the name of don Bernabé are actually included
in the main body of Zapata's text.[11] Interestingly, one of the documents in the collection

---

[6]See Libro de Informaciones de Novicios (note 2 on p. 22).

[7]We know from Zapata and the Annals of Tlaxcala, this volume, that he was ordained and said
mass for the first time in 1685. On the title page he did for Zapata's work in 1689, he is called cura
beneficiado of San Lorenzo Quauhpiaztlan in Tlaxcala. In a devotional drama he wrote and signed
in 1714, he called himself the cura beneficiado of the pueblo of Santa Cruz, also in Tlaxcala. John
Carter Brown Library, Codex Indigenous Number 16. I do not yet know why he left the Franciscan
establishment, though mention of the matter may well be buried in the Franciscan archive.

[8]For more on the honor and prestige attached to holding the position of cura beneficiado as
opposed to a simple curate, see Schwaller 1987.

[9]We know about don Manuel's "finishing" the manuscript because he explicitly described his
own role in a note at the front. The handwriting and ink colors used on that page match some of the
marginal notes and small illustrations found inserted throughout the manuscript.

[10]The use of the loanword *rey*, properly "king," to mean viceroy was quite widespread in Nahuatl, but is seen above all in relatively provincial situations and genres outside the mainstream of
Nahuatl document production. See also Lockhart's discussion in the following chapter, pp. 53–55.

As I say, there is a change from *virrey*/*visorrey* to *rey* around 1630, but the overall pattern is
more complex. Usage in earlier entries especially may be attributed to copying literally from the
texts of predecessors. From the 1550s through 1580s, *rey* is seen in only a minority of cases, but
does occur four times. From 1589 through 1624, only *virrey*/*visorrey* occurs. From 1629 through
1650, only *rey* is seen. Then from 1653 through the end, *virrey*/*visorrey* is again the exclusive term.

[11]See Zapata's entry for 1683 for a definite example.

of nineteenth-century copies gives evidence of having been transcribed from an original produced by some earlier resident of Topoyanco, which the set in this volume then absorbed through the copying process, in that it is almost identical to this one, except that some entries are a bit fuller; it also ends sooner, not long after the death of don Bernabé, don Manuel's father.[1]

After 1669, the words in our set of annals apparently become those of someone else, presumably someone of don Manuel's generation. The *rey* becomes the *virrey* again, and some details a bit chattier than before are now included. For 1685, the text says, in an unusual formulation, "the son of don Bernabé Salazar, named don Manuel de los Santos, was consecrated as a secular priest." Eventually, the document almost becomes a record of who currently fills the position of parish priest of Topoyanco. It seems virtually certain that it was not don Manuel himself who was writing this later section, but rather some relative who was proud of him, because the record notes in 1715 that don Manuel has died, and the vocabulary and tone do not shift noticeably at that point. Furthermore, the writer's level of education was appreciably lower than that found in work signed by don Manuel. An excellent example occurs at the entry for 1710, when the author begins to put "17010," "17011," "17012," etc., having grown used to writing the zeroes in preceding dates such as "1709."[2]

Original composition aside, it is entirely unclear who might have copied out what and when. In the 1680s, the glyphs lose all their charm and detail and become stick figures, and the writing, although not dissimilar to the earlier style, becomes somewhat more labored and difficult to read, as though someone were attempting to imitate the earlier writing but couldn't quite do it. Or perhaps it was the same man and he was merely trying to save paper, as the writer squeezes more entries onto a page than he had previously, with unhappy results as to clarity. He might simply have been growing old, or losing his enthusiasm and thus growing careless. The situation may have been very complex, with more than one writer involved in the same pages. It was typical for some Nahua annalists to lay out the year line before they began to write, leaving the amount of space they thought they would need (though this did sometimes lead to cramped entries). It is thus quite possible that some older relative drew the glyphs past the point at which he stopped writing, then left the work of actually writing out the entries to someone else, as the handwriting seems to deteriorate as early as the 1660s, before the glyphs are reduced to shadows of their former selves. There are even certain places where additions have been inserted and the writing looks like it might be that of don Manuel himself, though most of it is certainly not his production.

Linguistic evidence within the text itself supports the idea of multiple passings of the torch from generation to generation. To begin with, it contains a most remarkable phenomenon: the writer never once records a noun with a vowel stem as ending in the

---

[1] AAMC, Anales de Puebla y Tlaxcala, no. 1, part 3.

[2] This same person may possibly have been the one to have added an odd opening section pre-1519. Besides having the dating wrong, it does not include the appealing pictographs, but rather primitive copies of them. On the other hand, that section could simply have been faithfully copied by the main author as an addition he discovered the existence of after he began working.

generally-accepted *tl* consonant. Rather, he always spells out the full original ending "tli" or abbreviates it as "tl." with an obvious dot or period. Thus, for example, he puts "xihuitl." or "xihuitli" but never the more common *xihuitl* (year). He has "acatli" or "acatl." but never *acatl* (reed). The later writers of the text continue to reject word-final *tl* at the end of a vowel stem. This might stem from two possible causes: a distinctive local pronunciation and/or an isolated, somewhat less educated or perhaps self-taught original writer who was not fully familiar with standard practice and passed on his idiosyncrasy to other family members. Interestingly, the last abbreviation, that is, the last use of the dot to replace a word-final "i," occurs in 1638, close to a point where a significant stylistic change in the content also occurs, as I noted above. In earlier written Nahuatl, the practice of using dots between phrases had been common, with the intention of indicating breaks between nuclear phrases so that the clause divisions would be more evident. However, the idea was always employed erratically; in Stage 3 it gradually faded away almost completely.[3] The traditionally-minded don Juan Zapata in his manuscript used such dots with great frequency, and in the early segments copied from older texts, I have even seen occasional use of a dot to replace a word-final "i," especially where the pronunciation of the full form would have been necessary in real speech. Perhaps some early Tlaxcalan student had misunderstood what he was seeing, or combined it in his mind with the other more common practice of using dots-turning-to-dashes to indicate the elision of parts of words in abbreviations with superscriptions. The old-fashioned dots might well not be continued when a new writer apparently began to produce the records.

In the entries for the late 1660s, when yet another writer seems to have taken over if we listen to stylistic changes, an additional linguistic shift occurs as well. In many earlier Nahuatl texts, unlike later ones, the preterit formation is not normally marked with the prefix *o* unless it is meant to indicate the perfect tense ("has gone," for example, or the pluperfect "had gone," as opposed to "went"), and that is certainly the case at the start of this text. Beginning in the later 1660s, however, the writer begins to employ the preterit *o* far more frequently than not. In the entry for 1663, for example, the parish priest of Topoyanco dies and it is expressed as follows, without *o*: "momiquili gora topoyanco." Two years later, in the entry for 1665, the king, Philip III, also dies, and it is expressed as follows, this time using the *o*: "omomiquili Dotlahtocahtzin Rey pelipeh tercero." After this, people die both ways, but there is a preponderance of the latter formation. While this evidence is not conclusive, it is certainly supportive of the generational timeline I have sketched above.

We will probably never know whether don Manuel added here and there to the text or drew any of the glyphs himself. It seems clear, however, that someone close to him was responsible for the ultimate redaction. His entire family was apparently to some extent involved in the keeping of history. His father, as we know, collaborated with don Juan Zapata. Don Manuel himself at the very least collected historical annals, and it was through him—perhaps through his death—that a number of sets ended up in the hands of Europeans. Given his residence first in Tlaxcala, then in Puebla, then once again in

---

[3]For discussion and examples of this phenomenon, see Lockhart 2001, pp. 109–10. See also the treatment of the absolutive ending in the Annals of Tlaxcala in Lockhart's chapter here, pp. 57–58.

Tlaxcala, it may even be thanks to him that certain events are reported in both sets of annals in this volume; certainly someone with some connection to the Topoyanco annals was carrying information to and from Puebla. The clincher, perhaps, is that don Manuel is known to have been a mentor to several younger men in the Salazar family, one of whom even took over his first parish when he left it.[1]

Another set of annals, now existing only as two nineteenth-century copies, was written by one Marcelo Salazar ("nehuatl Marcelo Salazar," or "I, Marcelo").[2] He included a list of the Mexica kings, then launched into a text about Tlaxcala which is strikingly similar to the one in this volume, except that the entries are somewhat shorter, include more regular information on bishops, and do not end in 1720. Instead, this Marcelo Salazar began to add his own entries in the 1720s. They included regular commentary on the affairs of Topoyanco and were quite chatty; he even complained about the price of paper. In 1734, he recorded the death of his mother, María Concepción, without any title, possibly indicating that he was of a lower social status than some of the other Salazars of Topoyanco, and certainly that he was not don Manuel's younger brother—or at least not his full brother, as don Manuel's mother was doña Felipa Isabel, daughter of cabildo member don Francisco Andrés.[3] He could have been an illegitimate son of either don Bernabé or don Manuel; there would have been nothing unusual in that. Perhaps such details do not matter, except that they may illustrate how someone could have been fully versed in the annals tradition and yet not formally educated. What is clear is that this man was in some way connected with the Salazars and shared their love of history. They traced their antecedents back to the tlatoani who ruled in Quiyahuiztlan at the time of conquest and had continued to take an active role in the altepetl's governance ever since. The family was closely bound to Tlaxcala's history as it had unfolded since the coming of the Faith; they clearly considered it their duty to keep the memory of that past alive.

What exactly the past suggested to them is an interesting question. For the writer (or writers) of the annals presented here, history is mostly an internal affair. Even in the

---

[1] The latter, probably a younger brother, was el bachiller Nicolás Simeón de Salazar y Flores. Parish records indicate professional connections to other relatives named bachiller Josef Luis de Santiago y Salazar and bachiller Antonio Marcial de Salazar. See Riley 2007, p. 317. Probably in many types of original records all three of these personages bear the don as don Manuel does. Riley has also found a 1723 petition by one don Antonio Simón Rico de Salazar for the native nobility of Tlaxcala to be allowed to found a militia regiment (p. 324).

[2] A manuscript which we no longer have with us, now called "the Bartolache Annals," was summarized and excerpted by Josef Ignacio Bartolache in *Manifiesto satisfactorio anunciado en la Gazeta de México* (México, 1790). He saw it in the Real y Pontifica Universidad in 1787, and copied an introductory paragraph in which a first person author ("nehuatl Marcelo de Salazar") tells us he copied out the words of the old wise ones ("in huehuetixtlamaque"). There are two existing copies of another slightly different original, also now lost, both of which reference Marcelo de Salazar as author. One was copied by Ramírez in AAMC, Anales de Puebla y Tlaxcala, no. 1, part 1, and the other by Federico Gómez de Orozco, and is now in the BNAH, Colección Antigua 872, part 2. It is the latter copy which I read.

[3] See Zapata, p. 616, and Libro de Informaciones de Novicios (see n. 2, p. 22). By this time the women in quite prominent indigenous families were often without the doña or a lineage name, just like María Concepción; don Manuel Salazar's mother had a similar basic name, but her possession of the doña puts her on a higher level.

1680s, there were, after all, only eleven Spanish citizens living in Topoyanco.[4] Governors come and go, taxation rolls are maintained, festivals are prepared for arriving viceroys. When the outside world is mentioned, it is usually because Tlaxcalans are going there: as fighters alongside the Spaniards, as emissaries to the Spanish king, as settlers of new towns (like Puebla). Topoyanco is mentioned occasionally from the beginning, and after the provincial alcaldes were created the name of the one residing in Topoyanco is given from time to time. Toward the end, the name and the doings of the curate of Topoyanco figure prominently, not so much in a religious sense as in a patriotic one. The leadership of Topoyanco is essentially what is being recorded here. In 1669, for example, the Franciscans come down hard on the curate acting as parish priest, don Antonio Torres, for confessing people when, they say, he does not have the right to. In colorful speech reminiscent of earlier styles, he argues vociferously that he does, and it is clear that the writer of the annals is taking his side for reasons that were more political than spiritual. Even here, the text remains essentially an internal political history of Topoyanco.

It is a relatively predictable history, though punctuated by exciting or tragic events. In this it closely resembles the much longer and more detailed set of Tlaxcalan annals written contemporaneously by don Juan Buenaventura Zapata y Mendoza. It differs from that text, however, in that the larger entity of Tlaxcala itself seems less important than the more immediate history of the writer's own locale, Topoyanco. The names of the governors of the entire altepetl are given faithfully, but almost never their subaltepetl affiliation, and the names of the alcaldes are very rarely specified—unless they are local. This may be due not only to the writers' less cosmopolitan perspective, but also to the fact that the writers, and surely the final one, were living in a time when the ancient political principle of rotation was deteriorating, at least at the gubernatorial level. This certainly would have dampened enthusiasm for supporting the larger entity, or made such support less meaningful if one were from the political clique currently in power. Since this set of annals continues for thirty years past don Juan Zapata's, we are able to see the extent of this pattern for the first time (see Table 1). When Charles Gibson made his chart of Tlaxcala's indigenous governors in the sixteenth century, he demonstrated that in that period they adhered strictly to the original arrangement of rotating the office every two years.[5] In the 1590s, they moved to a yearly rotation, but from 1614 Tizatla gained a near stranglehold on the governorshp and held it for most of the first half of the seventeenth century. After at last being ejected, Tizatla was largely excluded from the office for many years. The generation of don Juan Zapata made mighty efforts to restore the rotation of the governorship in a general sense, and with much success. Although certain men ruled for two or three years in a row, others for only one, the classic order of Ocotelolco, Tizatla, Quiyahuiztlan, Tepeticpac was unviolated in all the years from 1683 to 1699. Then after that, in the early eighteenth century, the governorship came to be passed back and forth between Quiyahuiztlan and Ocotelolco alone. The traditional order had disintegrated once again, much as in the early seventeenth century. The writer living in Topoyanco looked on and made no comment.

---

[4]Gerhard 1981, p. 548.
[5]For a complete chart, see Gibson 1967, pp. 224–28.

Table 1: Indigenous governors of Tlaxcala, 1599–1719

Date[a]	Name	Affiliation[b]	Date[a]	Name	Affiliation[b]
1599	D. Toribio González	Oco.	1680	D. Francisco Ruiz	Tep.
1600	D. Juan de Ribas	Oco.	1682	D. Manuel de los Santos	Oco.
1607	D. Juan de Vargas	Tiz.	1683	D. Diego Martín Faustino	Oco.
1608	D. Diego Muñoz Camargo	Oco.	1684	D. Diego de Santiago	Tiz.
1614	D. Gregorio Nacianceno	Tiz.	1686	D. Pascual Ramírez	Qui.
1637	D. Diego Jacinto	Tiz.	1688	D. Francisco Ruiz	Tep.
1640	D. Antonio de Guevara	Tiz.	1690	D. Buenaventura Jiménez	Oco.
1645	D. Diego Jiménez	Oco.	1692	D. Miguel de Celis	Tiz.
1647	D. Pedro Luis Rodríguez	Oco.	1693	D. Pascual Ramírez	Qui.
1648	D. Francisco de la Corona	Tiz.	1696	D. Josef Martín	Tep.
1650	D. Diego Jiménez	Oco.	1697	D. Buenaventura Jiménez	Oco.
1651	D. Juan Zapata	Qui.	1698	D. Miguel de Celis	Tiz.
1652	D. Felipe Ortiz	Tep.	1699	D. Pascual Ramírez	Qui.
1654	D. Juan de los Santos	Oco.	1702	D. Pedro de San Francisco	Oco. (T)
1658	D. Juan Nicolás Cortés	Tiz.	1704	D. Manuel de los Santos	Oco. (T)
1660	D. Bernabé Salazar	Qui.	1705	D. Pascual Ramírez	Qui.
1662	D. Juan Nicolás Cortés	Tiz.	1706	D. Pedro de San Francisco	Oco. (T)
1663	D. Nicolás Méndez de Luna[c]	Qui.	1707	D. Salvador Ramírez	Qui.
1670	D. Juan Miguel Hernández	Oco. (T)	1708	D. Pascual Ramírez	Qui.
1671	D. Francisco Ruiz	Tep.	1709	D. Felipe Jiménez	Oco.
1673	D. Nicolás Méndez de Luna	Qui.	1712	D. Salvador Ramírez	Qui.
1674	D. Juan Miguel Hernández	Oco. (T)	1715	D. Felipe Jiménez	Oco.
1675	D. Diego Martín Faustino	Oco.	1716	D. Pedro de Paredes [d]	Tiz.
1676	D. Diego de Santiago	Tiz.	1717	D. Salvador Ramírez	Qui.
1678	D. Diego Pérez	Qui.		(same through 1719)	
1679	D. Pascual Ramírez	Qui.			

[a]It is understood that each governor took office in the year given next to his name and served until the following year on the table.

[b]Oco. stands for Ocotololco (an accompanying T means Topoyanco), Tiz. for Tizatla, Qui. for Quiyahuiztlan, Tep. for Tepeticpac.

[c]For 1664, don Juan Zapata says that don Juan Miguel Hernández was governor. Zapata was a council member at the time, but Hernández was from Topoyanco, and our annalist is unlikely to have forgotten when his neighbor was governor. A likely explanation suggests itself: Zapata, at that time, was determined that the governorship should rotate, and he particularly disliked don Nicolás Méndez, who had been governor in 1663. He probably insisted to himself that Hernández was the rightful governor after a contentious election, but then gave up the matter when Méndez became further ensconced the next year.

[d]Paredes was a dynastic name in Tizatla, going back to the don Diego de Paredes who was governor in 1554–55 (TA, p. 137). Since Tizatla had been excluded from the governorship for nearly two decades, and for generations no Paredes had been governor, one wonders if another Paredes line might be involved. But the 1716 entry specifies that don Pedro was from Atlihuetzan, in Tizatla. Some tie with one of the then dominant subaltepetl is still possible; the mother of don Juan Zapata of Quiyahuiztlan was a Paredes, for example. Perhaps a family from Tizatla was allowed in briefly for appearances' sake.

Sources: Annals of Tlaxcala (this volume) for all dates and names. Altepetl affiliations from Zapata y Mendoza 1995. (Those who served as governors after Zapata's death had mostly been council members earlier in life and thus are listed with their affiliations at the time of their service in his volume.) Note: There are occasional discrepancies of one year between the annals of this volume and Zapata's; I have followed the annals of this volume.

Tlaxcaltecapan in Cuitlaxcohuapan: the world of don Miguel

IF THE SET OF ANNALS from Tlaxcala reveals itself to have been put in final form by a man living a rather tranquil life in a somewhat isolated region, the set from Puebla is entirely different in this regard. It ends in the early 1690s and was probably put in final format at that time. There are several sets in the Puebla corpus that date from this period, each with a slightly different ending, so most likely a "trunk" version was copied by several different people at about the same time. This makes sense, as the people of the city, who had been living in a sort of golden age in terms of Puebla's many artistic and industrial accomplishments, suddenly found themselves experiencing exceedingly trying times, a period which was certainly of a nature to make people think about the sweep of history and their own role in it. In 1691, the region experienced a particularly frightening solar eclipse. Within a few months, an epidemic struck and rains came in such force as to destroy the crops. The most serious riots in Mexico City's history occurred, and news of them was heard with a shudder in both Puebla and Tlaxcala. Meanwhile, because of the continuing disease, the death toll mounted.

The document that several people apparently copied in this dreadful period reveals itself to have been written "here in San Juan del Río" or "Tlaxcaltecapan" primarily in the 1670s and 80s, when the entries are longest and fullest, though it naturally includes material absorbed from earlier annals in the years up to then. The version published here of course had its own copyist, who was free to make changes, as they all were. His forebears were apparently among the first to settle Xonacatepec ("Onion Hill"), a neighborhood at the farthest reaches of Tlaxcaltecapan as it extended up and away from the river. That neighborhood had been transformed from grassland to settled streets in the 1610s when some Tlaxcalan-descended people from the town of Xonaca del Monte, on the skirts of Matlalcueye, had asked for lands and received them. Other than replacing a simple mention of the founding of Xonacatepec that occurs in other versions of the annals with an actual listing of the first founders, however, the copyist made no other related changes: the place is not mentioned anywhere else and certainly is not the central vantage point of the document.[1]

Again, knowledge of the document's context, of other related versions, may lead us to the probable original author, or at least household of authorship. Another extant manuscript, put in its final form in 1706, very close to the one in this volume in its wording, except that it does not begin until 1610 with the official founding of the greater

---

[1]I do not mean to indicate that the copyist actually scratched out an earlier entry on the founding of Xonacatepec or in any way made an obvious new insertion. But other versions in the AAMC only briefly mention the founding of the new barrio, whereas this set lists the names of the first founders in such detail as only direct descendants would have been likely to recall. For more on Xonacatepec, including its settlement and the building of its church, see Toussaint 1954, p. 209, and Marín Tamayo 1989, p. 69. Tlaxcaltecapan continued to grow to the northeast even before Xonacatepec's founding. The area was sometimes called "El Alto," because it stretched up and away from the river. It had only two small churches even after many years and was known for being home to a number of mestizos and other mixed people.

altepetl, was relatively recently found in the cathedral archive in Puebla.[1] That set of annals contains gorgeous illustrations in traditional red and black ink: where the present writer renders a skeleton as a stick figure, for example, the writer of the other set presents a skeleton that promises to jump off the page. The illustrations appear at the same points in the document, and represent the same subjects; it is just that one set was done by a talented artist, and the other set by someone barely able to represent the notion of what he was seeing. One might think, then, that the manuscript in the Puebla cathedral archive was the original (albeit with the sixteenth century section lost) and the set presented here the copy. But it is not so. A close reading demonstrates that the set presented here was indeed a copy of something: sometimes the author starts at the wrong point, then scratches out a sentence, and proceeds, before including the previously-started material at the proper place. More often than not, however, the annals in this volume have fuller entries, while those from the Puebla cathedral archive often offer obvious paraphrases. There is only one conclusion to be drawn: the two authors independently copied from the same source (or different copies of the same source). One was more interested in reproducing all the text; the other was more interested in vibrant artwork. This book includes the set that provides fuller text. However, the other is useful, not only in demonstrating the richness that the original illustrations likely displayed, but also in that it occasionally provides an letter, syllable, clause, or sentence missing from the text I have transcribed. The importance of this supplementation extends to identifying the probable author, or at least the correct household, as will shortly be seen.

There is no question that the original writer was highly active in the 1670s and 80s, for it is in that period that the entries become fullest and deepest and are very obviously a reflection of the writer's own experiences. It is equally clear that the writer had a particular interest in architecture and building, judging from the inordinate number of references he makes to that subject. This manuscript, likely to have been copied out by a close connection of the writer, was found in the archive wrapped in an architectural drawing dating to approximately 1700. Still, none of this immediately suggests any particular name. Several individuals are referred to in the text as being active in the cabildo at that time and more than one of these as being part of building projects; it seems at first impossible to distinguish who specifically might have been behind this text.

A search for sentences or clauses about potential authors found in the beautifully illustrated set of annals but not in this one helps to reveal what we want to know: between the two annals sets, there are enough references to don Miguel de los Santos, who was

---

[1]The document essentially ends in 1692, but a few further notes are made until 1706, and then "don Francisco Sanches Tocis [?]" signs his name, with the year 1725. One may hazard the guess that the intention of "Tocis" is Tecciz, in view of the priest don Pedro Sánchez Tecciztzin, apparently of Topoyanco, mentioned in the Annals of Tlaxcala, this volume, for the years 1703 and 1710. At the end of the eighteenth century, Joaquín Alejo Meabe, parish priest of San Dionisio Yauhquemecan, Tlaxcala, found, copied, and translated the document. He was apparently Hispanic, but this project and others which he did demonstrate that he genuinely knew Nahuatl. The original manuscript and his copy of it survived together in a church archive in Puebla until the twentieth century. They are now in the possession of the cathedral. A change in church staffing recently made it possible for the document to be placed at the disposal of researchers, and thus a facsimile was published: Gómez García et al. 2000.

elected governor in 1685, to demonstrate a pattern. Although don Miguel is referred to only slightly more frequently than some other prominent figures, the *way* in which he is mentioned is consistently different. He does not just become governor like all other governors who have come before and will come after. We are given details, told not only that he erected a new stone cross for the indigenous cabildo, but also where he put the old wooden one. While governor, he sends someone to Mexico City to seek a particular record book that was carried off there by a previous census taker. The writer of the annals is intimately familiar with that story; he is aware of the census-taker's name and well versed in tribute payment categories.[2] Don Miguel even tells off the alcalde mayor when the latter attempts to make all indigenous people living in the central area of the city move back to the barrios. After the period in which don Miguel is governor, he is not simply named as the man who will administer church renovations; rather, he does his work beautifully, while those who come after him leave disasters in their wake. He not only consults with Spanish artisans about building projects, he is part of conversations which he reports. Again he confronts a difficult Spanish official, this time one who is trying to extract a bribe. We find none of this kind of detail consistently surrounding references to anyone else. While it is most probable that don Miguel himself wrote the words, it is also perfectly plausible that some close connection did so.[3]

It was indeed a proud moment in Tlaxcaltecapan's history. In 1685, when don Miguel becomes governor, we learn that he is the first governor from his district ever to serve. This at first seems surprising, since the Tlaxcalans were the first to settle and were close to the Franciscans, but in fact it is logical. The people of the centrally located San Pablo barrio had as their patrons the Dominicans, who were very influential in the city. (Even the bishop Juan de Palafox, a regular who was known for trying to curb the orders, was supportive of them, helping them found a new convent.) Some of San Pablo's residents, we must remember, apparently came with the original Spanish settlers who set out from Mexico City, and others were among early Tlaxcalan settlers who did not come in the train of the Franciscans but were powerful and independent enough to settle on their own land to the north of the city. Perhaps not surprisingly, the cabildo building itself was located in the barrio of San Pablo, as was the city's only hospital dedicated to the care of

---

[2]Most of the material in this paragraph is documented in the annals in this volume, but for this remarkable detail, see Gómez García et al. 2000, p. 64. In the entry for 1685, we find: "Sano iPan xihuitl in otlatitlan Don Mig de los Santtos Jues Gr in mexico in ocanatto Libros de cuentas yhua tesasion inic otepouh Jues D fernando delgado inic omoyectlali in tlacalaquili muchi otzinquis inic mi [?] miec ocatca in sen tlaxilacali Yhuan inic oquitlapopolhuiq̄ in Ye huehuentzitzin yhua ye ilamatzitzin inic quintocaYotia Reservados." ("In this same year, don Miguel de los Santos, judge-governor, sent to Mexico City to get the books of accounts and rates from when the judge don Fernando Delgado took a census and put the tribute right; it was all reduced because it had been too much [in every tlaxilacalli? in the whole tlaxilacalli?], and they pardoned the old men and the old women [from paying tribute], calling them the exempted.") Note that although the word *tlaxilacalli* for a constituent district of an altepetl, though it is not found in the Annals of Puebla in the present volume, in fact appears in this closely related version.

[3]The writer was someone who knew the details of don Miguel's life, and who was not equally proud when the next governor was elected from San Juan del Río a few years later; thus at the very least, he was a family member.

the indigenous. The subaltepetl of Santiago did not have a history of illustrious connections or a comparable collection of architectural monuments, but it had a substantial population. Given Cholula's proximity, more migrants seem to have come to Puebla from that area than from Tlaxcala; at the end of the eighteenth century their barrio of Santiago would have far more indigenous citizens than any other section.[1] And finally, the Franciscans, the allies of the Tlaxcalan settlers, had significantly lost in power after 1640, when parishes (formerly called *doctrinas*) were taken out of their hands and given over to secular priests; they had not, after all, been able to be very effective patrons of their Tlaxcalan neighbors. To the people of Tlaxcaltecapan, with their long sense of history, and their pride in having been the first to settle and help build the town, it was profoundly gratifying, at long last, in 1685, to have one of their own elected as supreme indigenous leader.[2]

No wonder that don Miguel—or some eager member of his extended family—had such a strong need to record the events of his day, putting in copious details of a kind seen in few other annals. It is even possible that it was at this point that the family took a much simpler, previously existing set of annals and put it into its present form, though most likely they had been working on it just as it is for a number of years, don Miguel having been an active community leader for a long time. To make the times even more compelling, the community in this period was embarked on a major renovation of its church.[3] Perhaps to modern ears this may seem a relatively minor affair, but it was not so to those concerned. The church represented their altepetl of Tlaxcaltecapan. It was a beautiful and lofty emblem of their contribution to a universe that was greater than themselves, but of which they were an integral part. Such events certainly called for the keeping of an elaborate and dramatic xiuhpohualli. In after years, numerous people in the barrio San Francisco made copies of the precious history.[4]

To a significant degree the document is a "classic" set of annals, recording the ongoing, unbreakable chain of local political authority, and thus the very existence of the altepetl. In line with the strong general Nahua interest in numerical order, seen for example in Chimalpahin as well, the governors are always listed with their ordinal number. "He was the third governor." "He was the fourth." (See Table 2.) This was so no matter what crisis or crises had occurred, or how contentious an election was.

Despite their classic nature, however, in certain regards these annals depart dramatically from any kind of an insular indigenous world. The writer—let us call him don Miguel, as it almost certainly was he, and certainly someone closely identified with his

---

[1]Contreras Cruz, Téllez Guerrero, and Pardo Hernández 1999.

[2]Only further research can fully clarify the relationships between the three indigenous altepetl and their constituent parts. When the city was founded, San Francisco consisted essentially of San Juan del Río, in the vicinity of the monastery, but as the city grew, African, Spanish and other indigenous neighborhoods sprouted up nearby, all becoming part of "San Francisco." It is not clear whether "Tlaxcaltecapan" expanded or remained an alternate name for San Juan del Río.

[3]Toussaint 1954, pp. 202–03.

[4]Krug in "Nahuatl Annals" has proven that no fewer than three of the sets of annals included in the AAMC shared a common root source with the version presented in this volume, and of course we have seen that the Puebla cathedral archive's version (Gómez García et al. 2000) did as well.

Table 2: Indigenous governors of Puebla to 1692

Place in order	Date of election[a]	Name
First governor	159?	D. Juan Bautista
Second governor	1603	D. Juan Calzón
Third governor	1610	D. Juan Bautista
Fourth governor	1629	D. Diego Pérez
Fifth governor	1639	D. Bartolomé Cortés
Sixth governor	1652	D. Blas de Galicia[b]
Seventh governor	1679	D. Josef de Ribera[c]
Eighth governor	1681	D. Juan Andrés
Ninth governor	1682	Mateo Jaén
Tenth governor	1684	D. Felipe de Santiago
Eleventh governor	1685	D. Miguel de los Santos
Twelfth governor	1686	D. Miguel de la Cruz
Thirteenth governor	1687	D. Josef Lázaro[d]
Fourteenth governor	1688	D. Juan de Galicia
Fifteenth governor	1691	D. Diego de León
Sixteenth governor	1692	D. Juan de Galicia

[a]It is assumed that a given governor served from the date of election until the date of the next election, but that is not positively known in all cases.

[b]Expelled in 1677, with a vacancy following.

[c]Murdered in 1679, with a vacancy following.

[d]Died that year; his son of the same name finished out the term.

Sources: Annals of Puebla (this volume). Mentions of the first governor and the governor serving in 1692 are found in Spanish documents and cited in Leicht 1967, p. 178.

interests—was a cosmopolitan individual. Puebla was the lynchpin of the main thoroughfare, the trunk line, between the coast and the capital; what happened in those two relatively faraway places was part of the people's consciousness. When it is rumored that the blacks of the capital are on the edge of rebellion, the story is alluded to. When pirates attack and hold Veracruz, it becomes one of the most frightening events of the writer's life, judging from his tone. Crimes against the Christian church are described with avid interest, whether or not they take place in Puebla. Nor is don Miguel's involvement with the wider world limited to a few highly sensationalized events. On a regular basis, he is involved with the Spanish world—in participating in ceremonies, making purchases, working with craftsmen. All the evidence indicates that he is a practical and successful man negotiating effectively in a busy urban environment; he also clearly prides himself on this being the case.

Indeed, don Miguel sees himself no less as a citizen of the wider entity of Puebla than as a member of his indigenous altepetl. He frequently adopts the perspective of a Puebla townsman, putting the city's general business over and above indigenous matters. Certainly crimes against the public, often committed by non-Indians against non-Indians, take up a substantial portion of his record: hangings and public burnings are described in excruciating detail. And he takes pride in each and every viceregal visit to the city, noting it happily when that visiting dignitary admired the beautiful churches. (Of course he seems most delighted when a viceroy visits the barrio of San Francisco, even mentioning where he went on foot and where he rode in the coach.) When the bishop of Tlaxcala, resident in Puebla, is named interim viceroy, the indigenous citizens are so delighted at the honor done to their home community that they partake in the general joy, even mounting their horses for racing and doing acrobatic tricks, a form of celebration far more typical of Spaniards. Don Miguel seems perfectly content when, during his term of office as governor, the alcalde mayor decides to organize public events of his own which partially coincide with San Juan Bautista's feast day, the celebration of which would normally have been orchestrated by Tlaxcaltecapan. (He makes no comment about the fact that the alcalde's celebrations consist of publicly torturing dogs, cats and other animals, but seems to treat it as a notable spectacle.)

And there is other, more subtle evidence of the indigenous community's degree of immersion in the wider, Hispanic world. Analysis of the language of the text in comparison to the Nahuatl of earlier eras reveals the depth of acculturation experienced by don Miguel and his peers, as will be demonstrated in the following chapter by my colleague Lockhart; readers will find loan verbs abundant, not simply loan nouns, and numerous expressions which have been re-envisioned in keeping with Spanish concepts, among other important elements. Comparison of the handwriting in this document with that in the Puebla cathedral archives would seem to indicate that literacy had been adopted as part of a way of life by a range of households. The writing in the latter piece is quite neat, even stylized, with relatively standard capitalization practices. These facts, as well as the copyist's fine European-style drawings, would seem to indicate that he had rather tight connections to the Spanish world, probably through the church. The copyist of the annals in this volume, on the other hand, is often less particular and sprinkles capital letters liberally, which indeed was the normal practice of writers of Nahuatl in his day. Let us look at two examples. First, the preterit marker *o* so frequently used by this time is very often capitalized, and the same treatment is occasionally extended to appearances of the letter *o* at the start of any word. (This widespread trait may go back to the fact that in some earlier Spanish writing a loop went up over an *o* so that it was a bit like a capital letter.) Second, the letter *c* is often capitalized if it appears twice within a single word. A double example of this is found almost immediately in the Puebla annals, in the entry for 1530: "yanCuiCan tlatoCatiCo mexico" ("He came to rule in Mexico City for the first time"). The phenomenon continues throughout the text, though not with absolute consistency. The word *cocolistli* ("sickness," as spelled in Stage 3), for example, almost always appears as "CoColistli," though there are exceptions. These traits and others, ultimately originating in a seventeenth-century Spanish change of calligraphic style, will be found in Stage 3 texts all over central Mexico and are another indication that Nahuatl speakers constituted a cultural area.[1]

Another aspect of the community's cosmopolitanism may be seen in don Miguel's treatment of his neighbors of African descent. Africans are known to have been present at the city's initial founding, functioning as skilled craftsmen. By the 1570s, large numbers of enslaved Africans had also been brought to the vicinity of Veracruz and Tlaxcala to work on sugar plantations. By the mid-seventeenth century, through flight, manumission,

---

[1]These phenomena are found well illustrated, for example, in the eighteenth-century wills of the Toluca Valley. See Pizzigoni 2007.

and self-purchase, many of their children and grandchildren had ended up in Puebla; only Mexico City had a larger population of free blacks.[2] A barrio inhabited largely by people of African descent existed next door to Tlaxcaltecapan. They had their own chapels and their own cofradías.[3] In 1683, when the pirates attacked Veracruz, a small, previously existing black militia was expanded and reorganized. They themselves seemed to want to be categorized as either *pardo* (tawny, mixed) or *moreno* (dark).[4] Our writer is hardly race-blind: he always mentions it when a person under discussion is *mulato* (a less positive Spanish term than *pardo*) or *tliltic* ("black," a direct translation of the Spanish *negro*), whereas he never calls a specific person indigenous, taking indigenous people as the point of reference. He does not seem to be actively hostile to either African-descended group, however, unless one counts recitations of their known crimes as hostility. This may be seen as merely a reflection of reality, however, since many runaway slaves living in remote rural areas as well as impoverished freed slaves did in fact turn to crime, for obvious and understandable reasons. In reporting two burnings of mulatto homosexuals, don Miguel may share the stereotyped notion of Spaniards of his time and place that mulattoes were associated with homosexuality, but it is hard to say, since he viewed it as his duty to report without much comment on any execution. We perhaps do see some corporate hostility when the cabildo ejects a Mateo Jaén, apparently of mixed African and indigenous descent, along with other members not fully indigenous, and don Miguel may show personal animosity in not according him the title don even when he was governor, the only one of the long list to be so treated. In any case, if we can speak of a relative lack of overt hostility, it is particularly noteworthy in view of marriage records indicating that significant numbers of urban indigenous women married blacks and mulattoes in this same period.[5] At the very least, we can say that don Miguel was well aware of sharing his world with Afro-Mexicans: he mentions them at least as often as he mentions residents of San Pablo or Santiago, the other two indigenous altepetl.

Yet if don Miguel was an astute citizen of the world, bilingual in a figurative and almost certainly a literal sense, he was at the same time profoundly religious. This is not surprising, as Puebla's founding was to some extent guided by the religious orders; it became the region's episcopal seat and in time boasted more churches than any other city in Mexico.[6] In his own immediate neighborhood, don Miguel was surrounded by no fewer than five churches (not to mention a string of chapels extending up the hill as far as

---

[2]To follow the work on Africans in early Mexico, see Aguirre Beltrán 1946, Palmer 1976, Cardoso 1983, Bennett 2003, Restall 2005, von Germeten 2006, Vinson and Restall 2009, and especially Restall 2009. In 1681, the parish of San José, which contained most of the indigenous quarters of San Francisco and San Pablo, contained about 1200 indigenous households and 800 households labeled "negros, mestizos y mulatos" (Gerhard 1981).

[3]The Franciscan monastery contained a chapel dedicated to San Benito de Palermo and maintained by the black population. See Zerón Zapata, p. 82. The Dominican establishment likewise was home to a Capilla de los Morenos, where, it was said, all mixed peoples were welcome. See Toussaint 1954, p. 218.

[4]For a thorough study, see Vinson 2001, especially pp. 30–31, 46–47, 108–11, 202–03.

[5]Sierra Silva 2008. Sierra Silva is embarked on a much needed study of relations between indigenous and African peoples in colonial Puebla. See also Castillo Palma and Kellogg 2005.

[6]See the illuminating map in Toussaint 1954.

he could see). The sound of church bells ringing became a part of his consciousness. He always knew what time of day it had been whenever an event occurred, sometimes down to the quarter hour. And he always knew which saint's day it was. Church festivals seem to have been the central signposts in his life. In his yearly entries, who the bishop is—and what he says or does—seems to be more important than events relating to the local Spanish magistrate or even the viceroy.

All the religious movements of his time seem to have touched don Miguel. He takes part in the cult, now traditional among both Nahuas and Spaniards, of saints who were patrons of local churches and of their constituencies. He is swept off his feet by the new wave of "missions" brought from Europe by the Franciscans and Jesuits, revivalist campaigns with a full panoply of drama, music, extravagant testimonials, and priests going into the streets ("No one wanted to go to sleep"). The proto-national cult of the Virgin of Guadalupe, growing since mid-seventeenth century, had also reached don Miguel, for the date of the supposed apparition is recorded in the entry for 1530.[1] Yet nearly all the members of the Tlaxcala-Puebla family of annals (including the Tlaxcalan text in this volume) refer to the incident, as a result of the constant borrowing from one another, so that the entry perhaps does not show anything particular about the author. Only one other entry, dated 1653, mentions Guadalupe, and in the part written in don Miguel's adulthood, he reports on the saints of Puebla only. In his own mind he seems to imbue the images of those saints (including Mary, and indeed most of them are female), with lives of their own. They go up and down hills almost of their own volition; only rarely are they explicitly carried. "There she slept," he says of Mary, when she is left in a particular church overnight.

Cosmopolitan though our writer was, he certainly had imbibed the superstitions of his world. Earthquakes and comets, for example, are always unsettling to him; sometimes they are seen as omens of subsequent events. The closing paragraph of the text describes a solar eclipse which was widely believed to be a harbinger of the terrible epidemic which followed—and which almost certainly had begun by the time the writer described the occurrences. When the darkness covering the sun finally recedes, the narrator seems to imagine that it takes the form of a black man, like one of the anthropomorphic deities of old, suddenly falling downward. Yet his vision was not necessarily indicative of older indigenous patterns of thought; the concept of omens, for example, was certainly shared by Spaniards of the time as well. So was his whole view of saints. It is difficult to determine to what extent don Miguel's immersion in a wider contemporary world had shaped him in this regard and to what extent he was following older norms.

The close degree of contact with the wider world had in some ways, of course, profoundly altered native ways. Given the nature of the xiuhpohualli, this is most obvious in our source as regards the relationship between political and social life. In Tlaxcala in this same period, the self-consciously traditionalist don Juan Zapata still envisions cabildo membership as the prerogative of senior members of each teccalli. He calls them "tlahtoque" (plural of the old *tlatoani*, long used for ruling bodies in general). He regularly

---

[1]In 1738, a later possessor of the manuscript used the 1530 entry to calculate on a blank folio how many years had gone by since the Virgin's apparition.

distinguishes between indigenous people who are *pipiltin*, nobles, and *macehualtin*, commoners. The annals of Tlaxcala in this volume waver in this regard: the later writers do not use *tlatoque* in their own era, for example, but they faithfully copy it in earlier segments. But for don Miguel in Puebla, the break with the past is more definite. The whole vocabulary for indigenous nobility is absent, not even used for governors and cabildo members, who are simply elders or leaders. The words *tlatoani* and *tlatoque* are reserved throughout for Spaniards or the deity. *Macehualli* exists only in the plural mock reverential form that throughout the Nahuatl-speaking world had come to mean indigenous people in general, including those of highest rank. The Tlaxcalan annals are much the same, but do contain hints and relics of the older meaning of "commoner."[2]

It is not that a sense of respect for prominent members of the community has disappeared. The use of the title "don" is still strongly indicative of perceived rank. It attached to certain offices with great regularity, and was equally regularly withheld from lesser officials, as will be discussed in the next chapter. Some of these figures may well have been the descendants of pipiltin who migrated from Tlaxcala (the Galicia family, for example, was well known there), but even if so, the notion of the teccalli and all its attendant terminology had long since disappeared; in Puebla, people no longer spoke in those terms, not even those of highest rank and most punctilious about distinctions.

With the disappearance of the idea of traditional indigenous nobility from the annals, native women also recede into shadow. From a male history-keeper's point of view, a female commoner would rarely matter enough to mention, but a *cihuapilli*, a noblewoman, could. She might on rare occasions rule, or more often, help to establish the legitimacy of a particular lineage. When the son of Diego Múñoz Camargo, the famous Tlaxcalan mestizo historian, decided that he wanted to be accepted by his paternal grandmother's indigenous community, he attained his goal by marrying doña Francisca Maxixcatzin, who had inherited the rulership of Ocotelolco. Don Juan Zapata does not fail to mention her, as well as other important political connections established through female lines. But for the equally communicative don Miguel, with the various teccalli now no more than a blurry communal memory—if they were remembered at all—women's political importance has disappeared. In fact, the only women he mentions in his text *are* of the status of a cihuapilli—but they are all Spanish, the wives and daughters of kings and viceroys.

Yet despite all the forms of cultural contact and the resulting changes—or indeed, perhaps because of them—the sense of being *indigenous* has if anything, it seems to me, only been enhanced. On the most basic level, we see a process of altepetl formation. In the course of the sixteenth century indigenous residential agglomerations of often quite miscellaneous origins worked and prayed together to the point that they began to think of themselves as cohesive altepetl, and then the three altepetl that had arisen in this fashion accepted an overarching identity embracing all indigenous people, of whatever subethnicity and geographic origin, who lived in the city of Puebla. They formed, in short, a complex altepetl in the ancient indigenous style, which in due course, early in

---

[2]All of this terminology is listed and explained in greater detail in Lockhart's chapter on language, pp. 60–61.

the seventeenth century, was formally recognized by Spanish authority.

And there are other more subtle ways in which a sort of indigenous identity manifests itself in the text. We have already seen the readiness with which don Miguel's anger at any interfering Spanish authority is touched off. Even epidemics are not merely mentioned, as they are in the Tlaxcalan annals, but the ethnicity of the victims is often specified: in the early macro-epidemics indigenous people, and in things of don Miguel's own time, which he saw and which drew his comments about their frightful nature, sometimes other ethnicities as well. Of the cough epidemic of 1686 he says, "Very many people died of it, indigenous people as well as Spaniards and all kinds of people." Don Miguel's perception of ethnicity was nuanced. The 1682 bread crisis was a head-on conflict between Spaniards and indigenous people and is explicitly so recognized. Yet the real villains were the Spanish members of the attempted monopoly combine, and don Miguel proudly notes that other Spaniards took the side of the indigenous, also gloating over the (Spanish) alcalde mayor's punishment of the perpetrators of the plot.

Upon the election as governor of don Nicolás Méndez, the son of a Portuguese man and an indigenous noblewoman, the author of this volume's Annals of Tlaxcala does not refer to the fact that he is a mestizo. The more fulsome don Juan Zapata does allude to it in his own annals of Tlaxcala, but only seems troubled by it when he becomes personally angry at Méndez. In the Puebla annals, on the other hand, the author is consistently more threatened by the possibility of people of mixed descent gaining control of the cabildo. In 1684, the members send to Mexico to get an order to have all such outsiders expelled. Other indigenous had demanded the like in other situations—it happened in Tlaxcala as well at about the same time—but there seems to have been more determination in this case, and the members did succeed in obtaining their order, and carried it out, even expelling the part-African Mateo Jaén, who had risen as high as governor only two years before.

In 1686, our author at one point calls don Juan de Galicia simply "the mestizo" when he tries to become governor, but he was in fact a member of a prestigious indigenous family, unlike Mateo Jaén. The generalized resistance to him that our annalist reports (he makes it clear that don Juan also had supporters in the community, though he belittles it) was probably mostly a reflection of the fact that an older relative of his, don Blas de Galicia, had clung to power for 25 years after assuming the governorship in 1652; he had to have made enemies. One clique supported him; a larger clique didn't. Still, it seems the suspicion of the younger man was truly somewhat related to his mixed blood status: our author does not seem hostile to the older don Blas, for example, only indirectly alluding to a great crisis in 1677. (We only know for a fact that he was expelled from office by his own people due to a Spanish record of the event.)[1] A descendant in whose keeping the present set of annals later resided wrote on the outside of the packet, "Sr Dn Blas de galisia, Gobernador de la ciudad de los angeles, digo yo, francisco gomes." ("Sr. don Blas de Galicia, governor of the city of Los Angeles; so say I, Francisco Gómez.") So the family or faction storing this copy did not pass down any hostility to the senior Galicia, just to the junior one, the mestizo.

---

[1] Leicht 1967, p. 178.

Both Galicia family influence and don Juan's access to Spanish patronage must have been significant; he was elected governor, after all, in 1688, and though he served for only a year, was re-elected in the crisis of 1692.[2] In defense of those who resisted him merely because he had a Spanish parent or grandparent, we should remember that in a multicultural urban environment, their concerns were not entirely groundless. If they let people into their midst who had close ties to powerful outsiders, it would only be a matter of time before those outsiders—who had enormous capital at their disposal, both real and cultural—supplanted them, and with them would go their language, their customs, and their history. This younger don Juan had established a household in Analco,[3] a more recently formed largely Tlaxcalan neighborhood just to the south of Tlaxcaltecapan, so the governorship was not quite returning to San Pablo de los Naturales. Even this, however, was not enough to mollify our don Miguel. He wanted a fully indigenous governor. If he died in the epidemic that began in 1691, as seems possible, even probable, given the end date of the manuscript, then he never knew that don Juan de Galicia was elected again in 1692 in the midst of all the troubles. Perhaps it is as well.

In his time on earth, don Miguel had certainly done his part to keep Nahua traditions alive. He did so not merely in his political activities, but also in his writings—in his choice of genre and topics, as well as in his vocabulary and syntax, as Lockhart indicates in the following chapter. Equally importantly, even in the midst of his urban, cosmopolitan lifestyle, he retained his interest in the same sorts of public events that his ancestors had likewise found compelling. He had retained, in short, a highly traditional sense of what mattered. That he was bent on commemorating the foundation and ongoing political life of the altepetl—his own subaltepetl, as well as the complex altepetl of which it was a part—is already clear. But the phenomenon went beyond even that, was both broader and more specific.

The subjects don Miguel treated were almost all modern iterations of ancient themes. The old xiuhpohualli were records not only of the installation of kings, but also of their ceremonial anointing and later of their deaths. In don Miguel's text, readers will find a litany of high appointments—of kings, queens, viceroys, alcaldes mayores, archbishops, bishops and indigenous governors—punctuated by mentions of the deaths of such important people. We can assume that the old pictoglyphs reminded performers to speak of the sacrifices made or the songs chanted at kings' coronations and funerals, and likewise here we often hear of the processions, the prayers, once even of the number of candles needed. During a precontact king's period of rule he was responsible for mammoth building projects requiring communal labor—palaces, temples to the gods, water works. One of don Miguel's favorite subjects in his annals is, of course, building projects: now they mostly relate to churches or convents, but water projects have not lost their fascination. Wars once dominated political life. That is no longer true in don Miguel's time, but he finds plenty of enemies to dwell on in his writings. Rioters in Mexico City, savage Chichimeca, rebelling slaves, dangerous criminals, pirates, and infidel English all must be defeated, and regularly are. Generally there are no prisoners of war to bring home, as there once were, but when English women prisoners are brought back to

---

[2]Ibid.   [3]Ibid.

be distributed as laborers, it is a matter to be mentioned, though they are not indigenous and don Miguel himself may never have seen them. The natural world looms as large as it ever did, with epidemics, floods and meteorological phenomena serving as defining experiences and also as omens. We can almost feel that a pantheon of gods still watches over these dramatic events encircling mortals, for don Miguel seems to feel the presence of each and every saint who marches through his pages.

Even when don Miguel reports on peculiarly Spanish activities, he often does so in a style of his own. Through him, we learn for the first time of a campaign of burnings of accused homosexuals. For the first one, the church organized an elaborate procession before the burning. Don Miguel does not talk about the affair in terms of sin, but speaks of it rather from the perspective of a connoisseur of public ceremonies. He says that the *tlapitzalli* (a traditional Nahuatl word for any wind instrument) "was not blown as it is when someone is hanged, but as when a feast day is celebrated." It was almost as if he were an ethnographer in that moment. This was not the awed reaction the priests were likely hoping for, or may even assumed they would elicit. But this time, the pen was in an indigenous man's hand.

Notes on transcription and translation

IN MY TRANSCRIPTION, I have attempted to be entirely faithful to the original documents as regards every character, mark of punctuation, and abbreviation. As is standard, the strings of letters that appear in the original texts have been re-spaced to make words in conformity with modern grammatical understandings. I have not attempted to maintain the original divisions, which not only represent an obstacle to modern readers but are also arbitrary and hard to detect reliably. My only real doubt about how to proceed has arisen in the area of capitalization (see p. 34): it is quite possible that another transcriber would have made different decisions in this regard at certain points, as the letters don't usually vary in shape, only in size along a continuum, but I believe I have succeeded in capturing the general impression the texts give.

Only in one respect is my transcription somewhat unusual by current scholarly standards: I have had access to other versions of the same sets of annals, as discussed above, and sometimes, in the case of the Annals of Puebla, when the copyist has accidentally failed to include a syllable or a word, and I have found the missing piece present in the parallel text, I have included it, but always inside brackets and in italics. This is possible to do in my work, though it is not generally possible in most other philological studies, because of the close degree of relationship among the Tlaxcala-Puebla family of annals. In nearly all cases I feel certain that the letters inside brackets were actually present in the manuscript from which our present version was copied.

In my translation, I have tried to downplay word-for-word literalism and use good idiomatic English phrasing that best represents what the writer was trying to convey to a well versed Nahua audience. What I hope to do is to introduce a greater sense of nuance and implication, wherever I feel certain that I have grasped them. For many generations now, scholars translating texts from European and Asian languages have worked to improve the degree of nuance they are able to convey; scholars of indigenous languages of the Americas still have a long way to go in this respect. Of course I have tried to be as faithful as possible: the last thing I want to do is to introduce unintended meanings. But at the same time I have assumed it is important to put things in such as way as to communicate the full intent. It seems to me that a too-literal approach, rather than being more faithful to the original, is actually less so, in that the resulting stilted phrasing or [to us] inexplicable metaphors end up infantilizing speakers who were actually eloquent and sophisticated. I have occasionally introduced footnotes whose sole purpose is to clarify my process of thought. I hope that those notes may be helpful to fellow Nahuatl scholars.

For non-readers of Nahuatl or relatively new students I include the following list of words, where the choices I have made in the translation seem to me to require comment.

Place names:

Cuitlaxcohuapan. This was the indigenous name for the place selected for the settlement of the Spanish city Puebla de los Angeles. Its etymology is obscure. The older form, still occurring occasionally in the texts, is Cuetlaxcohuapan, and most agree that the name's first element is *cuetlaxtli*, "cured hide, leather." A 1534 Spanish statement analyzes the word as "río de cueros," "hide river,"[1] but that interpretation ignores the *co* universally given as part of the name. Since *cohua* is "to buy," one thinks of a place of buying hides, which makes sense in that the region was known for trade, as it was located in a neutral zone between the altepetl of Tlaxcala, Tepeaca, and Cholula, but the verb cannot be integrated into the construct morphologically. We are left with *cohuatl/coatl*, "serpent," as a possibility for the second element. "Hide serpent" does not recommend itself as a Nahua notion, and the "snakeskin" sometimes put forth reverses the structure of the compound. If the first element were *cuetlachtli* instead of the very similar *cuetlaxtli*, we might have the more idiomatic construction "wolf serpent." The orthography *-cohua-* could hide an elision, i.e., *cohua-a-*, thus allowing for the notion of water or a river in the name. In any case, in both sets of annals in this volume, the writers refer to the city in question throughout as Cuitlaxcohuapan, not Puebla, and in the English translation I have followed their example. I risk confusing some readers, but hope to demonstrate the tenacity with which the people stuck to their own place name.

Mexico. When our annalists refer in the originals to "Mexico," they are using a Nahuatl word, meaning "place where the Mexica are," and they mean the city, never New Spain as a whole. In my translation, for clarity's sake, I have put "Mexico City," believing as I do that this does not essentially alter their idiomatic usage, though they do not explicitly refer to a city; the reference is to the composite entity including preconquest Tenochtitlan and the postconquest Spanish capital called the Ciudad de México, Mexico City.

Tepeaca and other local place names. One of Cuitlaxcohuapan's closest neighboring communities—indeed, one of those that contributed land upon the city's foundation—was the altepetl of Tepeyacac. The final "c" was often rendered in rapid speech as a glottal stop, and Spaniards soon began to spell the word as they were hearing it, that is, as "Tepeaca." The writer of the annals of Puebla, despite his literacy within the Spanish world, clung tenaciously to the Nahuatl rendering, "Tepeyacac." Despite the desire I have

---

[1] López de Villaseñor 1961, p. 64.

expressed above to remind readers consistently of the persistence of such Nahuatl forms, I have, after internal debate, elected to render the town's name in my translation as did the Spaniards, rather than the Nahuas, so as to ensure that readers will always understand the reference made and be able to locate it on other maps. This is perhaps especially important in this specific case, as readers might otherwise confuse a mention of "Tepe-yacac" with the place of that name now called "Tepeyac," near Mexico City, which is also mentioned in these annals, as it is the location of the Virgin of Guadalupe's supposed apparition. Even where it may be less important, however, I have followed the same guiding principle in regards to other local place names, in general rendering them as they appeared in the Spaniards' parish census of 1681 and have most often continued to appear since. Thus, for example, readers will find "Nopalocan," though a rendering more faithful to the Nahuatl would be "Nopallocan," and "Totimehuacan" rather than "Toto-mihuacan." The variations in the spelling of some names, such as the latter, may also be ascribed to slightly shifting regional and perhaps even personal pronunciations of certain words, but the issue is deeper than that; the alternate versions generally reflect Spanish efforts to spell the Nahuatl words as they heard them.[1] There is no perfect way to handle the situation, and I have violated my own rule on occasion. In 1681, for example, the Spanish priest reported on the numbers of parishioners in "Huexotzingo," which is so wrong according to Nahuatl orthographic rules that I could not follow him and have put "Huexotzinco" everywhere instead, just as our annalists did.

Social categories:

Macehualli. The predominant meaning of this word before the conquest was "com-moner." It originally meant "human being," and could be used as a residual category for people who would be outside of any more specific categories established, or in reference to the total population of an entity. It is translated as "commoner" in most scholarly work, and not inaccurately (although when possessed it meant someone's vassal or subject of any rank). In the two texts included in this volume, the writers in almost every case of the word's use did not simply mean to refer to "ordinary people" or "commoners." Instead, they were referring to their own broader ethnic grouping, including those of high rank, in opposition to people labeled Spanish. They meant, in other words, those whom we would today call indigenous people. They had not embraced the word *indio* that the Spaniards used to describe them, though the term was known to them—perhaps because they also knew about its pejorative connotation. In the early years after the conquest, they had been hard put to come up with any term that would work to categorize them-selves all together in opposition to the outsiders. They had never previously thought of themselves as a unified set of beings, except insofar as they were "human," but that word would not distinguish them from the Spaniards. At first, they gropingly used the term *nican tlaca* ("here-people, local people").[2] Over time, they worked out different linguistic strategies. In the annals of the Tlaxcala-Puebla valley, as in numerous other places in the Nahuatl-speaking world, the word *macehualli* resolves the difficulty. I have not wanted to translate it as "Indian," out of concern that it might appear to readers that they were

---

[1]See Gerhard 1981.

[2]This concept is explored in Lockhart 1993.

actually using that word.[3] But the terms "people" or "commoners" do not convey what they clearly meant to convey. I have thus settled on "indigenous people" or sometimes "natives."

Quixtiano. This is, technically speaking, the Nahuatl rendering of the Spanish word *cristiano*, or Christian. In later generations, of course, Nahuas became deeply familiar with the word *cristiano*, reborrowed it in an easily recognizable form, and today use it constantly. By the time that began to happen, however, the term *quixtiano* had fossilized as a word for "Spaniard." In some parts of Mexico, it remains in common parlance to this day, side by side with *cristiano*.[4] We find it used in such a way in the two texts in this volume. There seems to me still to have been a whiff of "Christian" in its use, entirely absent from the alternate term *caxtiltecatl*, Castilian, or *español*, but in my translation I have nevertheless used "Spaniard" because the authors certainly did not mean to imply an opposition to pagans, Jews, or any other religious group. We must remember, after all, that the Spaniards themselves in sources of the conquest sometimes say "españoles" and sometimes "cristianos," with the same meaning.

Chino. The Spaniards used this term to describe people from Asia or of Asian descent in general. Most often, they were really talking about people from the Philippines, where they were established. Speakers of Nahuatl picked the word up and used it to describe those in their own community who were of partially Asian (again, generally Filipino) descent. However, both Spaniards and Nahuas sometimes used it in reference to people who were mixed in other regards, leading to a suspicion on my part that it may have designated a mixed person of no particular provenance but the set of whose eyes was reminiscent of Asia. (It is used that way in certain Nahuatl-speaking Mexican pueblos today.) One scholar has noted that in colonial Puebla, it was often a colloquial term for a person of mixed indigenous and African descent,[5] and that is how it seems to be found in the Puebla annals. Because it would seem to be impossible to come up with an English term to convey all this, I have simply retain the word *chino* in the translation.

Mestizo. The Spanish word *mestizo* technically referred to a person who was part indigenous, part European, and that is the way it seems to be used in the Puebla text. There it occurs mainly in reference to the high-ranking mestizo don Juan de Galicia, whose mother was likely indeed Spanish, and in careful lists of non-indigenous people to be kept out of indigenous cabildos, with mestizo put between Spaniard and mulatto. It was sometimes used more loosely, however, and we cannot be sure of the type and degree of mixture manifested, for example, in the mestizo Felipe who was hanged in 1687. (The term fails to appear in the spare Tlaxcalan text at all.)

Mulato and *tliltic*. The Nahuas used the Spanish term *mulato* to designate a person of mixed African and European descent, and they probably extended it to people of mixed African and Indian descent, just as the Spaniards did, though this text does not provide

---

[3]The word *indio* does not occur a single time in either of our texts, which is normal for a Nahuatl document of any kind. There was to my knowledge only one exception. The Tlaxcalan annalist don Juan Zapata did use the term *indio* so he could reserve the term *macehualli* for indigenous commoners in opposition to indigenous noblemen. See Townsend 2009.

[4]Personal communication from Jonathan Amith.

[5]Aguirre Beltrán 1967, p. 167; see also Castillo Palma and Kellogg 2005.

proof of that. The word *tliltic* is Nahuatl for "black," and the writers of these annals used it in the same sense that the Spaniards used *negro* to describe a black person. The Afro-Pueblans with whom the indigenous lived and worked used the meliorative terms *pardo* and *moreno* to express these two concepts, and the Spaniards at times used those words interchangeably with *mulato* and *negro*.[1] In the Puebla text a *mulato* can be called "light" or "dark," almost as if the writer were merely describing racial characteristics or color, but I think the two categories are in fact used here as they were in the Spanish and Afro-Spanish worlds, to refer to distinct social groups, the former assumed to be more acculturated than the latter, and did not perfectly reflect phenotype. I have translated the words as mulatto and black with the assumption that they were being used to label social groups.[2]

---

[1]For full discussion see Vinson 2001. They tended to use the latter two terms when there was a negative implication (as in commentary on criminals) and the former in more positive contexts (as in commentary on the militia).

[2]See Lockhart's following chapter for a treatment of many of the ethnic terms from the perspective of language evolution.

The Language of the Texts

James Lockhart

THE TWO NAHUATL TEXTS published here are as different in their language as they are in other ways. At the same time, being in the annals genre, from the same general region, and composed at close to the same time, they have much in common, and it would be well to examine them closely for what they can tell us about the Nahuatl of their time and place. First let us look at the text from Puebla, which is much more extensive and also better developed in various respects, making it possible to detect things that are present in the Tlaxcalan text only as the barest hints or not at all.

Language contact phenomena

WHAT STANDS OUT most clearly as a distinct, readily identifiable topic are the results of Spanish linguistic influence, which seen as a whole we can call contact phenomena; that aspect, then, will be treated first and foremost. As is by now well known, the Nahuatl language went through three clear successive stages in relation to Spanish, first a brief time of no real borrowing of Spanish words (Stage 1), then a hundred years, up to around 1640 or 1650, of borrowing large numbers of Spanish nouns (Stage 2), followed immediately by Stage 3, with a series of new developments indicative of quite large-scale bilingualism on the part of the indigenous population. They include: the borrowing of Spanish verbs; borrowing of Spanish particles (prepositions, conjunctions, adverbs); calques and equivalence relationships using native vocabulary; new kinds of loan nouns and more ready adoption of them; plurals of inanimate nouns; and the acquisition of Spanish sounds not in the original native repertory.

The Puebla text. All in all, our Puebla text is perhaps the most comprehensive single illustration of Stage 3 Nahuatl extant, and this despite the fact that it was written quite early in the period, in the 1670s and 80s it seems. The annals genre gives adequate scope for the whole range of phenomena to show themselves, and location in one of New Spain's two major urban centers also favored the flourishing of contact phenomena. (New annalistic writing in Nahuatl in and around the other such center, Mexico City, had virtually come to a halt by the onset of Stage 3.)

Our list of Stage 3 traits in the Puebla text can begin with a glorious and exceptional outpouring of loan verbs not matched in any other known Nahuatl source. They follow Nahuatl's universal strategy for taking in Spanish verbs, first anticipated in a document of Mexico City in the last decade of the sixteenth century but not becoming a regular mechanism of the language until the 1640s and 50s. The infinitive of the Spanish verb is taken as a stem, which is integrated with the verbal base *-oa* (preterit *-o[h]*, future *-oz*, etc.), and the resulting construct functions like any of the *-oa* verbs with native stems that form a large class in the Nahuatl language. Here is a list of the loan verbs in our text:

consagraroa, to consecrate (used twice)
canonizaroa, to canonize (used twice)
coronaroa, to crown, used once meaning to install a king in office and another time to top off an edifice
culparoa, to blame, accuse, implicate

obligaroa, to oblige oneself in the legal sense
pregonaroa, to proclaim, issue a proclamation
sustentaroa, to sustain, maintain something one has started
visitaroa (used twice), to inspect, visit

Perhaps the reader will not be too greatly impressed by 8 loan verbs in 12 attestations in a text of 30 folios. But consider that the last full counting of loan verbs in the entire corpus of Nahuatl texts came to only 40, of which the Puebla text's examples represent a full 20 percent.[1] Quite a few additional attestations have been seen since then, but to give some notion of the rarity of this kind of concentration, a body of 98 Nahuatl testaments from the Toluca Valley, mainly written in the eighteenth century, contains a total of only 4 loan verbs.[2]

The examples here correspond well with Nahuatl's general tendency to resort to verb borrowing above all to reproduce special Spanish ecclesiastical, legal, and economic terminology. But from the beginning certain -oa verbs belonged to a broader, more popular domain, and so it is here too, with *sustentaroa*, to keep something up (and also to sustain oneself in life, get one's daily sustenance, which the loan verb as used by the writer probably also meant, though that is not specifically seen in the text). Here *visitaroa*, arising within the framework of official inspection, is perhaps beginning to come close to simple "visit" as well.

A general characteristic of Stage 3 Nahuatl is that whereas in earlier times words were borrowed in order to name something strikingly new and different for which no adequate word existed, in this age of much bilingualism vocabulary was often introduced even if reasonable equivalents already existed, simply because the Spaniards were employing it and it was useful in reporting things from the Spanish context. Thus the native *teochihua*, "to bless or consecrate," is used in the text with virtually the same meaning as the introduced *consagraroa* (it is true that at an earlier time this meaning of *teochihua* may have itself been a neologism). Simple *itta*, "to see," is often used in Nahuatl generally and also here in the meaning "to inspect, look into," little different than *visitaroa*.

When we come to the other outstanding diagnostic characteristic of Stage 3 Nahuatl, loans of particles (uninflected words), the Puebla text presents an unusual profile. There are 14 attestations of loan particles, even more than with verbs (though not an overwhelming number because generally speaking particle attestations are considerably more common in Nahuatl texts). But these examples are all of a single word, the loan particle *hasta*, uniformly written here as "asta," with the meanings "until, as far as, down to, even." The reason for the dearth of other loan particles is a mystery, especially since *hasta* has become so basic in the writer's speech. Looking to the Toluca Valley testament corpus again for perspective, we find 8 loan particles, compared with 4 loan verbs. The two most common particle loans in Nahuatl generally were *hasta* and *para*, "(destined) for, in order to," but overall *para* seems to have been even more common; in the Toluca Valley corpus it outnumbers *hasta* by 52 to 5.[3] Yet here it is entirely absent.

But despite being limited to a single word in this category, the Puebla text shows that word's fullest integration. *Hasta* is used constantly, with no restraint, and it has pushed competing native expressions almost completely off the scene. Sometimes loan particles in Nahuatl take on a life of their own, veering from Spanish meanings and usage, but such is not the case here. The word is used exactly as in Spanish: spatially, to express that

---

[1]Lockhart 1992, pp. 305–06.   [2]Pizzigoni 2007, p. 34.
[3]Pizzigoni 2007, ibid.

a movement proceeds as far as, up to, a certain location (thus a procession goes "asta yglesia mayor," "as far as the cathedral," f. 12); temporally, until a certain time ("asta ypan nahui ora teotlac," "until four o'clock in the afternoon," 30v);[4] figuratively ("asta axnotzitzin," "down to the poor little donkeys, even the donkeys," f. 19).

The Puebla text also illustrates well some of the general facts of the Nahuatl of the time in the realm of calques and equivalence relationships, where native vocabulary is used to represent a Spanish phrase or word instead of employing a loanword. Thus the rather extreme example *tle opanoc* (not in our texts) says literally, in terms of traditional meanings, "What passed over (the river, a plain, etc.)?" But in this case *pano*, to go over a surface, has become the equivalent of the Spanish verb *pasar*, and the meaning is "¿Qué pasó?," "What happened?" The phrase is a calque; but by the time of Stage 3, Nahuatl had gone beyond ordinary calques to what are called equivalence relationships, in which a given native Nahuatl word can automatically represent any meaning of the relevant Spanish word.

Though coming into its own in Stage 3, the formation of equivalences began already in the later part of Stage 2, especially with the best known example, Nahuatl *pia* for Spanish *tener*. Well endowed with ways to express possession, Nahuatl even so did not have a verb meaning exactly "to have" in the sense so dominant in modern European languages and represented in Spanish by *tener*. Before the Spaniards came, the Nahuatl verb *pia* often meant "to take care of," "to have custody of (for someone else)," quite far from "to have," especially in the sense of "to own" that is well developed in European languages. It did, however, also mean "to hold, have in one's control," and from there it began to become an equivalent of *tener* not only in the meaning of owning but in any idiomatic meaning that Spanish assigned to *tener*. Our Puebla text has good examples of these things. Thus objections were raised to a candidate for the indigenous governorship on the grounds that "amo quipie ycaltzin," that "he doesn't have a house," i.e., doesn't own and occupy one (f. 15).[5] The verb *tener* was and is widely used in Spanish in a multitude of expressions indicating age, measurements, and other things, and Nahuatl followed suit in that too. Here we have "ynic huecapan quipia cenpuali yhuan nahui bara," in Spanish "tiene 24 varas de alto," "it has, i.e., measures 24 varas in height" (f. 12). Not that *pia* had lost all of its older senses; when several times the text speaks of a person having an office for a given time using *pia*, it can be thought of as "held" rather than "had," and that meaning was fully traditional. After all, *tener* itself originally meant "to hold," and something of that was still left in its use in Spanish.

---

[4]Another instance of *hasta* with a temporal meaning, unlike most uses of the word in the text, contains a hint of older expressions: "oquimohuiquili yn onpa mexico asta oc omotlatitlanili caxtillan," "they took him to Mexico City until such time as they sent to Spain," f. 20. Here the native particle *oc* retains the meaning of provisionality, meanwhile, until such time as; a fully traditional expression here would probably have run "inic oc omotlatitlanili Caxtillan," or "ixquich cahuitl inic oc omotlatitlanili Caxtillan."

[5]In Nahuatl generally, the verb *pia* often appears in the variant *pie* just as it does here, with the [a] raised to [e] by the influence of an unwritten [y] between the two vowels, or possibly by the height of the [i] itself. The expression used here says more literally "he doesn't have his house." The possessive prefix is a vestige of an earlier Nahuatl expression for ownership or possession, which was of the type *onca icaltzin*, "there exists his house," in effect "he has a house."

Another widespread equivalence relationship, so far attested only for Stage 3, is the one already alluded to of *pano*, "to cross a surface," and the popular Spanish verb *pasar*, "to pass (in many meanings), to enter, go somewhere, to happen." It too is illustrated in the Puebla text. Thus "oc opanoc yn ilhuitzin San Ju⁰ baptista," "meanwhile the feast day of San Juan Bautista had passed" (f. 16). Or "opanoc macuilli tonali," "pasaron cinco días," "five days passed" (f. 23v).

In addition to the common equivalence words *pia* and *pano*, another verb in the Puebla text gives indications of something similar, but it is not as well known from elsewhere and does not appear to have spread to all senses of the Spanish verb. In the text the native verb *quiça* repeatedly means the same thing as the Spanish verb *salir*,[1] in a way not clearly associated with the usual meanings of the native word, but always in the restricted sense of someone turning out to be selected in a process of election or appointment. Thus "oquis gobernador yn D. Ju⁰ andres," "salió gobernador don Juan Andrés," "Don Juan Andrés came out as, turned out to be, governor" (f. 15). Or "oquis yncapitan se tliltic," "a black turned out to be their captain" (f. 18v).[2]

As we see, many equivalence relationships involved verbs, for Nahuatl seemed to remain especially reluctant to borrow verbs that were extremely frequent in everyday speech. Some such relationships, however, employed a native particle or particle-like word instead of a verb. Thus a common equivalence in Stage 3 Nahuatl involved *quenami*, originally meaning "something that is in a certain manner," most often used interrogatively ("what is it like?"), which became the equivalent of Spanish *como* in the specific sense of "as, in a certain capacity." In the Puebla text we find that in an emergency the bishop attired himself "quenami se soldado," "como un soldado," "as a soldier" (f. 18v). The most common equivalence of this type in countrywide Stage 3 Nahuatl used *ica*, the third person singular possessed form of the relational word *-ca*, originally indicating primarily instrumentality, which was made equivalent to the Spanish preposition *con*, "with." Few entirely unambiguous examples appear in our text, though several passages could be so interpreted, and one seems definite: "ocasique yca sihuatl," "they caught him with a woman" (f. 21v).

An equivalence relationship is a kind of frozen and generalized calque. More specific calques are also found in the Puebla text, as they are in other texts of Stage 3. As in most cases of this period, they are only partial, for Nahuatl now had no hesitance about borrowing any noun that might be involved, and only the verbal part of the Spanish expression would be conveyed through a native word in a new sense. Thus "quartoz

---

[1] The verbs *quiça* and *salir* have a very different orientation in that the Nahuatl verb basically means to come out, with the viewer already outside, and *salir* is basically to go out, with the viewer still inside. Nevertheless, in many other respects the two coincide closely. Another possible *quiça/salir* equivalence with a slightly different slant is "amo yuhcatzintli omoquixti yn itlaçoxayacatzin," "the precious face [of the saint] didn't turn out right, or as it was before" (f. 28).

Another probable related calque uses *quixtia*, the causative of *quiça*, as the equivalent of Spanish *sacar*, "to take out," in the meaning of "taking," that is, making, a copy or image. The example, "yn quimoquixtilia ytoca diego de la siera," "the maker is named Diego de la Sierra," is on f. 29.

[2] The meaning "to turn out" was a natural one for *quiça*. Since its basic meaning was to come out, to emerge, the only thing necessary was to take emerge in a figurative sense. The same usage occurs once in the Tlaxcalan text too: "oquizqui capitan" (f. 17).

oquinchiuhque," "los hicieron cuartos," "they quartered them [after hanging]" (f. 11). The expression is used several times. Another is "oquimacaque termino," "les dieron término," "they gave them a deadline" (f. 17). Or "oquima[ca]que garrote," "le dieron garrote," "they garroted him" (f. 21v). But otherwise either full calques or semi-calques of this type seem to be missing and could not be said to play a large role in the author's strategies. (Consider, however, "calaque en cabildo," "they entered in session" [f. 23v].)

Massive borrowing of Spanish nouns was already the prime characteristic of Stage 2 contact phenomena. In Stage 3 generally, various new types of noun loans appeared, especially some having to do with close kin relationships, as well as nouns that already had close equivalents, and a general loosening and hastening of the process took place so that almost any Spanish noun could be borrowed ad hoc. In the Puebla text this last principle reaches the ultimate. The writer uses words that surely few Nahuas, even in urban Puebla, were familiar with, or even perhaps few Spaniards, but that were necessary vocabulary for speaking of certain domains, especially the author's favorite subject of architecture, where we see things like "media naranxa," "dome"; "lanternilla," an aperture for light at the top of a dome; "bobeda," "vault"; "cornija," "cornice"; "sotabanca," "pediment."[3] At times the writer seems to be showing off; in reporting the emergency with English invaders in Veracruz he lists by Spanish name almost every sort of military equipment one could think of, from the old-fashioned "pora," *porra*, "mace," to the new-fangled *carabina*, "carbine."[4]

The principle of following Spanish usage in adopting new loans can result in an old loan being displaced by a new one. Through most of the text the word for cathedral is *iglesia mayor*, "main church," which Spaniards in all parts of the Indies had used in that sense up to this time. But in the last part of the text the loanword "catedral" appears, and after a brief transition it becomes predominant, surely reflecting the fact that the Spanish community of that time was adopting the more specific and pretentious word.[5]

The author of the Puebla text seems to have reached the point of assuming that any special Spanish word that he needs will be understood by his audience, and surely he

---

[3]This word today and even in some older reference works is given as *sotabanco*, but the form with -*a* may have had some currency too at one time. Also, *linternilla* is the common form rather than *lanternilla*; yet the latter probably once existed in Spanish.

[4]Karttunen and Lockhart 1976 gives a list of loanwords on pp. 74–77 identified as "c. 1700," all of which were culled from the Puebla annals in this volume. The list contains 95 loan nouns as well as the same 8 loan verbs as dealt with here. Both the standard spelling and one of the forms occurring in the text are given. Not all the loanwords in the text are included, only those thought to be attested for the first time in the Nahuatl corpus, so that the most common loans stemming from Stage 2 are missing, as well as important Stage 3 loans appearing in earlier texts, including something as much used in the text as *hasta*. But for that very reason the particular nature of the text's loan vocabulary emerges clearly.

Pp. 112–16 of the same publication contain a selection from the Puebla annals in transcription and translation. Although mainly agreeing with what is found here, the translation contains several unclarities and errors that have been overcome through research done by my colleague Townsend, so that it should be viewed as superseded by the present translation of the same passages. The remarks on the language of the text on pp. 112–13, however, remain of interest.

[5]An isolated instance of "catedral" is found in the entry for 1681, but all the rest are from 1689 forward. The change indicates that often the author was writing entries close to the time of events.

shows no reticence about using anything at hand. Many of his loan nouns seem to be taken on the spur of the moment, and as already implied, we surely cannot assume that they were all common currency among the whole Nahua population. In many cases they may have originated in what the writer heard in Spanish conversations. He himself clearly understood Spanish well, and there must have been others like him.

But what of the most famous new noun loans of Stage 3, for close kin relationships, substantially reorganizing the conceptualization of Nahua kinship? As it happens, following the traditional conventions of the annals genre, the writer has no occasion to mention his relatives (at least as such) or to dwell on private matters in his circle. We are left only with what emerges in wider spheres: mainly words for father, child, grown daughter that even in most Stage 3 Nahuatl did not change from the traditional native form. One or two congruent facts do come out, however. On f. 8v the writer speaks of a curate and "yhermanotzin," "his brother," using as a loan the Spanish word for a brother in general rather than one of the native words that specify the age of the sibling relative to the person from whom the relationship was reckoned and that person's gender, but do not specify the gender of the sibling if younger. Another instance goes even further beyond traditional usage with kinship, referring to "ome hermanoz," "two brothers," whereas in traditional Nahuatl every kinship term had to be in some form possessed, and there were no blanket expressions like brothers, sisters, etc. Note that both these examples refer to Spaniards and are probably reported from conversation in Spanish.

In Stage 2 it was common to indicate in some way the newness of a loan and the awareness that another Nahua might not understand it, either by supplying some native approximation or by indicating in some fashion that that is what the Spaniards say. The most frequent of these expressions was *in quitocayotia*, "what they call . . ." Our writer generally speaking bypasses any such devices. Nevertheless, a vestige remains. Despite listing so many Spanish weapons with no explanation, the writer speaks of the "nechichiuhtli yn quitocayotia yn caxtilteca armas," "the gear that the Spaniards call arms" (f. 19v). Similarly he speaks of the region "yn quitocayotia mal pays," "that they call the badlands" (f. 25v). And once he even gives a quite full Nahuatl explanation: "in hui tlacnopilhuistli yn itoca Jubileo," "the great boon called plenary indulgence" (f. 16v).

As mentioned just above, Stage 3 loans often involved common Spanish expressions for which Nahuatl had already attained good equivalents. The Puebla text contains examples. Older Nahuatl annals standardly use the word *tlayahualoa*, literally to go around, in the meaning to go in procession. Here we uniformly find the noun "prosesion," often with the verbs *quiça*, "to come out," and *yauh*, "to go." The old verb is used in only a few passages, and in one of these it refers to going about inside the church when it was raining in lieu of a regular procession (f. 30). The word "sermon" also replaces older ways of speaking of preaching and sermons. Some of the loans betray the decay of the traditional vigesimal numbering system when it came to higher numbers. Both *mil*, "thousand," seen as "mill" and even "mitl"[1] (ff. 7v, 3), and *millones* (f. 4v) occur in the

---

[1]Probably a copying error, not a merging of [tl] and [l]. The writer retains *tzontli* for 400 and counts numbers to 400 in twenties. On f. 9v see "Sentzontli yhua caxtolpuali pesos," "700 pesos," one 400 plus 15 twenties. Later Nahuas often thought in hundreds and lost the meaning of *tzontli*.

text. Loanwords for ethnic types are based on normal Spanish usage, as they had been in Nahuatl since early in Stage 2, with additions whenever they occurred among Spaniards.[2] We do see a new word, corresponding to Mexican Spanish *gachupín*, a derogatory term arising sometime in the seventeenth century for peninsular Spaniards. The word is commonly thought to be of Nahuatl origin. The form used here is "cachopopin" (f. 29), possibly an error and at any rate not transparent as to its elements. Conceivably it is borrowed back from Spanish.

A large proportion of the loan nouns in the text has to do with locating things in time. Loanwords for the days of the week and months of the year are rife, and had been common in Nahuatl texts of all kinds from early in Stage 2. A little newer, but also already seen in Stage 2, are expressions on the order of "ypan ome ora teotlac," "at 2 o'clock in the afternoon" (f. 15). Here specifications of the time of day are found on every page, sometimes down to the half hour and even quarter hour, using the loanword *cuarto*. Days are commonly located on the church calendar by phrases on the model of "ybisperas san agustin," "on the eve of [the feast day of] San Agustín" (f. 17).

One might begin to wonder if loans had any limit at all for this writer and his peers. Yet when we look at the text's loan nouns as a whole, most of them, as in Stage 2, still denote concrete objects, people in certain offices, occupations, and social categories, or well delineated actions and procedures. Abstract nouns beyond the realms of religion, law, and economics hardly appear, and the vocabulary for ordinary thoughts and actions remains overwhelmingly indigenous.

A minor but suggestive aspect of Stage 3 contact phenomena in the Nahuatl-speaking area overall is the use, under the influence of Spanish practice, of some plural endings with inanimate nouns, which lacked them in traditional Nahuatl and indeed mainly continued to lack them. In interpreting such plurals in texts of the eastern region of Nahuatl speech the problem arises that it seems, from various sources, that a tendency to mark plurals of inanimate nouns existed there before contact; it is to be seen already in sixteenth-century texts. With the Puebla text, inanimate plurals are in any case barely present. One could mention "ymahuan," "his hands" (f. 19v), and "ycxihuan," "his feet" (f. 20), for in traditional Nahuatl the body parts were treated as inanimates. These examples could equally well represent a tendency of eastern Nahuatl or the influence of Spanish plurals, *manos* and *pies*.

Our last Stage 3 trait is the acquisition of Spanish sounds not present in traditional Nahuatl, something we can judge only by a text's orthography. Letter substitutions representing existing Nahuatl sounds that approximate absent Spanish sounds are good evidence that the writer has not acquired those sound segments. (Thus "paltolome" for Bartolomé would indicate that [b] and [r] have not yet been adopted by the person who wrote the word.) Spellings that are like those used by Spaniards are more indicative of Spanish-style pronunciation. Though nothing can be deduced from a single example, and almost any text will spell words the Spanish way at least part of the time, when a mass of words in a text uniformly follows conventional spelling, the impression mounts

---

[2]The major exception is that *tliltic*, "black," both generally in Nahuatl and here, replaces a loanword from *negro*. But the loanword does appear here once in the margin (f. 18v).

that the writer is pronouncing them using normal Spanish sound segments. In the case
of the Puebla text, the spelling is spectacularly good compared to what we usually see.
Ultimately the reader draws the conclusion that the author spoke a reasonable Spanish
and was using a pronunciation of loanwords in Nahuatl closely approaching that of those
words in Spanish. Most of the variations in his spellings were normal in the Spanish
writing of the time, such as between *b* and *v*, "birrey" or "virrey" (viceroy), "barrio" or
"varrio," and have no deeper meaning. Another example is the wavering with *e* and
i, "trenidad" and "trinidad" (Trinity), or "besitador" and "visitador" (inspector). One
variation common in the text, between single and double *r*, as with writing both "bario"
and "barrio," may indicate that the writer was weak in making the distinction between
flap [r] and trilled [r̃]. From hints in the whole Nahuatl written corpus it seems that [r]
and [r̃] were the very last Spanish sound segments to be fully mastered, at all levels.[1]

One kind of marked variation in spelling in the text has rather a different significance.
We see "Dios" but also "Dioz"; "marso" but also "março"; plural *s* written part of the
time as *z*, forms such as "limozna" for *limosna*, "offering." In the sixteenth century,
Spanish *s* had represented a sound approaching [sh], and in Stage 2 Nahuatl writing, *s*
was sometimes the equivalent of *x*, which was the normal Nahuatl representation of [sh].
Around the time of the onset of Stage 3, Spanish *s* had come to be pronounced [s], the
same as *z* had been. Now, in both Spanish and Nahuatl writing, *s* began to take over from
z, so that people would write "crus" instead of *cruz*, "cross." In early Stage 3, a mixture
of *s* and *ç/z* will often be seen in Nahuatl texts, the writers frequently putting *z* for *s* as
if to try to make sure that the [s] sound was being indicated. Before long *s* gained a
thorough dominance. In our writer's practice, *s* is used consistently for [s] in native
vocabulary. By the time he was active, the late seventeenth century, we would expect the
same to be true in his writing of loan vocabulary, but it is not; rather he constantly
switches back and forth between *s* and *z* in syllable-final position (less often *ç* in syllable-
initial position). Some of the above may too technical for many readers, but the point is
that nothing about the Puebla writer's practice with *s/ç/z* casts doubt on his acquisition of
Spanish sounds; rather it confirms his following contemporary Spanish pronunciation
closely.

Yet if we examine the entire text carefully, we will find several exceptions, cases in
which loanwords are written with distinctly non-Spanish spellings. How can this be
reconciled with the writer's general orthographic practice? The explanation is simple.
These words are older loans with Stage 2 pronunciations containing typical substitutions;
some of them also acquired meanings at considerable variance from the original meanings of the Spanish words.

In several such cases Spanish *s* is replaced by *x*, which as we have just seen was a
quite good match for the Spanish pronunciation of *s* in Stage 2. These forms and
meanings were frozen in Nahuatl before the advent of Stage 3, so that the *x* in them no

---

[1]Although the version used here is copied from an earlier draft and would in the first instance
speak of the pronunciation of the copyist rather than that of the author, this is a careful copy made
in the close proximity of the author. A similar orthography is seen in a related text (Gómez García
et al. 2000) that Camilla has used in interpreting the primary text.

longer changed in response to the switch to *s* [s] generally. Prominent among these words is "caxtiltecatl," the primary term used for Spaniard, especially for the Spaniards as a group. The word is only half a loan, being a native formation based on "Caxtillan," "Spain," from Castilla, which also occurs in the text.[2] Also common in the Puebla text is "quixtiano," originally an approximation of *cristiano*, "Christian," with *r* omitted in a consonant cluster as often, and *x* for *s*. The form, which continued to be common wherever Nahuatl was spoken, took on the meaning "ethnic Spaniard," starting from the fact that it was one of the main words the Spaniards used for themselves in the earliest days. Once we see "xinola," another widespread and long-lasting early form, based on *señora* but soon coming to mean "Spanish woman" (here [i] replaces unstressed Spanish [e] as it often did, [ñ] is reduced to [n], and [l] replaces the [r] that was missing in Nahuatl). Yet another famous form is "xolal" for Spanish *solar*, "house lot," with the usual [l] for [r]. The *x* in "axno" for *asno*, "donkey," also indicates an older loan, and *caballo*, "horse," a ubiquitous early loanword, appears once in the old form "cahualo."

The form "melio," based on *medio* and meaning half a real, occurs several times (along with standard "medio"), for at first Spanish [d] in medial position was sometimes replaced by [l]. Thus virtually all the unorthodox spellings in the text represent fossilized older loans found across the entire Nahuatl-speaking area. Possibly the form "toltilla" (also written "tortilla") is different, an additional hint of a continuation in the writer's speech of the Nahua struggles with [r].

The Tlaxcalan text. As we have seen, there is a great deal to be said about contact phenomena in the Puebla text. The same is hardly true of its Tlaxcalan counterpart. The topics of loan verbs and loan particles are quickly disposed of, for the text completely lacks both. It seems to be the same with calques, and very nearly so with equivalence relationships, though in some quite obscure passages an *ica* affected by Spanish *con* may be hiding, and *quiça* for *salir* in the sense of to be chosen for an office appears here as well as in the Puebla text.[3] Loan nouns in the document include few if any that could not easily have been in a text of Stage 2. We might note that the Tlaxcalan text just once uses the term "espanoles" (f. 26) and does not contain the Puebla text's *caxtiltecatl*. It also has the interesting phrase "miyec omiqui cristiano" (f. 26v), apparently "many Christians died." Here we must wonder if despite the spelling, the intention might not be the same as with the Puebla text's *quixtiano*, so that the meaning in this passage would be that many Spaniards died. While at times employing standard versions of the loanword for viceroy,

---

[2]Caxtillan from Castilla was imagined to contain a stem *caxtil-* plus the frequent Nahuatl locative suffix *-tlan*, which becomes *-lan* before an *l* stem. Any locative word in *-tlan* has a corresponding inhabitant name consisting of the stem plus *-tecatl*, hence *caxtiltecatl*, an inhabitant of Caxtillan. It is quite unexpected that such an urbane document as the Puebla text should always use the older forms *caxtiltecatl* and *quixtiano* and not the *español* that for example had been the main term in the early seventeenth-century Mexico City annals of Chimalpahin.

[3]A dubious case is the Tlaxcalan text's occasional use of *inahuac*, usually "close or next to," in the meaning "with," as in "omomictique ynahuac motesoma ytlacahuan," "they fought with the subjects of Moteucçoma" (f. 10), and "mixnamique macehualtzitzintin ynahuac al^calte mayor," "the indigenous people argued with the alcalde mayor" (f. 25v). I am unsure whether these passages (and some parallels in the Puebla text) represent the extended use of *-nahuac* often seen on the Nahuatl periphery, or an alternate calque on Spanish *con*.

the Tlaxcalan document quite frequently uses *rey*, literally "king," in that meaning. This usage was widespread and can be found occasionally in texts produced by the well educated, but one can say that it is all in all something from popular vernacular. It never occurs in the Puebla text.

We also find the apparent adjective "depossitado" (f. 25v), conveying that a body was left deposited (in temporary burial). Loan adjectives are rare and ambiguous in Nahuatl; the Puebla text lacks a single one except in set loan phrases like *alcalde pasado*, past alcalde, or *altar mayor*, main altar. We might note that though the Tlaxcalan text does have quite a few such phrases, they are not as well developed. Thus once we see the phrase "gobernador ocatca," "late or former governor, or who was governor" (f. 29), and not *gobernador pasado* as in the Puebla document.

Early Stage 2 loans sometimes contained a Spanish plural even though the singular was meant. Except in some frozen forms, this practice had virtually disappeared by Stage 3, and no unanalyzed plurals are found in the Puebla text. The Tlaxcalan text has "ce soldados," "a soldier" and "clerigos" in reference to a single secular priest (f. 10), but these examples likely stem from literal copying of early entries first generated many decades before, and nothing similar is found in more contemporary passages.

It must be said that in principle the loans for indicating time and date are about the same as those in the Puebla document, not only loan vocabulary for the days of the week and the months of the year, but for indicating the time of day, as in "ypan nahui ora," "at 4 o'clock." The half hour is indicated less often, however, and the quarter hour not at all. The use of *víspera* in dating is also known. Similarly, as in the Puebla texts, the Spanish decimal *mil*, "thousand," is used instead of traditional vigisemal terms for rendering higher numbers (f. 17v).

In the matter of marking inanimate nouns plural, the Tlaxcalan text does have two prime examples, the collapse in an earthquake of *teopantin*, "churches," and *torretin*, "towers" (f. 28v). But since the finer points of Stage 3 Spanish influence are so conspicuously missing from the document, these forms probably simply reflect the original eastern Nahuatl propensity to mark more plurals on nouns than central Mexican Nahuatl.

If we are left with little to say about the Tlaxcalan text in the above categories of interest, on the other hand its orthography cries out for comment. It is again the opposite of the Puebla text, so remarkable for its conventional and basically consistent spelling of loanwords. In the Tlaxcalan document the spelling of Spanish loans and names seems to have gone wild. The same word may be spelled any number of different unconventional ways, even in close conjunction (in addition to a good many words spelled in the conventional Spanish manner). The reader may feel like bursting into laughter at many of the forms. They do, however, make sense, and they tell us much. First, they inform us that the writer (or writers) was without very much training, for even in the early times of Nahuatl alphabetic writing when no adjustments to Spanish pronunciation had been made, many skilled notaries of Tlaxcala came far closer to Spanish spellings than what we see in this text. Second, they tell us that the writer or writers had acquired virtually no Spanish sounds that were not already in the traditional Nahuatl repertory. Both primary and hypercorrect letter substitutions are rife, from the first page to the last. Here are some examples of primary substitutions:

p for *f*	pernantes	Fernández
p for *b* or *v*	panteras	banderas
	pispera	víspera
t for *d*	tienta	tienda
c for *g*	carçia	García
l for *r*	lodrigo	Rodrigo

Equally prominent and well developed are the secondary or hypercorrect substitutions:

b for *f*	biscal	fiscal
b for *p*	albarecion[1]	aparición
d for *t*	desurero	tesorero
g for *c*	gora	cura
r for *l*	Reros	reloj

Add some superficially odd forms like "pohuete," *puente*, "bridge," indicating that the writer pronounced the word, of one syllable in Spanish, with two syllabic vowels connected by a glide; he has also omitted a syllable-final *n*, a strong tendency of mundane Nahuatl texts in general.

Overall, then, the writing of loanwords and Spanish names in the Tlaxcalan text is a very strong indication that the writer or writers had acquired no Spanish sound segments at all, that rather he or they were still fully at the level of Stage 2 in this respect. And indeed, except for the external appearance of the writing with its many capitals and the height of some of the characters, and of course the subject matter going on into the eighteenth century, the text belongs, in respect to Spanish contact phenomena, typologically more to Stage 2 than to Stage 3.[2] But before attempting to draw broader comparative conclusions, let us go on to a bit of examination of the language of the texts in ways going beyond contact phenomena.

Signs of eastern Nahuatl in the texts

A QUESTION that arises is to what extent our two texts belong to the eastern branch of Nahuatl, of which the language used in Tlaxcala is best known, with some indications of similar phenomena in places such as Huexotzinco and Cuauhtinchan. This eastern variant and the variant found in the Valley of Mexico were identical in many respects, but to the extent that they differed, the Tlaxcalan form (so for the moment we may call it) retained some archaic features that, as in many peripheral areas of Nahuatl speech, remained the same as earlier while the speakers in the central valley made innovations.

---

[1]This form also has an unexpected intrusive *l* and a quite rare substitution of *e* for *i*.

[2]To judge to what extent the text in this volume is typical of the Tlaxcala of its time, we can look to the partly contemporaneous corpus of Zapata, at a much higher level, fully comparable to the Puebla text in quality or vision and on an even larger scale. It must be taken into account that Zapata, an early patriot of Nahuatl culture, was deliberately trying to minimize Spanish contact phenomena. Even so, he let slip some loan verbs (*prendaroa*, "to hock" [p. 292], and *presentaroa*, "to present" [p. 488]), which are missing in our Tlaxcalan text here. Like the latter and unlike the Puebla text, he frequently uses *rey* to mean viceroy. My impression is that more of his Spanish names and loanwords are written in a standard fashion than in our Tlaxcalan text. Nevertheless, he repeatedly shows all the kinds of "Stage 2" spellings in evidence there. Some examples: "Brobiçia" for *provincia*, "province"; "fonifacio" for Bonifacio; "Christa" for Tristán; "Olalde" for "Olarte"; "Bose" for Ponce; "tisiepre" for *diciembre*, "December"; "fefero" for *febrero*, "February."

The known features are quite miscellaneous, and we had just as well test our texts against them one trait at a time.

Preterit verbs in Nahuatl had once borne a suffix -*qui* in the singular. In the central valley that suffix had virtually disappeared from finite verbs. But in Tlaxcala, as seen in the Tlaxcalan Actas, it was retained in situations where the verb would otherwise be monosyllabic. Thus in central Nahuatl the preterit of *quiça*, "to come out, etc.", was *o-quiz*, whereas in Tlaxcala it was usually *oquizqui* (the preterit sign *o-* does not count as part of the verb). Where does the Puebla text stand on this question? In a word, -*qui* predominates, but the reduced version is also found. With the verb *pehua*, "to begin," there are no less than 27 forms with -*qui*, just one without. But with the example just used, *quiça*, the reduced form wins out, attested 9 times to only 5 with -*qui*. And so it goes, with more than enough -*qui* to show a strong influence of eastern Nahuatl, but also enough reduced examples to show either some central Nahuatl influence or that the kind of Nahuatl spoken by the writer was itself evolving.[1]

The picture in eastern Nahuatl was the same in respect to essentially the same -*qui* when used as a suffix of future verbs; this -*qui* too had disappeared from central Nahuatl. The Puebla text offers one test of the matter, the future of the verb *ca(h)*, which is *yez* in the reduced form, *yezqui* in the Tlaxcalan form; the text contains 2 examples of each variant.

The Tlaxcalan text, which after all actually was written in Tlaxcala and also patently did not suffer from excessive outside influence, comes down much more clearly on the side of the archaic -*qui*. Five eligible verbs in the text have attestations of the -*qui* form and none at all of the reduced form, the most impressive being *miqui*, "to die," with 18 -*qui* attestations.[2] One verb, *pehua*, to begin, has 9 -*qui* forms and 1 reduced form, the only one in the whole text.

A form very popular if not universal in sixteenth-century Tlaxcala was *nochi* instead of *mochi*, "all." The Puebla text indeed has *nochi* in 10 attestations, but standard central Nahuatl *mochi* wins out mightily with 67.[3] Again the Tlaxcalan text is much more clearly Tlaxcalan, with 7 *nochi* and only 1 *mochi*.

Central Nahuatl had changed many sequences that were originally [ya] to [ye], whereas they tended to remain [ya] in Tlaxcala. For example, central *ye*, "already," was mainly *ya* in Tlaxcala, and central *miec* or *miyec*, "much," was often *miac* or *miyac* in Tlaxcalan writing. Yet the Puebla text has almost innumerable examples of *ye* and only one (f. 20v) of *ya* with the same meaning. Surprisingly, the result is the same in the Tlaxcalan document: 5 *ye* and no *ya* at all. Just so the Puebla text gives *miec* repeatedly and never the variant with *a*; the Tlaxcalan text has *miyec* twice and also lacks the *a* variant. Perhaps this facet of eastern Nahuatl was undergoing rapid change.[4]

---

[1]With *ana*, "to take," 11 examples with -*qui*, 1 without; with *miqui*," to die," there are 4 reduced forms, 2 with -*qui*; with *yauh*, "to go," 3 forms with -*qui*, 1 without; with *neci*, "to appear," and *huetzi*, "to fall," both have one of the two versions each.

[2]The other verbs are *neci, quiça, yauh, huetzi*.

[3]Often spelled *muchi*. The frequent plural of both forms adds -*n*, but only once the -*ntin* that predominates in central Nahuatl. *Mochtin* occurs three times.

[4]The Puebla text even has examples in which [ya] has become [ye] in words where central

Central Nahuatl had innovated separate first person reflexive prefixes, *no* singular and *to* plural, whereas Tlaxcala and the whole Nahuatl periphery stayed with the earlier universal *mo* reflexive prefix. The Puebla text in fact has the expected Tlaxcalan *mo* in the first person plural (f. 26v), but there are no other relevant cases, nor do any appear in the Tlaxcalan text.

Nahuatl had two forms of the impersonal of the verb *yauh*, "to go." In central Nahuatl *huilohua* was greatly predominant, and *yalohua* was a rarity. In peripheral regions, however, the situation was often very different. The preterit impersonal of *yauh* is used quite frequently in both texts to indicate that parties went to carry out various assignments, and the form used is always *yalohua* in both texts, never central Nahuatl's *huilohua*.[5]

In the Valley of Mexico the preterit of the auxiliary form of this same verb *yauh* was usually written *-tia*, with the alternate *-ta* much less common and rather looked down upon. In Tlaxcala *-ta* was dominant (this is one case in which the Tlaxcalan variant is not older). The Puebla text has *-ta* three times, but *-tia* four times. Once again the Tlaxcalan text is more eastern, with two examples of *-ta* and none of *-tia*.

Over centuries if not millenia the Nahuatl language has had in operation a process in which a progressively weakening vowel changes from [a] to [e] to [i] (is raised) and then may disappear, depending on the context. In peripheral areas this process often moved more slowly than in the center. In eastern Nahuatl specifically, some vowels that had become [i] in central Nahuatl could still appear as [e]. Thus in the well known letter of Huexotzinco we see *elnamiqui*, "to remember," instead of the central standard *ilnamiqui*.[6] The Puebla text participates in this tendency to a certain extent, although as usual with it, central versions also occur. In the Valley of Mexico, "inside" was mainly *itic*, with the older *itec* seen far less. In the Puebla text *itec* appears 9 times, *itic* 5.[7] Also, in the same text we see an *e* before the applicative *li* of verbs that had become *i* in central Nahuatl: "Oquimotelique" (f. 18v) for standard *oquimottilique*, "they saw it," and "nechmotelis" (f. 19v) for standard *nechmottiliz*, "he is to see me."[8] The smaller and less varied Tlaxcalan text has no test of either of these matters.

A topic discussed also in the general introduction may relate to retarded reduction in the eastern region. Standard older Nahuatl used *-tli* as the singular absolute of nouns after a consonant stem (*pan-tli*, banner) and the reduced *-tl* after a vowel stem (*a-tl*, water). Usage in the Puebla text conforms to this model so well that any exceptions may be errors. With the Tlaxcalan text, however, essentially *-tli* is retained in all cases, not

---

Mexico retained [ya]: "tlayehualoa," to go around, standard central version *tlayahualoa*; "yecana," to lead, central version *yacana*, and other examples. In fact, one can say that the Puebla text shows a strong tendency for [ya] to move to [ye], more so than in central Nahuatl generally speaking. The phenomenon is observed in the Tlaxcalan text as well, if less fully illustrated.

[5]*Yalohua* is also attested generally in eastern texts, as in the Tlaxcalan Actas (TA, pp. 107–08) and Zapata (p. 202). We find the related *yaya* imperfect form of *yauh* in the Puebla text (f. 4, also in Zapata, p. 98). The greatly predominant form in the center was *huia*. *Huia* occurs in our present texts as well, however, and also in eastern texts more generally.

[6]Lockhart 1993, pp. 288, 294. It is true that *elnamiqui* is sometimes seen in the center as well.

[7]*Itec* occurs also in the Tlaxcalan Actas (TA, p. 93).

[8]Standard *tili* in formally applicative verbs is seen many times through the text, but in all other instances the *ti* derives from the *tia* of a Class 3 verb and not from *ta* as here.

only with the word *xihuitl*, "year," at the beginning of each entry, but with all other nouns having vowel stems throughout the document.[1] Such is the situation hypothesized for Nahuatl as a whole at a time that one would imagine to have been some generations before contact.

In central Nahuatl, the standard plural of the word *tlacatl*, "person," was *tlaca (tlacah)*. In the Puebla text it is usually the reduplicated *tlatlaca* (often in the probably mock reverential form *tlatlacatzitzintin*), unless in reference to the people of a group, as in "San cosme tlaca," "the people of San Cosme" (f. 7), or in the phrase "huehuey tlaca," "adults" (17v). *Tlatlaca* is also attested once in the Tlaxcalan text (23v). The form is apparently specifically characteristic of eastern Nahuatl, for we find it in Zapata as well (pp. 204, 642); Zapata also confirms the Puebla text's unreduplicated "huehuey tlaca" (p. 98). Apparently reduplication was used only when the word was unmodified.

In sum, the evidence, considerable if fragmentary, indicates that the language of both our texts continues with a number of traits that were characteristic of eastern and specifically Tlaxcalan Nahuatl in the sixteenth century. In the Puebla text, most of these features are mixed with and in some cases overshadowed by traits typical of the Valley of Mexico. The apparent reason is that Puebla as New Spain's second city was the center of constant movements of people in and out, the dimensions of which we can hardly judge, but in the varied and cosmopolitan Nahuatl of the Puebla text we see the result. In the Tlaxcalan text, as one might expect, Tlaxcalan traits are much more dominant, and the document is far more one-dimensional. One would imagine, however, that the location might not be the entire explanation, for the Tlaxcalan text embodies a very reduced conception of the annals genre, giving us little material, and the writer or writers were people of little training and narrow horizons. Yet it seems to me that the annals of the well trained and well connected Tlaxcalan don Juan Zapata y Mendoza, who conceived the genre broadly and produced a large corpus, share many of the same traits.[2]

---

[1]That is, if "xiuitl." and "xiuitli" mean the same. The dot is sometimes more like an undotted i. The forms with dot/period and with *i* are in strictly complementary distribution, that is, it is either one or the other throughout, and as is pointed out in the introduction, in the latter part of the text we find *i* only. Also, the text contains many other nouns with vowel stems, all of which have -*tli*.

Texts such as the Tlaxcalan Actas or the Huexotzinco letter show no sign of unorthodoxy with the absolute ending. A possibility, as envisioned in the introduction, is that the relatively uninstructed writer or writers betrayed a tendency in speech that was not usually written down. The use of a dot instead of *i* with *xihuitl* may imply that the final vowel was very weak.

The Tlaxcalan annalist Zapata also shows a quirk with the absolute ending, but in the opposite direction, often omitting *i* after a consonant stem: "tochtl" for *tochtli*, "rabbit," "metztl" for *metztli*, "month," or "piltzintl" for *piltzintli*, "child." Possibly the vowel of the absolutive was extremely weak in all contexts. (As it happens, the Puebla text has a very few such cases, including "metztl" and "telpochtl.") In any case, the majority of the absolutives in Zapata are standard.

[2]Here I will give some attention to the orthography of the two texts in respect to native vocabulary. The phenomena observed have to do partly with purely orthographic style, partly with the reflection of pronunciations; it is not always possible to be sure which aspect is involved.

Both texts evince a relatively standard Stage 3 orthography with native words, but as usual the Puebla text is more characteristic of its time. A general tendency of Stage 3 was to write double consonants, above all *l*, as single. While both documents follow the pattern, the Puebla text does so much more strongly. We find *tonalli*, here meaning day, as "tonali" 189 times, "tonalli" only 4

Vocabulary and discourse

OF COURSE PHENOMENA of Spanish contact and regional dialects are far from the only language topics in our texts that invite study. What of the nature of the authors' general discourse? To what extent did it retain the turns of phrase and key terms of the sixteenth century? The Tlaxcalan text virtually bans anything beyond the most skeletal utterances, so that the general speech of the author or authors largely escapes us. The Puebla text, on the other hand, provides a generous sample of speech in a number of realms. The repertory of expressions cannot be examined here in all detail, but perhaps a quick look at a few aspects will give some provisional notion. The Puebla author retains the impressive core of the Nahuatl language's resources little different and hardly reduced from what one might find in, say, the Tlaxcalan Actas of the mid-sixteenth century. However, some specific important aspects of that vocabulary are now missing, and the absence means more than simply a word change; it signifies different conceptual organization of important branches of life.

---

times. It is the same with *calli*, "house." And with the frequent *hualla*, the preterit of *huallauh*, "to come," only "huala" occurs. In the Tlaxcalan text, although "huala" appears 20 times, there are 7 attestations of "hualla" and 10 of the unassimilated "hualya." Against 5 "tonali" there are 2 "tonalli." The biggest difference, indeed a reversal, comes with *calli*: 58 "calli" to only 3 "cali." Also, in the Tlaxcalan text many standardly single *l*'s, especially in verbs, are doubled.

Without demonstrating it in detail, I will assert that whereas the Puebla text is generally consistent in writing [s] as *s* in native vocabulary, the Tlaxcalan text has much *c*, *ç*, and *z* alongside *s*, once more closer to Stage 2.

A purely visual double *t* was thought elegant by some writers in Spanish of the time, and we find a great deal of it in the Puebla text (as in "ttemictti," f. 9v, for *temicti*), though not to the exclusion of single *t*. In the Tlaxcalan text there are only one or two examples of the practice.

The Tlaxcalan text alone carries its extensive hypercorrect letter substitution with loanwords on into native vocabulary. The phenomenon seems restricted to *d* for *t*, as in "deocali" for *teocalli*, "temple," or "depeyacac" for Tepeyacac. It was more common in the eastern region than in the center to recognize the glottal stop in writing, as *h*. In the Puebla text, however, this *h* is used moderately, whereas it is seen in the Tlaxcalan text much more frequently. With *iquac*, "at that time," the forms "ihquac" and "iquac" (and some other spellings) constantly alternate through the document. Any word apparently beginning with a vowel in older Nahuatl actually began with a glottal stop, which was only rarely written down, but the Tlaxcalan text has this *h* quite frequently, as in "hobispo" for *obispo*, "bishop," or "honcan" for *oncan*, "there."

Both texts generally retain the standard writing (and hence possibly pronunciation) of syllable-final consonants to a greater degree than is sometimes seen at this time in other regions. The omission of syllable-final *n*, rife in the Nahuatl corpus generally, is barely a factor in the Puebla text (though it does occur, as in "ypa" for *ipan*, "in, on it" [f. 15v and elsewhere]); in the Tlaxcalan text it is more common, but surely does not exceed expectations for a Nahuatl text.

In many places, syllable-final [w] was losing its rounding in Stage 3 and becoming [h], expressed in writing *-uh* as *-h* or in other ways. In the Puebla text we see little hint of the phenomenon other than the case of "tlilihqui" for *tliliuhqui*, "dark, blackish" (f. 28v) ("otlaSencah," f. 14v, looks like an error). The Tlaxcalan text also usually has the full *-uh*, but *-h* does occur three times in the word *itequiuh*, "his term," as in "ytequih" (f. 26). However, the standard form of the word is equally frequent, and nearly all other such words are written with *-uh*; the exceptions are "opequi" for *opeuhqui*, "it began" (f. 25v), and "otepoh" for *otepouh*, "he counted people" (f. 26v).

Syllable-final [ts], standardly written *tz*, is occasionally found weakened to [s] in much Nahuatl writing. The same is seen at times in both our texts, with *s* instead of *tz*. In the Tlaxcalan text, "mestli" for *metztli*, "moon" (f. 27); in the Puebla text, "omixquesque" for *omixquetzque*, (*cont'd*)

Terminology of rank. I will discuss one such aspect, because it can be easily detected and investigated. In the sixteenth-century Nahua world, in both east and center, a vocabulary of social rank, which coincided quite closely with political rank, was crucial to sociopolitical organization and appears in the sources on every hand. The key terms were *tlatoani*, ruler, with *tlatoque*, rulers but also the members of a ruling body or cabildo members; *teuctli*, lord, head of a lordly house; *teteuctin*, lords, but also describing the officeholders as a group; *pilli*, noble, and *pipiltin*, again used for the cabildo members or for the whole nobility and directing group; *cihuapilli*, noblewoman; *macehualli*, commoner and person obliged to carry out a series of physically taxing duties for the altepetl.

None of these terms occurs in the Puebla text in reference to indigenous people even a single time except the last, and that in a different meaning.[1] Prominence and office-holding have been redefined. The title of an office, given with a Spanish loanword, is constantly repeated with an individual's name. Holders of high office bear the title don, which goes far toward doing what *teuctli* and *pilli* once did but is acquired in a different way. When the cabildo members are spoken of as a group, the Puebla text calls them *huehuetque*, elders (ff. 15v, 22v) or *teachcahuan*, leaders or again elders (f. 21). These are traditional terms but were originally used more at the subdistrict level and had no connotations of nobility. They now mean prominence; the whole notion of nobility seems in abeyance.

One might think that this state of things came about because the original indigenous migrants to Puebla were mainly humble people, and indeed that may have contributed,[2] but in point of fact the same kind of change in terminology was occurring throughout the Nahua world around the time of the onset of Stage 3, though not always as consistently as here. As we have seen, the Tlaxcalan text is too sparse to test most such questions, but in view of the concentration on high indigenous officials, perhaps it is significant that also there the traditional vocabulary of high social rank is entirely missing. Some groups of prominent indigenous figures are indeed called *tlatoque*, but such passages are found

---

"they were appointed" (f. 17).

In standard Nahuatl the sequence *l-tl* is supposed to assimilate automatically, becoming *ll*, but in some texts from all regions it fails to do so. In the Puebla text we find both "hualathui" (f. 10), assimilated, and "hualtlathui" (f. 24v), unassimilated, for *huallathui*, "at dawn." The Tlaxcalan text also has an example of *l-tl*: "ohualtlamelauque" for *ohuallamelauhque*, "they came straight." I am not sure whether these spellings have any implications for pronunciation or not.

A noticeable tendency in the Puebla text is to write *hui* for standard *huei* [wēi and the related k^wēi], though not to the exclusion of the orthodox spelling. The phenomenon, also seen in other regions, appears in "chicui" for *chicue(y)i*, "eight," 5 times, and once in "hui" for *hue(y)i*, "large" (f. 16v); it probably represents actual pronunciation.

[1]*Tlatoani* and its plural *tlatoque* occur several times in the text, but aside from being used once in reference to God (f. 30) and once to a nobleman from Spain (f. 20v), they seem to refer to members of the Spanish cabildo or prominent local Spaniards generally (ff. 15v, 29v); the word may serve as the equivalent of *caballero*, "gentleman" ("caballeroz" actually occurs once in much the same context as *tlatoque* [f. 12]). Perhaps the clearest case is that of the Spaniard don Tomás de Mármol, called a "tlatohuani," said to be of high parentage in Puebla (f. 20v); the intention must be caballero or señor.

[2]Yet the list of the first settlers of Xonacatepec (f. 5) shows some individuals with quite illustrious names (outnumbered by those with modest appellations, but that would be true anywhere).

only in sixteenth-century entries that were copied from earlier sources. In entries for the first decade of the seventeenth century the term is used three times for the cabildo membership as a whole. It does not occur again.[3]

The old word for the mass of the population, those who worked the land and did all kinds of duties for the nobility and the altepetl, was *macehualli*, which apparently originally meant human being and even in the sixteenth century could (used in the plural or the singular as collective) have the sense of "the people" in general. As the old sociopolitical terminology faded, by the early seventeenth century the word was beginning to mean "indigenous person" (mainly used in the plural). Very often seen is *macehualtzitzintin* with a mock reverential, meaning "the poor indigenous people." This form tended to become frozen, largely losing the coloring of humbleness and pitifulness, and becoming the usual way of referring to indigenous people either as a whole or in groups. The word in this form is standard fare in the Puebla text, virtually the only version ever used (generally "masehualtzitzintin" with the Stage 3 *s*, occasionally omitting the final *-tin*). It no longer has any implication of low social rank; it is used even in association with the cabildo and its members, the highest-ranking indigenous people in local society (f. 23v).

In the Tlaxcalan text the standard Stage 3 form *macehualtzitzintin* occurs once (f. 25v), in an entry for 1675, apparently with the usual meaning of indigenous people in general, just as in the Puebla text. But other forms coexist. On f. 26 the simple singular "macehuali" is used as a collective, definitely with the meaning of indigenous people, for it is put in direct contrast with Spaniards. The form "masehualtin" appears once (f. 12v), without the mock reverential; it might mean either commoners as a social rank (especially since the entry is for 1557) or the general indigenous population. Another time we find the singular "maçehualtzintli," which could be either a poor commoner or a poor indigenous person and indeed seems to mean both, for it is in an entry ostensibly dated 1510 that is based on the mid-seventeenth-century Miguel Sánchez/Laso de la Vega story of the apparition of the Virgin of Guadalupe and is used in reference to Juan Diego.

Naming patterns. A corollary of the general decline of traditional rank designations in Nahuatl was the evolution of a complex naming system capable of making many distinctions. The Puebla annals show the system operating in its classic form by mid-seventeenth century, if not before. The text is not generous with names of indigenous people, however, and is barren of names of indigenous females; not a single indigenous woman is even mentioned as an individual, much less named. We owe the bulk of the names in the Puebla text to two sources alone: listings of indigenous officials and of people who were hanged. This at least gives us a notion of naming patterns at the upper and lower levels.

Briefly, the mature pattern for indigenous names as it existed in the Nahua world and well beyond involved the virtual absence of names from indigenous languages and a hierarchy that proceeded from, at the lowest level, two first or Christian names (by origin names of saints); next highest, a series of names taken from religious concepts (such as de los Angeles); of these de la Cruz was especially salient, and for some reason de

---

[3]We will not forget, as emphasized in the general introduction, that the great Tlaxcalan annalist Zapata assertively retained the entire panoply of traditional rank terms.

Santiago had about the same cachet, as did the entire name of a saint as a unit, such as Miguel de Aparicio; higher yet, Spanish surnames, with patronymics like Hernández having an aura unlike their nondescript flavor in Spanish, and at the very top surnames that were distinguished in Spanish too either in general or as borne by high-ranking individuals, such as Guzmán, Cortés, Mendoza, Mendieta.

If we take the governors of indigenous Puebla, they show the whole gamut of name types from lowest to highest, with little obvious change across the seventeenth century. All except one bear the don, which in most cases must have come along with the governorship. Thus the name of the first governor, don Juan Bautista, was undistinguished; in 1681 don Juan Andrés's name was equally so, and the same in 1687 with don Josef Lázaro. At the medium level were our don Miguel de los Santos and don Miguel de la Cruz in the 1680s; the name of don Felipe de Santiago in 1684 has the same aura, perhaps a touch higher in tone. In 1629 the governor don Diego Pérez had a Spanish patronymic as a second name. Several higher-level surnames appear from early to late, some of them specifically associated with high-ranking indigenous families in Tlaxcala and probably elsewhere: Calzón, Cortés, Galicia. Others seem to be simply good-sounding Spanish surnames, like Ribera and León (though they may have a background unknown to me). The chino Mateo Jaén has a very reasonable Spanish surname but, in view of his ethnicity and probably also other qualities that we cannot judge, was not accorded the don, at least not by our annalist. As we have seen, all other governors were called don.

Offices below the rank of governor did not always command the don, though its use seems to increase with time. The first deputies of the governor lacked the title; most of the later ones received it (the very last did not, however). An alcalde might have the don or not; those in offices lower than alcalde rarely did, and surprisingly, though in most indigenous polities the fiscal of the church came with time to be at least equal in rank to an alcalde and hardly behind the governor, in the Puebla text none of the six fiscales mentioned are don, from the first in 1561 to the last in 1690.

People without the don would acquire it with high office, perhaps also sometimes aided by seniority. In the case of governors the title was retained thereafter; with holders of other offices not necessarily. Our probable annalist was just Miguel de los Santos in 1667 as regidor, became don as governor in 1685, and keeps the don in later entries. Melchor de los Reyes was interim governor in 1684 without the don, but the second time that he served in that capacity in 1686, he received it. Diego de León, who lacked the don as fiscal in 1686,[1] received it as alcalde in 1688 but did not keep it as a past alcalde in 1690, though he regained it as governor in 1691. It seems that very few men bore the don before acquiring it through office—a general pattern in indigenous central Mexico by Stage 3—but there were apparently some exceptions for scions of well established lineages. The mestizo don Juan de Galicia, probably son of a famous former governor, had acquired the don even before holding office.

Going beyond officeholders, those mentioned as first settlers of Xonacatepec in 1603 bear an assortment of names ranging from the most humble, including Baltasar Conetzin (with an indigenous second name) and a Juan Lucas, through Juan Hernández with a

---

[1]Gómez García et al. 2000, for 1686, corresponding to f. 24 in the Puebla annals, this volume.

Spanish patronymic, to the prestigious surnames of Cortés, Rojas, and Luna.

With those hanged, the ethnicity is consistently given only in the case of mulattoes and blacks. We must recognize the indigenous people among those executed solely by the character of their names,[2] and indeed the majority have the most common name type for humble people, two first names as with Juan Francisco or Juan Miguel, and we see a few indigenous second names as in the case of Andrés Pochtli (for indigenous names seem to have held on longer in the eastern Nahuatl region than in the center). Some went by a single name, like the Gabriel hanged in 1665, and some have only a first name plus an occupation, like Juan Pastelero in 1671. But some Santiagos were hanged too; someone with the splendid name of Francisco Espinosa was hanged in 1654 along with three other people who were clearly indigenous, and perhaps he was indigenous also.

As for the Tlaxcalan text, naming patterns of the seventeenth and early eighteenth centuries fall in the same general range as in Puebla, though even less well illustrated beneath the level of high officials. The governors of Tlaxcala exhibit all the same name types as those of Puebla. We see a few humble names, as with don Diego Jacinto, governor in 1637–1639; some middling names such as don Gregorio Nacianceno (that being a complete saint's name), who regardless of the name had the longest tenure of any governor; several patronymics, as with don Diego Pérez in 1678; and quite a few impressive names like Celis, Cortés, Paredes. The difference was in the fact that a good many of the names had become dynastic, with an aura of nobility and antiquity no matter what their nature otherwise. Thus the simple patronymic Jiménez not only was borne by the governors don Diego in 1645 and 1650, don Buenaventura in 1697, and don Felipe in 1709 and 1715, all of them of Ocotelolco, but went back to the famous Ocotelolcan Juan Jiménez, prominent in many capacities on the cabildo of Tlaxcala in the years around mid-sixteenth century. The name had an extra flavor from the beginning, for it was taken from a locally active Franciscan friar. Don Nicolás Cortés of Tizatla, governor in 1658 and 1662, was a descendant of Baltasar Cortés (don late in his life), a sixteenth-century cabildo member and governor. Other such names were Téllez de Guevara, Salazar, and Paredes (of which line a scion was governor as late as 1716). We also see the rise of a new dynastic name; from Quiyahuiztlan don Pascual Ramírez was repeatedly governor starting in 1679 and ending in 1708; don Salvador Ramírez followed, holding the office in 1707, 1712, and 1717.[3]

So ingrained was the contemporary system of names and titles in the writer of the Tlaxcalan text that he imposed it on historical figures in the time before it was formed; since in his time any indigenous governor and any Spanish alcalde mayor would be called don, he (or possibly a predecessor) gave the title to many people who lacked it in their lifetime or received it only later. Such ex post facto titles are lacking in the Puebla text, I think not so much because of the patently greater acumen of the writer, who was actually

---

[2]In the case of those hanged in 1665 who are called *chololteca*, Cholulans, the meaning appears to be specifically indigenous inhabitants of Cholula.

[3]The name Ramírez was not new on the cabildo, however. On many of the founders of dynasties see TA, pp. 134–39: Baltasar Cortés, p. 135; Juan Jiménez, p. 136; don Diego de Paredes, p. 137; (don) Hernando de Salazar, p. 138; Antonio Téllez, p. 138.

not well informed on the sixteenth century, but because, in view of Puebla's different evolution, almost no names of indigenous people surface before 1600.[1]

One aspect in which the Tlaxcalan system differed from that of Puebla and indeed from many indigenous districts in central Mexico is that names of indigenous origin retained some prestige for figures at a high level. Though such names are no more than an undercurrent here (better developed in the fuller annals of Zapata), one notes that the governor of 1678 is called don Diego Pérez Cuixcoatzin, and a priest of indigenous origin, said to be the grandson of Tecciztzin, is called once don Pedro Sánchez (1703) and again don Pedro Tecciz (1710) (ff. 28–28v).

The Tlaxcalan text delivers almost no useful information about the naming of people below cabildo level.

Elements of rhetoric. The great mass of devices of elevated or polite language so characteristic of Stage 2 or sixteenth-century Nahuatl is nearly absent from the Puebla text, starting with the famous double phrases and extended metaphors. A single traditional "diphrasis" occurs, "ȳ tloque nahuaque totecuiyo Dioz," "the master of the close and the near, our lord God" (f. 30v), going back to a precontact expression indicating the omnipresence of the deity, then adapted as a standard epithet of the Christian God. This is a relic of the specifically religious fancy language that was so prominent in early ecclesiastically sponsored texts but which generally speaking showed little sign of penetrating to the Nahuas in general, and one is surprised to find it even once in a text with very strong Stage 3 characteristics. The only other thing with a somewhat similar flavor is "yn çemanahuac tlatoani dioz," "the universal ruler God" (f. 30).

Some hint of the same method may remain in a phrase on f. 18v, "yn estandarte de sangre ynn ayc quisani yn ayc mosohuani," "the standard of blood that had never been brought out, never been unfurled." But one will look in vain for anything else of the kind, and though the method of phrase doubling is effectively captured in this passage, its vocabulary does not involve any of the many well established set pairs in older rhetoric.

Even such things are lacking as the pervasive use of -*yollo* to indicate emotional states and volition, as in *quinequi iyollo*, "his/her heart desires it," meaning in effect he/she wants it, or *iuh ca iyollo*, "thus is his/her heart," meaning that is the way he/she feels.[2] On the basis of early Tlaxcalan texts, it may be that Tlaxcala was never quite as given to high-flown rhetoric as some other regions. Yet that is likely an illusion caused by the selection of texts that has chanced to come down to us. The famous Huexotzinco letter to the crown of 1560[3] contains a great feast of double phrases and metaphors.

In any case, a well developed traditional native vocabulary and syntax remain in the Puebla text as the medium in which the rest floats; for example, the entire system of

---

[1]Many examples of anachronism with the don are given in the notes to the body of the Tlaxcalan text. Note that the more sophisticated Zapata, who also had far better sources, did not award the don posthumously, but stuck closely to the usage of the time recorded.

[2]See Carochi 2001, pp. 440–41, or Lockhart 2001, p. 97. The element *yol-* appears several times in the Puebla text, but within verbs frozen in a certain configuration with a certain meaning, as in *yolcuitia*, originally to declare the heart, hence to make a declaration or acknowledgment, and from Stage 2 Nahuatl forward meaning to confess (one's sins).

[3]Lockhart 1993, pp. 288–97.

predication and subordination is still intact; the elaborate series of auxiliaries and pur-
posive motion forms is prominent, handled faultlessly; complex reverential verbs are still
common. Tradition is especially visible in certain domains. Thus the vocabulary and
idioms for telling of the great old staples of Nahuatl annals—eclipses, storms, and
earthquakes—are not only overwhelmingly native but can be matched almost word for
word in passages of Chimalpahin and other earlier authors. An eclipse is still expressed
as the sun or moon being eaten (*qualo*), and a comet is a star that smokes (*popoca citlalin*); its tail may be called its smoke (*ipocyo*). Yet "cometa" appears once as well (f.
27), and the tail is sometimes called a tail just as in English. These terms in any case were
not taken as literally as we, who are not so used to them, imagine them to have been.
Equally traditional vocabulary was used for rain, snow, and wind storms, but the terms
were closer to the ones we use ourselves, and *tlalolini*, "for the earth to move," is a
straightforward description of what happens in an earthquake. Loanwords were not
intentionally avoided, it seems, as we see from the case of *cometa*, and if a storm happens
to rip off a weather vane, the object will be called by a loanword.

The Puebla text also contains the traditional set of phrases in annals that serve as
exclamation points, often on the occasion of these same natural phenomena, but also with
other kinds of crises and disasters, and further in a positive sense with spectacles and the
like: it was frightful (*temamauhti*), never was the like seen (*aic iuhqui motta*), there was
nothing but weeping (*çan choquiztli mania*), it was splendid (*mahuiztic*), etc., and for
particularly alarming eclipses or winds, that people were afraid the world was about to
end (*tlamizquia cemanahuac*). All this and more is traditional annals fare from much
earlier, still very much alive and used just as in older texts.

The Puebla text combines the actual speech of urban indigenous people with traditional elements in a natural, efficient, rather amazing way. Its language is surely as well
adapted to its situation and purpose as were annals of precontact times and the sixteenth
century. The one thing that has been greatly reduced, as also with the great contemporary
Zapata y Mendoza in Tlaxcala, perhaps because it was no longer in keeping, perhaps
because in Puebla it was going the way of the old terminology of rank, is the close first-
person recording of conversations (of which the general introduction contains good
descriptions). Yet traces remain in examples such as the direct-speech reaction of the
viceroy when he hears news of the fake inspector general (f. 19v), or a friar's first-person
report of having visited heaven in a vision (f. 20v), or various lesser fragments.

The Tlaxcalan text is so skeletal that the near absence in it of even the modest rhetoric
of the Puebla document is not surprising. We do find at least one dialog hinted at (f. 25)
and the same expressions for eclipses, comets, earthquakes, and storms.

BOTH TEXTS, then, show us a late seventeenth-century Nahuatl that was still in touch with
its origins. Characteristics of the eastern region since precontact times are seen in both
sets of annals, but in a more unadulterated form in the Tlaxcalan set, whereas the Puebla
text mixes in many traits from the central region. More contact with the outside is also
seen in the Puebla text when it comes to Spanish contact phenomena, which represent a
full illustration of Stage 3, while the Tlaxcalan text lags behind with many Stage 2 traits.

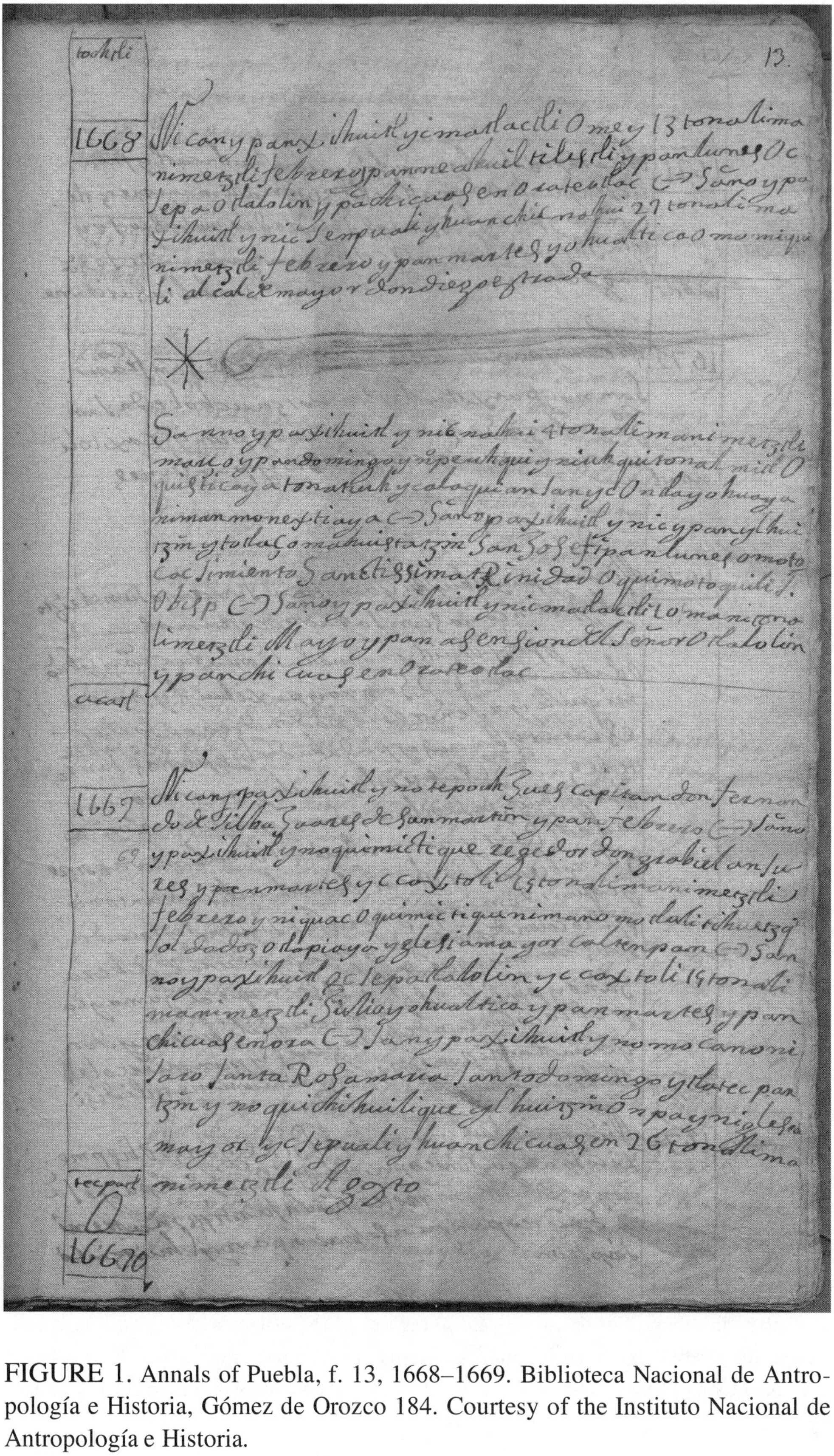

FIGURE 1. Annals of Puebla, f. 13, 1668–1669. Biblioteca Nacional de Antropología e Historia, Gómez de Orozco 184. Courtesy of the Instituto Nacional de Antropología e Historia.

Annals of Puebla

————————————

[*f. 1*]   cuatesontzitzintin
11   frai Jua de balos[1]
12   frai andres de Cordova
          Ca yehuantin huel achtopa hualmohuicaque quihualmohuiquilique yn iteoyotzin
          yn t^OCui Dioz

————

~~Ca~~tecp

————

1526

————

canli

————

1527

————

tochtli

————

1528

————

acatl

————

1529

————

tecpatl

————

1530[2]   NiCan ypan xihuitl huala presidente yanCuiCan tlatoCatiCo mexico[3] Sanno y-
          pan xihuitl yn huel yanCuican hualmohuicac teOpixcatlatoani OBispo ytocatzin
          frai Juan de sumarraga san fransisco teopixqui[4] yn huel yCuac monextitzino yn
          totlasonantzin de guadalupe[5]

————

cali

————

1531

————

tochtli

————

1532

---

[1]The first ten names on the list of the "apostolic twelve" (the initial Franciscan contingent
arriving in 1524) apparently appeared on a previous page, now lost.

[2]At this point a change in the writer's dating schema becomes evident. He originally had
"1510" and then wrote over it to render it "1530." He amended dates by adding twenty years all the
way through 1565 (previously 1545), then returned to 1546 and covered the recent period again,
with different entries. Upon closer inspection it becomes evident that the entries for 1526, 27, 28
and 29 had originally read "156, 157, 158, 159" and then each had been amended by insertion of a
small "2." Several sets of the Tlaxcala-Puebla family of annals manifest this error: someone

[*f. 1*]   Tonsured Ones
11   fray Juan de Palos[1]
12   fray Andrés de Córdoba
          These were the very first who came. They brought here the holy things [sacra-
          ments] of our lord God.

———

Flint-knife

1526

———

House

1527

———

Rabbit

1528

———

Reed

1529

———

Flint-knife

1530[2]   Here in this year came the president [of the Audiencia], who came to rule in
          Mexico for the first time.[3] In this same year for the very first time came the
          priestly ruler, the bishop, named fray Juan de Zumárraga, a Franciscan friar.[4] At
          this very time our precious mother of Guadalupe appeared.[5]

———

House

1531

———

Rabbit

1532

———

assumed early on that Cortés arrived in 1500 and carried out the conquest in 1501, rather than 1521.

[3]Don Sebastián Ramírez de Fuenleal, president of the Second Audiencia (1530–1535).

[4]Fray Juan de Zumárraga was actually present as first bishop of Mexico from 1527 to 1547. (He was consecrated in 1528.) In 1547 he became New Spain's first archbishop and served for one year.

[5]The Virgin of Guadalupe was purported to have made her appearance at Tepeyac in 1531, but this was a story originating in the seventeenth century. See Sousa, Poole, and Lockhart 1998.

———— [*f. 1v*]

acatl

————

1533   NiCan ypan xihuitl yn omotlali altepetl quitlalique tlaxcalteca nican cuitlax-
        coapā[1] motenehua siudad de loz angeles[2]

————

tecpatl

————

1534

————

cali

————

1535

————

tochtli

————

1536

————

acatl

————

1537   Nican ypā xihuitl huala virrey don antonio de mendoza[3]

————

tecpatl

————

1538

————

cali

————

1539

————

tochtli

————

1540

————

acatl

————

1541

————

[1]Indigenous people did not normally say Puebla (de los Angeles) for that city but used this indigenous word, presumably the name of the site before the Spanish city was founded there. The older form was Cuetlaxcohuapan, which still appears in our texts at times, but the weakened Cui-tlaxcohuapan predominates. See introduction, p. 41.

——— [*f. 1v*]

Reed

1533   Here in this year the altepetl was established. The Tlaxcalans established it here at Cuitlaxcohuapan,[1] called the city of the angels.[2]

———

Flint-knife

1534

———

House

1535

———

Rabbit

1536

———

Reed

1537   Here in this year the viceroy don Antonio de Mendoza came.[3]

———

Flint-knife

1538

———

House

1539

———

Rabbit

1540

———

Reed

1541

———

[2]Different Spanish sources give various founding dates: 1530, 1531, or 1532. Other Nahuatl annals in the region mention 1531. However, the entries that follow (until the writer backs up from the 1560s to the 1540s) are almost all three years behind reality, so most likely the annals here refer to the earliest events related to the founding, which occurred in 1530.

[3]Don Antonio de Mendoza, conde de Tendillas. He actually served from 1535 to 1550.

tecpatl

————— [f. 2]

1542

—————

cali

—————

1543   Nican ypan xihuitl yn opoliuhque xochipilteca yhuā ycuac Ohuiya Orisaba Bi-
        Rey don antonio de mēdoza

—————

tochtli

—————

1544

—————

acatl

—————

1545   Nican ypan xihuitl huala Señor OBispo Don Juanlian grases de aragon santo
        domīgo teopixqui yancuican huala nicā cuitlaxcoapā[1]

—————

tecpatl

—————

1546   Nican ypan xihuitl yn omochiuh huey cocolistli[2] yn icuac motlatlalo mixcoatl
        ytech ylhuicatl

—————

cali

—————

1547   quimichin[3]

—————

tochtli

—————

1548   Nican ypan xihuitl yn huel otlaquimichcualoc

—————

acatl

—————

1549

—————

tecpatl

—————

1550

—————

———————————————————

[1]Don Julián Garcés was the first bishop of Tlaxcala (1529–1542). His last visit could have been
no later than 1542, when he died. He played an important role in having the episcopal seat removed
from Tlaxcala to Puebla.

Flint-knife [*f. 2*]

1542

———————

House

1543   Here in this year the people of Xochipillan were defeated. And at this time the viceroy don Antonio de Mendoza went to Orizaba.

———————

Rabbit

1544

———————

Reed

1545   Here in this year the lord bishop don Julián Garcés of Aragon, a Dominican friar, came. He came here to Cuitlaxcohuapan for the first time.[1]

———————

Flint-knife

1546   Here in this year a great epidemic occurred;[2] at that time clouds kept running across the heavens.

———————

House

1547   Mice[3]

———————

Rabbit

1548   Here in this year things were really eaten up by mice.

———————

Reed

1549

———————

Flint-knife

1550

———————

---

   [2]There was a great plague from 1545 to 1548. Charles Gibson quotes an observer as saying that a thousand Indians died daily in the region of Tlaxcala. Gibson 1967, p. 138.

   [3]Possibly rats. Spanish records indicate a rat infestation in this year.

cali

─────── [*f. 2v*]

1551

───────

tochtli

───────

1552

───────

acatl

───────

1553   Nican ypan xihuitl huala biRey don luis de belasco[1]

───────

tecpatl

───────

1554

───────

cali

───────

1555

───────

tochtli

───────

1556

───────

acatl

───────

1557

───────

tecpatl

───────

1558

───────

cali

───────

1559

───────

tochtli

───────

1560   Nican ypan xihuitl yn ohuasico atl tecpāquiahuac tianquisco yn ocanato alcalde
         mayor Romano[2]

─────────────────────

[1]Don Luis de Velasco, conde de Santiago, viceroy of New Spain (1550–64).

House [*f. 2v*]

1551
———————

Rabbit

1552
———————

Reed

1553   Here in this year the viceroy don Luis de Velasco came.[1]
———————

Flint-knife

1554
———————

House

1555
———————

Rabbit

1556
———————

Reed

1557
———————

Flint-knife

1558
———————

House

1559
———————

Rabbit

1560   Here in this year water [from a conduit] reached the palace entrance in the mar-
        ketplace. The alcalde mayor Romano was the one who conducted [the water]
        there.[2]

———————————————

[2]Above the entry an elaborate fountain is drawn. Tello Román, alcalde mayor in 1556, was responsible for completing work on an aqueduct. See Zerón Zapata, p. 66.

———

acatl

———

1561

———

tecpatl

——— [*f. 3*]

1562

———

cali

———

1563

———

tochtli

———

1544 [*sic*]

———

acatl

———

1545   NiCan ypan xihuitl yn ohuasico atl san fransisco yn ocanato ytoca frai nicolas

———

tecpatl

———

1546   NiCan ypan xihuitl yn oyaloac a la florida[1] (–) Sanno ypan xihuitl yn omochiuh
         cocolistli yn opeuhqui ypan febrero yn omomiquili masehualtzintli ontzontli
         mitl[2] yc nochi yn Reyno

———

cali

———

1547

———

tochtli

———

1548

———

acatl

———

1549

———

tecpatl

———

[1]There actually was a major expedition to Florida in 1558, with the active participation of
Puebla's indigenous barrios (Carrión 1970, p. 18).

———

Reed

1561

———

Flint-knife [*f. 3*]

1562

———

House

1563

———

Rabbit

1544 [*sic*]

———

Reed

1545   Here in this year the water reached [the convent of] San Francisco. The one who brought it was named fray Nicolás.

———

Flint-knife

1546   Here in this year a party went to Florida.[1] (–) In this same year there occurred an epidemic which began in February. Eight hundred thousand[2] indigenous people died of it in all the realm.

———

House

1547

———

Rabbit

1548

———

Reed

1549

———

Flint-knife

---

[2]The form "mitl" was no doubt originally intended as "mill" for "thousand." On the epidemic see n. 2, p. 73 above.

———

1550   NiCan ypan xihuitl huala señor Obispo Don frai martin sarmiento san fransisco
        teopixqui[1]

———

tochtli [*sic*]

———

1551

———

tochtli
——— [*f. 3v*]
1552

———

acatl

———

1553   Nican ypa xihuitl yanCuiCā yalohac [*sic*] atatacoyan[2]

———

tecpatl

———

1554

———

cali

———

1555

———

tochtli

———

1556

———

acatl

———

1557

———

tecpatl

———

1558

———

cali

———

1559

———

———————————

[1]Fray Martín Sarmiento Hojacastro, bishop of Tlaxcala (1548–1558).
[2]*Atataca* is to do excavation related to water works. In the annals from the Valley of Mexico, it

1550   Here in this year came the lord bishop don fray Martín Sarmiento, a Franciscan friar.[1]

———

Rabbit [*sic*]

1551

———

Rabbit   [*f. 3v*]

1552

———

Reed

1553   Here in this year for the first time a party went to the place of excavations related to water.[2]

———

Flint-knife

1554

———

House

1555

———

Rabbit

1556

———

Reed

1557

———

Flint-knife

1558

———

House

1559

———

---

usually refers to the drainage of the central lake, or to the construction of dikes or canals. López de Villaseñor 1961 indicates significant activity related to water works in Puebla in the 1550s.

tochtli

———————

1560

———————

acatl

———————

1561

———————

tecpatl

———————

1562

———————

cali

——————— [*f. 4*]

1563   Nican ypa xihuitl yn omochiuh palasio mexico

———————

tochtli

———————

1564   Nican ypan xihuitl huala viRey marques de falses[1] tepoztica motlaquentiaya

———————

acatl

———————

1565   Nican ypan xihuitl yn omochiuh fiscal geronimo de S.tiago tlaxcaltecapā onca
       tlatzcantitlan tisatla[2] yn ayac gobernador San oc ye quitlatahuiaya yn altepetl[3]

———————

tecpatl

———————

1566

———————

cali

———————

1567

———————

tochtli

———————

---

[1]Don Gastón de Peralta, Marqués de Falces, viceroy of New Spain (1566–68). The Audiencia had been governing for a chaotic two years following the sudden death of don Luis de Velasco.

[2]On the importance of the barrio of Tlaxcaltecapan see the introduction, pp. 9–11 and 29–40 passim. Tizatla is part of Tlaxcala and contributed its share to the indigenous population of Puebla. If the existence of the barrio of Tlaxcaltecapan were not known, one could translate that Santiago was from Tlaxcalan country, from Tlatzcantitlan in Tizatla.

Rabbit

1560

—————

Reed

1561

—————

Flint-knife

1562

—————

House   [*f. 4*]

1563   Here in this year the palace in Mexico City was built.

—————

Rabbit

1564   Here in this year the viceroy, the marqués de Falces, came.[1] He was dressed in iron [decked out in full armor].

—————

Reed

1565   Here in this year Gerónimo de Santiago became fiscal in [the barrio of] Tlaxcaltecapan. He was from Tlatzcantitlan, in Tizatla.[2] There was no governor [yet]; in the meantime he was the one who spoke for the altepetl.[3]

—————

Flint-knife

1566

—————

House

1567

—————

Rabbit

—————————————

[3]Here we are being told that in this period before the full establishment of a confederation of three altepetl among the indigenous people under a governor, the *fiscal* or church steward (who was in general charge of church affairs), perhaps the one in Tlaxcaltecapan specifically and only for his own district, stepped in to fill the breach.

The word *rey* is seen between the lines above the phrase "ye quitlatahuiaya yn altepetl." No connection is yet apparent between this word, which in this text otherwise refers only to the Spanish king, and the rest of the entry.

1568   Nican ypan xihuitl huala biRey Don martin enrriques[1]

———

acatl

———

1569

———

tecpatl

———

1570   NiCan ypan xihuitl hualmohuicac Obispo D. fernande [Vi]llagomes auh atrisco
          omomiquilito Oyaya besita[2] Sanno ypan xihuitl yn oyaloac chichimecapan[3]
          yaqu[e] tlaxcalteca yhuan yaqui D. migel calson[4] yc oyaq̄ calS[. . .][5]

———

cali

———

1571

———

tochtli

———

1572
——— [*f. 4v*]
[acatl]

———

1573

———

tecpatl

———

1574

———

cali

———

1575   NiCan ypan xihuitl ohuala señor OBispo D. pablo gil de talauera atitlan mo-
          miquilico amo ohuasico nicā[6]

———

tochtli

———

1576   Nican ypan xihuitl yn omochiuh huey cocolistli ypan abl[7] [*sic*] yn omomiquili
          masehualtzintli ome millones yc moChi

---

[1]Don Martín Enríquez de Almansa, viceroy of New Spain (1568–80).

[2]Don Fernando de Villagómez was named as bishop of Tlaxcala in the 1550s but apparently did not actually arrive on the scene until 1570. He was present for only two years.

[3]Tlaxcalans went on numerous expeditions of settlement and conquest throughout the century.

[4]On the indigenous family name Calzón see the entry for 1603.

[5]The rotting away of the paper makes it impossible to read more.

1568   Here in this year the viceroy don Martín Enríquez came.[1]

Reed

1569

Flint-knife

1570   Here in this year the bishop don Fernando Villagómez came; he died in Atlixco
        when he was going on an inspection tour.[2] In this same year a party went to
        Chichimec country.[3] Tlaxcalans went, and don Miguel Calzón[4] went. The rea-
        son [Calzón?] went was [. . .][5]

House

1571

Rabbit

1572

--------- [*f. 4v*]

[Reed]

1573

Flint-knife

1574

House

1575   Here in this year the lord bishop don Pablo Gil de Talavera came. He got to the
        coast and died. He did not reach here.[6]

Rabbit

1576   It was here in this year that a great epidemic broke out, in April.[7] Two million
        indigenous people died in all.

---

[6]The Nahuatl could be taken to mean that the bishop died at a place called Atitlan. Spanish
sources confirm that he did not live to arrive in Puebla, but assert that his death occurred in 1544.
The confusion probably arose because the bishop who actually arrived in this period died after
holding office for only a very short time (see n. 1, p. 84). See Zerón Zapata, p. 50, and Schäfer
1942, vol. 2, pp. 600–01.

[7]A terrible epidemic from 1576 to 1581 is mentioned in many sources.

———

acatl

———

1577

———

tecpatl

———

1578   Nican ypa xihuitl hualmohuicac señor Obisp [*sic*] Dō antonio de morales y
         molina[1]

———

cali

———

1579

———

tochtli

———

1580[2]

———

acatl
——— [*f. 5*]
[acatl image]

———

1601   Nican ypa xihuitl yn omotlalique yanCuican alcaldes yeyntin yhuan regidores
         alhuasi [*sic*] mayores[3]

———

tecpatl

———

1602

———

cali

———

1603   NiCan ypan xihuitl yn omotlali gobernador D. Juan de Calso[4] yc ome go.[or]
         yhuan ycuac motlalique xoNacatepec[5] tlaca huel achtopa tlalmaseuhque ca
         yehuantin – Juan lucas – Juan cortes – baltasar conetzin lucas de luna – Juan
         hernandes Juan de rojas Ca yehuantin achtopa motlalique

———

tochtli

_____

[1]Don Antonio Ruiz de Morales y Molina became bishop of Tlaxcala in 1572 and apparently
died shortly thereafter.

[2]A gap of twenty years follows this entry. The same gap occurs in the most closely related set
of annals that we have (Gómez García et al. 2000). The missing years were apparently considered
in the year cycle, for starting with 1580 as a Rabbit year, 1601 indeed comes out as a Reed year.

[3]The three alcaldes would have been one each for the three subaltepetl that were evolving

—————

Reed

1577

—————

Flint-knife

1578.   Here in this year the lord bishop don Antonio de Morales y Molina came.[1]

—————

House

1579

—————

Rabbit

1580[2]

—————

Reed   [*f. 5*]

[Reed image]

1601   Here in this year three alcaldes as well as regidores and chief constables were installed for the first time.[3]

—————

Flint-knife

1602

—————

House

1603   Here in this year don Juan de Calzón[4] was installed as governor. He was the second governor. And at this time the people of Xonacatepec[5] settled [here] and obtained land for the very first time. Those who first settled were Juan Lucas, Juan Cortés, Baltasar Conetzin, Lucas de Luna, Juan Hernández, and Juan de Rojas.

—————

Rabbit

————————————————

among the indigenous population of Puebla. The other officers were no doubt also allocated among the three in some manner. In a literal reading, however, the passage could mean merely that it was the first time in office for each of the three alcaldes and other officials.

[4]Ordinarily *de* would not be used with the name Calzón; Nahuatl texts sometimes use too much *de*, by Spanish principles (they also frequently omit it where it is customary in the Spanish context).

[5]On the barrio of Xonacatepec see the introduction, p. 29.

1604   NiCan ypan xihuitl huala señor OBispo D. diego Romano[1] (–) Sanno ypan xi-
         huitl yn omochiuh cōgregasion nohuiyan quinechicoque tlatlacatzitzintin[2]

acatl

1605   NiCan ypan xihuitl huala biRey D. juan de mendoza yhuan marques de mon-
         tesclaroz y marques de caxtil[3]

tecpatl

1606

cali

1607

tochtli
                        [f. 5v]
1608

acatl

1609   NiCan ypan xihuitl momiquili ttotlatoCatzin Rey PHe Po III[4]

tecpatl

1610   Nican ypan xihuitl huala Don juan baptista tisatl[5] [sic] yc yey gobernador (–)
         auh Sanno yquac yn omochiuh cabildo sala Real ynic yey altepetl quichiuhque
         san fransisco san pablo santiago[6] (–) Sano yquac yn omochiuh biRey yn
         arsobispo mexico santo domingo teopixqui ytoCatzin Don frai grasia de quiera[7]

cali

---

[1]Don Diego Romano, bishop of Tlaxcala (1577–1607).

[2]The reduplicated *tlatlaca* is a common form of the plural of *tlacatl*, person, in this region. The
reverential with nouns such as *macehualli*, "commoner," or *cocoxqui*, "sick person," connotes the
subject's humility or pitiable condition, and I take it in that sense here.

[3]Don Juan de Mendoza y Luna, marqués de Montesclaros, viceroy of New Spain (1603–1607).
I do not find other titles attested, and the last title is somehow truncated; taken literally as it is, in
Nahuatl it would mean "marqués of chicken."

[4]Philip III died in 1621. This error is often found in the Tlaxcala-Puebla family of annals.

1604   Here in this year the lord bishop don Diego Romano came.[1] (–) In this same
        year a congregation was carried out. From everywhere they gathered the poor
        people[2] together.

———

Reed

1605   Here in this year came the viceroy don Juan de Mendoza y Luna, marqués de
        Montesclaros and marqués de Castil.[3]

———

Flint-knife

1606

———

House

1607

———

Rabbit   [*f. 5v*]

1608

———

Reed

1609   Here in this year our ruler King Philip III died.[4]

———

Flint-knife

1610   Here in this year don Juan Bautista from Tizatla[5] came as third governor. (–).
        And at the same time a cabildo was held in the *sala real*, so that they formed
        three altepetl, San Francisco, San Pablo, and Santiago.[6] (–) At the same time the
        archbishop of Mexico became viceroy. He was a Dominican friar named don
        fray García Guerra.[7]

———

House

---

[5]The word "tisatl" must have been intended to read "tisatla." Within the Tlaxcalan provenience
of the indigenous people in Puebla, Tizatla seems to receive mention especially often in this text.

[6]This then would be the formal establishment of three subaltepetl, though they are mentioned
before this time (see 1601). The sala real, "royal chamber," is where the Spanish alcalde mayor
held court.

[7]Don fray Francisco García Guerra, archbishop of Mexico (1607–1612), acting viceroy of New
Spain (1611–1612). Francisco was usually omitted and García treated as a first name, as here.

1611   Nican ypa xihuitl yn otlayohuac ybisperas san bernabe apostol ypan yey ora
        ypan tonali viernes yc matlactli[1] ___ tonali mani metztli junio

_____

tochtli

_____

1612   Nican ypa xihuitl huala BiRey marques de guadaCasar[2] (–) Sanno yquac yn
        oquichihuasquia yaoyotl[3] tliltique ypan jueves santo onpā mexico

_____

acatl

_____

1613   NiCan ypan xihuitl huala señor OBispo Don alonso de la mota[4]
        ———— [f. 6]
tecpatl

_____

1614   NiCan ypa xihuitl Oquisaco[5] japones yc matlactli omey tonali mani metztli ma-
        yo

_____

cali

_____

1615

_____

tochtli

_____

1616   NiCan ypa xihuitl yn otlacuiloloc ycapillatzin san Ju[o] baptista[6] yquac otlanqui
        pulpito ymactzinco frai fran[co] de luria yhuan frai sebastia maldonado huey
        guardian y senpoali yhuan nahui tonali mani metz [sic] Junio

_____

acatl

_____

1617

_____

tecpatl

_____

1618   Nican ypan xihuitl Opeuhqui yn icaltzin San[to] angel de la guarda ytencopa-
        tzinco omochiuhtzino Don alonso de RyBera yc matlactli tonali mani metztli
        março

_____

[1]The writer seems to have meant to specify the rest of the number, rendering it June 11, 12, 13,
or 14.
    [2]Don Diego Fernández de Córdoba, marqués de Guadalcázar, viceroy of New Spain (1612–21).
    [3]While *quichihua yaoyotl* means to make war even on the broadest scale and in the most formal
sense, in postcontact texts it at times seems to include phenomena such as fights, disturbances,
riots, anything involving group violence. Chimalpahin, living in Mexico City at the time, tells a
fuller story of the suspected plot on the part of Afro-Mexicans, showing strong skepticism about it.
He reports that 28 men and 7 women were ultimately hanged, though many died still swearing to

1611   Here in this year it grew dark on the eve of San Bernabé Apóstol, at 3 o'clock on Friday, the __th[1] day of the month of June.

————————

Rabbit

1612   Here in this year the viceroy Marqués de Guadalcázar came.[2] (–) At this same time some blacks were about to make war[3] in Mexico City on Holy Thursday.

————————

Reed

1613   Here in this year the lord bishop don Alonso de la Mota came.[4]
—————— [*f. 6*]
Flint-knife

1614   Here in this year a Japanese passed through[5] on the 13th day of the month of May.

————————

House

1615

————————

Rabbit

1616   Here in this year the chapel of San Juan Bautista[6] was painted. At that time the pulpit was finished under the direction of fray Francisco de Loria and fray Sebastián Maldonado, the chief guardian, on the 24th day of the month of June.

————————

Reed

1617

————————

Flint-knife

1618   Here in this year there began [the building of] the house [church] of the Santo Angel de la Guarda, It was done at the command of don Alonso de Ribera. [It was begun] on the 10th day of the month of March.

————————

their innocence. See Chimalpahin 2006. For a useful account of these events summarizing Spanish bureaucrats' reports, see Carrión 1970, pp. 21–23.

   [4]Don Alonso de la Mota y Escobar, bishop of Tlaxcala (1607–1625).

   [5]The form *quiçaco* is often seen when a ship lands at the coast, etc. In this case, Chimalpahin (2006, pp. 282–83) speaks of a Japanese ambassador who left the capital in May to go to Spain, which would have involved passing through Puebla.

   [6]A *capilla para indios* in the complex of the monastery of San Francisco (Zerón Zapata, p. 81), the focal point of the Tlaxcalan community's worship until they built a full church nearby (1643).

———

cali

———

1619

———

tochtli

———

1620   Nican ypa xihuitl yn opopocac sitlalin ypan ylhuitzin san diego (–) Sanno ypan
        xihuitl yn oquimictiq̄ totatzin onpa amosoc cuauhtla[1] ypā ylhuitzin san sebastian

—————— [*f. 6v*]

acatl

———

1621   Nican ypa xihuitl Ohuala BiRey D. diego del castillo meda y portugal de gelbes
        marques de pliego[2] motepoztlaquetiaya

———

tecpatl

———

1622   NiCan ypa xihuitl yn oquisaco huancho quihualhuicac chicahuac tlatlasistli miec
        yc momiquili Onpa oquitlatiq̄ huexotzinco[3]

———

cali

———

1623

———

tochtli

———

1624   Nican ypa xihuitl yn oquichihuilique yaoyotl biRey gelbes[4] yhuan quitlatiliq̄
        palasio (–) Sanno ypa xihuitl huala BiRey D. Rodrigo pacheco Osorio marques
        de seRalbo[5]

———

acatl

———

---

[1]Krug, in "Nahuatl Annals," compares three versions of this statement found in the area's
annals: 1) "oquimictique teopixqui amotzoc opā cuauhtla ytoca fray gaspar" 2) "oquimictiq̄ totatzin
onpa amosoc cuauhtla" (the same as the passage here) and 3) "hoquimictique se totatzin amosoc
cuauhtl[. . .] yhuan hoquimictique xonacatepec yei tlacatzintzintin calyecac hoquimictique" The
first entry is particularly helpful, as it demonstrates that the place name and the word "woods"
should be understood separately. The third entry makes the further clarification that three people
from Xonacatepec killed him [in front of?] the house [or church building?]. Trautmann 1980 lists
San Bernabé Amaxac or Amoxoc, which could be a candidate for the place mentioned, but much
more likely would be the parish of Amozoc (also called Amozoque) to the east of Puebla. Zapata
offers us Santa María Amozoc, a hamlet appearing only once in his whole manuscript, for 1679,
when another priest living there and known to him personally was transferred to a parish in Puebla.
An entry comparable to the present one is in the Tlaxcalan annals in this volume for 1620.

————

House

1619

————

Rabbit

1620   Here in this year a comet appeared on the feast day of San Diego. (–) This same
        year was when they killed our father [a priest] in the woods at Amozoc,[1] on the
        feast day of San Sebastián.

———— [*f. 6v*]

Reed

1621   Here in this year came the viceroy don Diego del Castillo Meda y Portugal de
        Gelbes, marqués de Pliego.[2] He was dressed in iron [wore armor].

————

Flint-knife

1622   Here in this year Huancho passed by. He brought with him a bad cough of which
        many died. They burned him at Huexotzinco.[3]

————

House

1623

————

Rabbit

1624   Here in this year they made war on viceroy Gelves[4] and burned his palace. (–) In
        this same year came viceroy don Rodrigo Pacheco Osorio, marqués de Ce-
        rralvo.[5]

————

Reed

———————————

[2]Don Diego Carrillo de Mendoza y Pimentel, conde de Priego, marqués de Gelves, viceroy of
New Spain (1621–1624). His wife was the high-ranking doña Leonor de Portugal, which perhaps
explains our writer's conception of the viceroy's surname.

[3]Other annals from the region make it clear that many died of the illness before the vengeful
burning occurred. The great impact of the disease, which took mostly children, is visible in a record
of deaths in Huexotzinco (John Carter Brown Library, Codex Indigenous 43, Los Difuntos). In
1619–1630 at least 3,000 died in that region alone. The illness would kill a town's small children,
and then return a few years later when new births had created another susceptible population. The
annals of Tlaxcala in this volume refer to the same topic under the year 1623.

[4]The phrase could also be translated "a riot broke out against the viceroy" (see n. 3, p. 88). The
viceroy and the archbishop were virtually at war with each other. For a recent analysis, see Cañeque 2004, pp. 63–65, 79–80.

[5]Don Rodrigo Pacheco y Osorio, marqués de Cerralvo, viceroy of New Spain (1624–1635).

1625   NiCan ipa xihuitl ynn otlayohuac ypan sauado ypan ylhuitzin santo tomas de
        aquino cuaresma ypan matlactli ora yhuan tlaco yn otlayohuac huel onesque yn
        sisitlaltin yc chicuey tonali mali [*sic*] metztli marso (–) Sanno ypa xihuitl yn
        omomiquili s^r Obispo D. alonso de la mota (–) sāno ypa xihuitl huala visitador
        oquinechiCoCo yn itlatqui gelbes
──────── [*f. 7*]

tecpatl

1626

cali

1627   NiCan ypa xihuitl hualmohuicac Sr Obispo D. gutierres fernandes de quiroz[1] yc
        caxtoli tonali mani metztli otubre

tochtli

1628

acatl

1629   NiCan ypan xihuitl ttenqui atl mexico ypan san mateo ybisperas (–) Sanno
        yquac canqui ytequiuh D. diego peres yc nahui gobernador

tecpatl

1630   Nican ypā xihuitl yanCuican Oquisqui prosesion animas ypan lunes santo yc
        chicuey tonali mani metztli abril ytencopatzinco frai geronimo majuelo ca nochi
        quisaco papaloteca tenantzinco tlaca San cosme tlaca cuauhtotohuacan tlatlaca
        San geronimo tlaca mochin quisaco yca tunica (–) Sanno pan [*sic*] xihuitl yaloac
        atatacoyā yc matlactli tonali mani metztli de disiembre[2]

cali

1631   Nican ypan xihuitl yn omolinitzino santissima crus huey milagro Oquimochi-
        huilitzino ylhuitzin[3] tlaxcaltecapan

tochtli

──────────────────

[1]Don Gutierre Bernardo de Quiroz, bishop of Tlaxcala (1626–1638).

1625   Here in this year it grew dark on Saturday, the feast day of San Tomás de
        Aquino, during Lent, at half past ten o'clock. When it was dark the stars
        appeared clearly. It was on the 8th day of the month of March. (–) In this same
        year the lord bishop don Alonso de la Mota died. (–) In this same year an
        inspector general came to collect Gelves's property.

——————— [*f. 7*]

Flint-knife

1626
———————

House

1627   Here in this year came the lord bishop don Gutierre Fernández de Quiroz,[1] on
        the 15th day of the month of October.

———————

Rabbit

1628
———————

Reed

1629   Here in this year Mexico City was inundated, on the eve of San Mateo. (–) At
        this same time don Diego Pérez took up his post as fourth governor.

———————

Flint-knife

1630   Here in this year for the first time the procession [of the cofradía of] Animas
        came out on Monday of Easter week, the 8th day of the month of April. At the
        command of fray Gerónimo Majuelo the people of Papalotlan, Tenantzinco, San
        Cosme, Quauhtotohuacan, and San Gerónimo all came out. They all came out in
        tunics. (–) In this same year, on the 10th day of the month of December, a party
        went to the place of excavation related to water.[2]

———————

House

1631   Here in this year the most holy cross moved. It performed a great miracle [on]
        its feast day[3] in [the barrio of] Tlaxcaltecapan.

———————

Rabbit

———————————————————————

[2]Doubtless having to do with the *desagüe* projects in the Valley of Mexico during this time of
great flooding. See also the (second) entry for 1553.

[3]Gómez García et al. 2000 has "omolinitzino Santisima Cruz ipā ilhuitzin" with *ipan*, "on."

1632   Nican ypan xihuitl ȳ cualoc tonatiuh yc caxtoli tonali mani metztli abril (–) San [*sic*] yquac[1] tlanqui yn icaltzin s.to angel de la guarda ypan metztli marÇo[2]

——— [*f. 7v*]

acatl

———

1633   NiCan ypan xihuitl tepouh jues don antonio de miranda solis (–) Sanno ycuac tlatlasistli quisaco ytoca chichimeco miyec tlacatl y omomiquili[3] (–) Sanno ypa xihuitl yn omoteochiuh rretablo capilla san juan baptista[4] capillero frai Juan ñuñes ypan metztli otubre alcalde marcoz bernal regidor mayor migel bueno alhuasil mayor bartolome agustin yn ipatiuh rretablo se mill yhuan chiconpuali pesos

———

tecpatl

———

1634   Nican ypan xihuitl xittin puentte atoyac[5] yc matlactli tonali mani metztli mayo (–) Sanno ycuac tlapan canpana yglesia mayor yc 22 tonali mani metztli Junio ipan corpoz rey[6] ytetzauh mochiuh huey CoColistli (–) Sanno ypa xihuitl yn opeuhqui huey CoColistli ypan abril miyec tlaCatl momiquili motocaya Semilhuitl napoali tlacatl ytzatzalan pipiltzitzintin auh yn achitzin omocauh ypan ytlasoylhuitzin San fran[co] auh yn capillero frai diego del Castillo teopixCatzintli tepan moquixtiaya motetlamaquiliaya techachan omotlali ospital ychan pedro Juares catca[7] (–) Sanno ypan disiembre chicahuac yeyecac

———

cali

———

1635

——— [*f. 8*]

Nican ypan xihuitl huala BiRey D. lopes dias de almendras marques de calderetta[8] (–) Sanno pa [*sic*] xihuitl yn omochiuh Jues alcalde maJor Don ju[o] de seruātes[9] Ottepouh

———

tochtli

———

1636   Nican ypan xihuitl Oquisaco Altepeatl ypan ybisperas Sa bartolome ypan Sabado ypan chiquasen Ora tteOtlac[10] capillero frai x̄tobal de bargas

---

[1]"San iquac" should read "sanno iquac," "at the same time." Across the text the writer makes the same error at least ten times in connection with specifying the same time or year, probably because of the commonness of this formula here. Henceforth I will omit [*sic*] in such cases.

[2]See also the entry for 1618.

[3]Nearly all the annals in the Tlaxcala-Puebla family mention this epidemic. See the next year's entry for the progress of the disease.

[4]See also the entry for 1616.

[5]The Atoyac frequently flooded in the rainy season.

1632   Here in this year there was an eclipse of the sun on the 15th day of the month of
        April. (–) At this same time,[1] the house [church] of the Santo Angel de la
        Guarda was completed, in March.[2]

——————— [*f. 7v*]

Reed

1633   Here in this year judge don Antonio de Miranda Solís took a census. (–) At this
        same time a cough called "the Chichimeco" broke out. Many people died.[3] (–)
        In this same year, in the month of October, the altarpiece of the chapel of San
        Juan Bautista was consecrated.[4] Fray Juan Núñez was chaplain; Marcos Bernal
        was alcalde; Miguel Bueno was regidor mayor; Bartolomé Agustín was chief
        constable. The cost of the altarpiece was 1,140 pesos.

————————

Flint-knife

1634   Here in this year the Atoyac[5] bridge collapsed, on the 10th day of the month of
        May. (–) At this same time a cathedral bell cracked, on the 22nd of June, Corpus
        Christi day;[6] it was the omen of a great plague. (–) In this same year, in April, a
        great plague began. Many people died. Each day eighty people, children among
        them, were buried. It let up a little on the precious day of San Francisco. And the
        friar in charge of the chapel, fray Diego del Castillo, went among the people. He
        held communion in various people's homes. A hospital was set up in the home
        of the late Pedro Juárez.[7] (–) In this same time, in December, strong winds blew.

————————

House

1635   [*f. 8*]

        In this year came the viceroy don Lope Díez de Almendras, marqués de
        Cadareita.[8] (–) In this same year don Juan de Cervantes[9] became judge and
        alcalde mayor; he took a census.

————————

Rabbit

1636   Here in this year the altepetl water came out on the eve of San Bartolomé, at 6
        o'clock in the evening.[10] The chaplain was fray Cristóbal de Vargas.

———————————————

[6]The meaning of the word "rey" is not clear; perhaps it is a reinterpretation of one of the old
ways of abbreviating Christo or Christi (such as $\overline{xpi}$).

[7]An alternative translation is "in what used to be the home of Pedro Juárez." It was the practice
in Puebla to turn large houses into hospitals in periods of epidemic. See Carrión 1970, p. 30.

[8]Don Lope Díez de Almendáriz, marqués de Cadereita, viceroy of New Spain (1635–1640).

[9]Don Julio de Cervantes Carvajal was alcalde mayor at this time (López de Villaseñor 1961).

[10]The entry apparently concerns some sort of municipal water supply, most likely a fountain in
a plaza, but the mention of the chaplain connects the project with the chapel of San Juan Bautista.

acatl

1637   Nican ypan xihuitl yaloac quauhtla Omotamachihuato tlali yquac huala alcalde
        corte ypan abril (–) Sanno yquac yn omotteochiuh Canpana yglesia mayor
        yttoCa D.Nā MaRya ypan lunes yc chicui tonali 8 mani metztli Junio[1] (–) Sanno
        yquac quinmiminque tlilttique senttepec maCuilttin[2]

tecpatl

1638   Nican ypan xihuitl yn omomiquili S.ʳ OBispo D. guttierres bernando de quiroz
        yc chicome 7 tonali mani metztli febrero ypan sabado tteotlac

cali

1689[3] Nican ypan xihuitl yn oSepayauh yc matlactli 10 ttonali mani metztli de enero
        (–) Sanno yquac peuhqui saranpio miec yc Omomiquili (–) Sanno ypan xihuitl
        yn ocāqui itequiuh D. barttolome corttes yc chicunahui 9 tonali mani metztl [sic]
        Junio ypā Jueves yc macuili 5 goberdor [sic]
        ———— [f. 8v]
tochtli

1640   Nican ypan xihuitl Ohualmohuicac S.ʳ OBisPo Don Juan de palafos de mendo-
        za[4] ypan maria magdalenā ylhuitzin ypan sabado yc senpoali yhuā ome 22 tonali
        mani metztli Julio (–) Sanno yquac huala biRey D. diego pacheco duque desca-
        lona marques de villenas[5] oc omocauh San antonio ye quin Juebes calac yn
        Siudad yc Senpoali yhuan chicome 27 tonali mani metztli Julio — Sāno ypan
        xihuitl yn opeuhqui yglesia mayor obra

acatl

1641   Nican ypan xihuitl yn ottechaque clerigos yca doctrina[6] Cura baesa ymatica
        quitlapo yn puerta santa crus del milagro ypan domingo yohuatzinco yc caxtoli
        omome 17 tonali mani metztli de Enero (–) Sanno ypan xihuitl yn omochiuh
        BiRey S.ʳ Obispo D. Juan de palafos[7]

———

[1]Spanish records indicate exactly the same date for the consecration of the bell (Zerón Zapata, p. 69).

[2]This sentence probably means that they were shot with arrows, but the missiles could be of other kinds. Centepec was located just to the west of the city.

[3]The original intention can only have been 1639, although the "8" is clear in the manuscript.

[4]Don Juan de Palafox y Mendoza, bishop of Tlaxcala (1639–1649).

[5]Don Diego López Pacheco Cabrera y Bobadilla, marqués de Villena, duque de Escalona,

———————

Reed

1637　　Here in this year a party went to the forest to measure land. At that time an alcalde de corte [criminal judge of the Royal Audiencia] came, in April. (–) At this same time the cathedral bell called doña María was consecrated, on Monday, the 8th day of the month of June.[1] (–) At this same time they shot five blacks at Centepec.[2]

———————

Flint-knife

1638　　Here in this year the lord bishop don Gutierre Bernardo de Quiroz died, on Saturday, the 7th day of the month of February, in the afternoon.

———————

House

1689[3]　Here in this year it snowed on the 10th day of the month of January. (–) At this same time the measles began, of which many died. (–) In this same year don Bartolomé Cortés took up his post on Thursday, the 9th day of the month of June, as the fifth governor.

——————— [*f. 8v*]

Rabbit

1640　　Here in this year, on the feast day of María Magdalena, Saturday, the 22nd day of the month of July, the lord bishop don Juan de Palafox y Mendoza[4] came. (–) At the same time came the viceroy don Diego Pacheco, duque de Escalona, marqués de Villena.[5] First he stopped at San Antonio. Only on Thursday, the 27th day of the month of July, did he enter the city. — In this same year work began on the cathedral.

———————

Reed

1641　　Here in this year the secular clergy took us over as to religious instruction;[6] the parish priest Baeza with his own hand opened the door of [the church of] Santa Cruz del Milagro early on Sunday, the 17th day of the month of January. (–) In this same year the lord bishop don Juan de Palafox became viceroy.[7]

———————

——————————————

viceroy of New Spain (1640–1642).

　[6]*Doctrina* was religious instruction, catechism in a broad sense, but the word also meant a parish with an indigenous population, and that may be the sense here, for the secular clergy was indeed taking over administration of many indigenous parishes from the mendicant orders.

　[7]From June to November 1642, the bishop of Puebla served as archbishop and acting viceroy of New Spain. When his replacement came he resigned and returned to his duties in Puebla.

tecpatl

_____

1642   Nican ypan xihuitl oc sepa quisaco cocolistli omotlali ozpital ycan alonso catca[1]
        yn omotocaya onpa santa crus del milagro yn tlatlacatzitzintin (–) Sāno ypan
        xihuitl Ohuala viRey Conde de salbatierra[2]

_____

cali

_____

1643   Nican ypan xihuitl yn omotocac Simiento Juan de Ryo Sann oc yxtlahuacan
        catca yn quimotoquili Simiento cura ytoca Sebastian de pedrasa yhuan yermano-
        tzin migel de pedrasa ypan ylhuitzin maria magdalena ypan miercoles Regidor
        mayor nicolas ypolito alhuasil mayor diego migel fiscal marcoz bernal

_____ [f. 9]
tochtli

_____

1644   Nican ypan xihuitl yn Omotepexihuique quapatlanque Opoztec yn cuahuitl ni-
        man yexcan Oquisqui[3] yquac yn ocalmamalihuac de lo rredioz[4] [sic] yc caxtoli
        ose 16 tonali mani metztl de ottubre ypan domingo teotlac miec tlacatl omo-
        miquilique (–) Sanno ypan xihuitl yn omomiquili Reyna donā ysabel de borbon[5]
        ynfanta de fransia yc caxtoli ose 16 tonali mani metztli otubre

_____

acatl

_____

1645   Nican ypan xihuitl yn oquimopopoztequilique S. Juan yhuan santo xp̄o onpa
        sentepec ypan lunes yc matlactli Ose 11 tonali mani metztli de disiembre otla-
        masehualoc

_____

tecpatl

_____

1646   Nican ypan xihuitl omochiuh BiRey y Señor Obispo ōpa huaXacac Don marcoz
        de torres[6]

_____

cali

_____

1647

_____

[1]The form "ycan" must be for "ychan," "(at) his home." As in the similar case in 1634, the
meaning could be "in what used to be Alonso's home."

[2]Don García Sarmiento de Sotomayor, conde de Salvatierra, marqués de Sobroso, viceroy of
New Spain (1642–1648).

[3]The "head-flyers" or *voladores de palo* were acrobats who would climb to the top of a high
pole set up for the purpose, attached by strong ropes or ribbons, and then come spiraling down
head-first bit by bit in various patterns. They still perform in Mexico.

Flint-knife

1642   Here in this year sickness broke out again. A hospital was set up in the late Alonso's home.[1] The poor people were buried at Santa Cruz del Milagro. (–) In this same year the viceroy conde de Salvatierra came.[2]

_____

House

1643   Here in this year the foundation for the church of [San] Juan del Río was laid. It was still only empty plain when the parish priest named Sebastián de Pedraza laid the foundation, along with his brother Miguel de Pedraza, on the feast day of María Magdalena, a Wednesday. The regidor mayor was Nicolás Hipólito; the chief constable was Diego Miguel; the fiscal was Marcos Bernal.

_____ [*f. 9*]

Rabbit

1644   Here in this year the head-flyers fell to the ground. The pole broke and then separated into three parts.[3] It was when the building of Los Remedios[4] was inaugurated, on the 16th day of the month of October, a Sunday in the afternoon. Many people died. (–) In this same year, the queen, doña Isabel de Borbón,[5] died, on the 16th day of the month of October. She was a French princess.

_____

Reed

1645   Here in this year they [accidentally] broke into pieces [images of] San Juan and Santo Cristo at Centepec, on Monday, the 11th day of the month of December. Penances were performed.

_____

Flint-knife

1646   Here in this year the bishop of Oaxaca, don Marcos de Torres,[6] became viceroy.

_____

House

1647

_____

_____

[4]This was the church of Nuestra Señora de los Remedios (Zerón Zapata, p. 89). It was in the indigenous barrio of Analco, where many Tlaxcalans lived.

[5]The wife of Philip IV. She was the daughter of Henry IV of France and Marie de' Medici and several times was left to govern Spain in her husband's absence. She did die in this year, and the funeral celebrations in Puebla surpassed any in recent memory. The indigenous cabildo participated in the procession. Hernández Yahuitl 1999.

[6]Don Marcos de Torres y Rueda, bishop of Yucatan, acting viceroy of New Spain (1648–1649).

tochtli

1648

---

acatl

1649   Nican ypan xihuitl yN OMO·TEOChihu [*sic*] yglesia mayor ypan marttes
        ylhuitzin san marcos yc senpoali yhuan macuili 25 tonali mani metztli a abril[1]
        Oquimoteochihuili S. obispo D. juan de palafoz[2] Sanno yquac yn otlatlaque
        judios mexico se yolticatca yn tlatlacac [*sic*] ytoca tremiño[3]
        ——————— [*f. 9v*]

tecpatl

1650   Ninan [*sic*] ypan xihuitl huala biRey D. luis enRyques de gusmā conde de alua-
        ro[4] yc caxtoli yhuan yey 18 tonali mani metztli Julio

---

cali

1651

---

tochtli

1652   Nipan [*sic*] xihuitl yn omochiuh capittulo general[5] ypan sabado yc Sempuali
        yhuan chicome 27 tonali mani metztli Enero Capillero frai mattias de sifuentes
        (–) Sanno ypan xihuitl Ohuala don blas de galisia ychicuasen 6 gobernador y
        ypan domingo quiseli yn ttopili ypan ylhuitzin San Juan yc sempuali yhua nahui
        24 tonali mani metztli Junio (–) Sanno ypan xihuitl yn oxitin coliuhqui miec
        oatococ[6] yhuan quixitini puentte attoyac ypan ylhuitzin San fransisco viernes —
        Sanno ypan xihuitl ttemictti armiJo quimicti don balerio ypan Semansanta [*sic*]
        (–) Sanno ypan xihuitl opopocac Sitlalin yn ipocyo ytztoya yttech matlalCue-
        yetzin[7] ypan disiembre

---

acatl

1653   NiCan ypan xihuitl yn otlalolin ypan ylhuitzin san anto pan [*sic*] viernes yc

---

[1]The text reads "a abril" because the writer started the word over at a line break. The phenomenon is common in this document. Henceforth I will add *sic* in the text but will not comment in a
footnote.

[2]The cathedral had been under construction for a century, and was mostly finished by the early
seventeenth century. Palafox pushed to complete and consecrate it (Zerón Zapata, pp. 55–56).

[3]Tomás Treviño. Some other Jews were burned in this period as well. See Liebman 1970. The
1596 burning of Luis de Carvajal is mentioned in a related set of annals in the AAMC (for background see Cohen 2001). As we have seen (n. 2, p. 84), the years 1580–1600 are missing in the
present set.

Rabbit

1648

─────────

Reed

1649   Here in this year the cathedral was consecrated on the feast day of San Marcos, Tuesday the 25th day of the month of April.[1] The lord bishop don Juan de Palafox consecrated it.[2] In this same year Jews were burned in Mexico City. One was alive when he burned; his name was Tremiño.[3]

─────── [*f. 9v*]

Flint-knife

1650   Here in this year the viceroy don Luis Enríquez de Guzmán, conde de Alvaro,[4] came, on the 18th day of the month of July.

─────────

House

1651

─────────

Rabbit

1652   Here in this year a general chapter meeting[5] was held on Saturday, the 17th day of the month of January. The chaplain [in charge of San Juan Bautista] was fray Matías de Cifuentes. (–) In this same year came don Blas de Galicia, the sixth governor. He received the staff on the feast day of San Juan, Sunday, on the 24th day of the month of June. (–) In this same year arches collapsed. Much was inundated.[6] And [the flood?] destroyed the bridge on the Atoyac on Friday, the feast day of San Francisco. — In this same year Armijo committed murder; he killed don Valerio during Holy Week. (–) In this same year a comet appeared. Its tail faced toward Matlalcueye.[7] It was in December.

─────────

Reed

1653   Here in this year there was an earthquake on the feast day of San Antonio,

─────────────────────

[4]Don Luis Enríquez de Guzmán, conde de Alva de Liste, marqués de Villaflor, viceroy of New Spain (1650–1653).

[5]The reference is apparently to the Franciscan order, especially since the writer's barrio was in the section of the city dominated by the Franciscan establishment.

[6]Given the next sentence, the reference is probably to the arches of a bridge. Grammatically, it is possible that only one arch crumbled. It is also possible that many people were drowned rather than things inundated, since here *miec* is sometimes a collective in speaking of people, and the verb could mean carried off by the water instead of drowned or inundated.

[7]Matlalcueye is the famous volcano/mountain now known in Spanish as "la Malinche."

caxtoli yhuan ome 17 tonali mani metztli Enero yohualtica ypan matlactli ose
11½ ora[1] yhuan tlaco (–) Sanno ypan xihuitl huala bRey [*sic*] D. fransisco
fernandes marques de alboorqueque[2] [*sic*] yc Senpuali yhuan macuili 25 tonali
mani metztli agosto (–) San ypan xihuitl yn omotlecolti totlasonantzin de
guadalupe tepeticpac quiauhticac yn omotlecolti[3] pan [*sic*] domingo yc senpuali
yhuan macuili 25 mani metztli disiembre

——————— [*f. 10*]

tecpatl
——————

1654   Nican ypā xihuitl yn opiloloque nahuintin yn iuh yalhua CatCa ylhuitzin maria
        magdalena hualathui Juebes yc Senpuali yhua yey 23 mani metztli Julio[4] achto-
        pa piloloc Ju⁰ fran^co niman Ju⁰ miguel Ocoton mecatl tlatzin[5] ohuetzico niman
        oc sepa otlecoc[6] momiq̄li niman fran^co espinosa Satepā diego alonso

——————

cali
——————

1655   Nican ypa xihuitl yn omic alcalde mayor D. diego oreJon ypan ylhuitzin San
        sebastian

——————

tochtli
——————

1656   Nican ypan xihuitl ohualmohuicac señor obispo don diego OSorio y llamas
        escobal[7] yc Sēpuali yhuā yey 23 mani metztli Junio

——————

acatl
——————

1657
——————

tecpatl
——————

1658
——————

cali
——————

1659   Nican ypan xihuitl yn omomictique tlilttique yhuā caxtilteca ypan Juebes Santo
        oncan y motlalia tlaxcalchiuhque auh yn señor obispo ōhualmoquixtia yglesi
        [*sic*] mayor oc sepa tetica Oquinmocalaquilique yn teopan yhuā Se Santo christo

——————————————

[1]The use of the fraction symbol ½ in this context is highly unusual.

[2]Don Francisco Fernández de la Cueva, duque de Alburquerque, viceroy of New Spain (1653–1660).

[3]Saints' images were spoken of and perhaps thought of as carrying out movements of their own volition. In effect, an image of the Virgin of Guadalupe was ceremonially carried to the top of the hill, and indeed the verb *tleco* can literally be so translated, depending on the intention.

[4]The annals of Tlaxcala in this volume also mention this event for the same year, adding that

Friday the 17th day of the month of January at half past 11 o'clock at night.[1] (–) In this same year came the viceroy don Francisco Fernández, marqués de Alburquerque.[2] (–) In this same year, our precious mother Guadalupe climbed up to the mountain top. It was raining as she went up.[3] It was on Sunday, the 25th of the month of December.

————— [*f. 10*]
Flint-knife

1654   Here in this year four people were hanged on the day after the feast day of María Magdalena, at dawn on Thursday, the 23rd of July.[4] First Juan Francisco was hanged. Then Juan Miguel; the rope broke and he fell down.[5] Then he climbed up[6] again and died. Then Francisco Espinosa, and afterward Diego Alonso.

House

1655   Here in this year the alcalde mayor don Diego Orejón died, on the feast day of San Sebastián.

Rabbit

1656   Here in this year the lord bishop don Diego Osorio y Llamas Escobar[7] came, on the 23rd of the month of June.

Reed

1657

Flint-knife

1658

House

1659   Here in this year blacks and Spaniards fought on Holy Thursday, where the bakers are set up [in the marketplace]. The lord bishop came out of the cathedral; with stones they forced them back in the church, along with a Santo Cristo

---

those hanged were thieves. The names of three of those hanged are typical for humble indigenous people. The expression *huallathui*, literally "as dawn is coming," or "when dawn came," can also mean at some time in the night before the day mentioned.

[5]The intention of "tlatzin" was apparently "tlatzintlan."

[6]Or was taken up.

[7]Don Diego Osorio de Escobar y Llamas, bishop of Tlaxcala (1656–1673). The annals of the region indicate that this bishop was well liked.

(–) Sāno ypan xihuitl yn omochiuh sāranpio miec yc omomiquili ypā otubre [*f. 10v*] Sanno ypan xihuitl yn omoteochiuh Retablo san juan de Rio yn ipatiuh Sentzontli yhua caxtolpuali pesos rregidor mayor juan agustin alhuasil mayor miguel de samora fiscal ju⁰ geronimo

tochtli

1660   NiCan ypā xihuitl yn ohuala BiRey D. ju⁰ de leybas de la serda marques del baño¹ (–) Sano ypa xihuitl yn omotocac simiento y canpanario omotoquili [*sic*] don p.⁰ prieto alCalde Ju⁰ geronimo fiscal Ju⁰ agustin (–) Sanno ypā xihuitl yn omotocac simiento calbario² oquimotoquilique san fran^co teopixque yhuan omenti clerigos se ytoca lisensiado martin fernandes yn oc se lisensiado don diego de bargas ypan lunes ybisperas san pedro yc puali [*sic*] yhuā chiCui 28 Junio

acatl

1661   Nican ypā xihuitl yn omo̶t̶e̶o̶c̶h̶i̶u̶h̶miquili alcalde mayor Conde de santiago³ ypan biernes yOhualtica yc caxtoli onnahui 19 tonali mani metztli nobiembre Sanno ypan xihuitl chicahuac omochiuh durasno se carga ypatiuh se yhuā melio

tecpatl

1662   Nican ypan xihuitl yn omoteochiuh tersera orden ypan domingo yc senpuali yhuan ome 22 de febrero (–) San ypan xihuitl y omotlayahualhui yn totlaso-mahuisnantzin yglesia mayor ypan sabado ylhuitzin San simon yc senpuali yhuan chicuey 28 tonali man [*sic*] metztli de otubre mochiuh nohuian Conbentos yhuan monJas seseyaca omochiuhta yn ilhuitzin (–) Sanno ypā xihuitl yn omo-chiuh maynalisitli [*sic*] ypatiuh ocatca yn tlaoli nahui peso 4 p⁰s⁴

cali

1663   Nican ypan xihuitl y mic alcalde mayor don felipe moral⁵ ypan martes teotlac yc senpuali yhuā [*f. 11*] chicome 27 tonali mani metztli março (–) San ycuac yn omoteochiuh San Roque⁶ yc se tonali abril ypan domingo (–) Sanno ypan xihuitl yn opiloloque omentin yc Senpuali yhuan chicome 27 tonali mani metztli Julio quartoz oquinchiuhque ypan otetlacuicuilique Sieniga Rey y tomin yn oquitecuilique auh yn intzontecon onpa quintlalito yn sienega biernes yn

---

¹Don Juan de Leiva y de la Cerda, conde de Baños, marqués de Leiva y Ladrada, viceroy of New Spain (1660–1664).

²A *calvario* was sometimes a tiny chapel and sometimes a cross set out of doors in a prominent place as a shrine. In the barrio of San Francisco, the Franciscans set up a *via crucis* extending from their establishment past the church of San Juan del Río and on up the hill, culminating in a cluster of chapels referred to simply as "El Calvario." It is most likely that this annalist is referring to a

[that he was displaying]. (–) In this same year, in October, measles broke out, of which many died. [*f. 10v*] In this same year the altarpiece of [the church of] San Juan del Río was dedicated. It cost 700 pesos. Juan Agustín was regidor mayor; Miguel de Zamora was chief constable; Juan Gerónimo was fiscal.

Rabbit

1660   Here in this year came the viceroy don Juan de Leiva de la Cerda, marqués del Baño.[1] (–) In this same year the foundation was laid for the belfry. Don Pedro Prieto, alcalde, laid it. Juan Gerónimo was fiscal, and Juan Agustín [was regidor mayor?]. (–) In this same year the foundation for the Calvario was laid.[2] Franciscan friars and two secular clerics, one named licenciado Martín Fernández and the other licenciado don Diego de Vargas, laid it, on Monday, the 28th of June, the eve of San Pedro.

Reed

1661   Here in this year the alcalde mayor, the conde de Santiago,[3] died, on Friday night, the 19th day of the month of November. In this same year peaches yielded abundantly; the cost of a load was 1½ reales.

Flint-knife

1662   Here in this year [the chapel of] the Third Order [of San Francisco] was consecrated, on Sunday, the 22nd of February. (–) In this same year our precious revered mother went in procession to the cathedral on Saturday, the feast day of San Simón, the 28th day of the month of October. Everywhere in each of the monasteries and convents his feast day was celebrated. (–) In this same year a famine occurred; the price of shelled maize was 4 pesos [a measure].[4]

House

1663   Here in this year the alcalde mayor don Felipe Moral[5] died, on Tuesday afternoon the 27th [*f. 11*] day of the month of March. (–) At this same time the [hospital] of San Roque[6] was consecrated on Sunday, the 1st day of April. (–) In this same year two people were hanged, on the 27th day of the month of July. They quartered them because they robbed people at La Ciénaga del Rey, taking money from them. Their heads were placed at La Ciénaga. It was a Friday when

chapel associated with the church for which the people of San Juan were responsible.

[3]Don Juan Altamirano y Velasco, conde de Santiago.

[4]No doubt per fanega.

[5]Don Felipe Morán de la Cerda.

[6]San Roque was a hospital for travelers. See Zerón Zapata, pp. 98–102.

opiloloque se ytoca Nicolas carrion yn oc se juan de grincola[1]

tochtli

1664   Nican iypā [sic] xihuitl yn omoteochiuh calbario ypan domingo yc caxtoli yhuan
        ome febrero (–) Sanno ypan xihuitl yn omochiuh birrey obispo don diego osorio
        y llamas de escobar[2] ypan lunes yohualtica ypan matlactli ora 10 yn ohuasico yn
        amatl nochin opapaque yn siudadanos oncan opeuhqui yn ahuili yn masehual-
        tzitzintin mochin mochi [sic] ynpan cahualo omahuiltique yn oasico yn amatl yc
        senpuali yhuā matlactli 3 [sic] tonali mani metztli Junio (–) Sanno ypa xihuitl yn
        ohuala virey D. antonio Sebastia de toledo de salasar marques de masera yc
        sempuali yhuan yey 23 tonali mani metztli septiembre[3] (–) Sanno ypan xihuitl
        yn opopocac sitlalin auh in ipocyo tlacpacopa ytztoya yn opeuhqui popoca ypan
        nobiembre yn omocahuato ypan Enero

acatl

1665   Nican yPā xihuitl huel temamauhtti y mochiuh yPan ylhuitzin San sebastian
        yohualttiCa huatlathui [sic] [f. 11v] Miercoles ypan yey ora yn ottopo ttePetl
        popocatzin yn iquac ottopon mochi quiquequenttihuetz y tletl yhuan muchi yn
        tlaltticpactli oolin yn opeuhqui yn popoca ypan Junio huel ttemamauhtti yn
        omochiuh (–) Sanno ypa xihuitl yn omottocac simiento San diego[4] yc senpuali
        oSe 21 tonali mani metztli enero (–) Sanno p̄a ypan xihuitl yn omanato canpana
        ypan chololan otli ypan martes yc Sempuali yhuan chicome 27 tonali mani
        metztli Enero niman hualathui Omoconsagraro ~~yttoca~~ ymaticatzinCo yn Señor
        Obispo D. diego Osorio OquicoSagraro ytoca y Campana Jesus NaZaReNo
        sanno pan [sic] febrero yc se tonali yn otlecoc ypan domingo yohuatzinco ypan
        chicuasen ora (–) Sāno ypan xihuitl yn opopocac sitlalin ypan cuaresma ypan
        marso yn ipocyo tlacpacpa ytztoya
        Sanno ypa xihuitl de 1665 yn omomiquili ttotlatocatzin yn Rey feliPe cuarto yc
        caxtoli yhuan ome 17 mani metztli Septtiembre ypan Juebes yohuatzinco ypā
        yey ora[5] sannopa [sic] xihuitl yn opiloloque chololtteca yc nahui 4 tonali mani
        metztli nobiembre ypan Juebes yn Se ytoca grabiel — yn oc Se juᵒ de s.tiago —
        ynic yey Andre pochtli [f. 12]
        Sanno ypa xihuitl[6] yn omochiuh Jura[7] ynic ome 2 tonali mani metztli Julio ypan
        ylhuitzin Santa ySabel oncan tianquisco omotlali tablado ca huel mahuistic yn
        omochiuh mochtin yn caballeroz oquisque AlcalDe mayor D. astasio coronel

---

[1]The name appears as "grinola" in Gómez García et al. 2000.

[2]The bishop of Tlaxcala, resident in Puebla and familiar to the people there, became acting
viceroy of New Spain in the middle of June and served until mid-October.

[3]Don Antonio Sebastián de Toledo Molina y Salazar, marqués de Mancera, viceroy of New
Spain (1664–1673).

[4]A chapel in the upper reaches of the barrio of San Francisco (Zerón Zapata, p.108). See also n.
2, p. 104.

they were hanged. One was named Nicolás Carrión, the other Juan de Griñola.[1]

Rabbit

1664   Here in this year the Calvario [chapel] was consecrated, on the 17th of February. (–) In this same year bishop don Diego Osorio y Llamas de Escobar became viceroy.[2] It was on a Monday night at 10 o'clock that the letter arrived. All the citizens rejoiced. Then began the celebration. All the indigenous people celebrated on horseback. The letter arrived on the 30th day of the month of June. (–) In this same year came the viceroy don Antonio Sebastián de Toledo de Salazar, marqués de Mancera, on the 23rd day of the month of September.[3] (–) In this same year a comet appeared; its tail faced up. It began in November and ended in January.

Reed

1665   Here in this year something very terrifying happened on the day of San Sebastián, during the night, very early [*f. 11v*] Wednesday at 3 o'clock, which was that Popocatepetl exploded. When it exploded, fire quickly covered it all, and the whole earth shook. It began to smoke in June. What happened was really terrifying. (–) In this same year the foundation of San Diego[4] was laid, on the 21st day of the month of January. (–) In this same year a bell was taken to the Cholula road, on Tuesday, the 27th day of the month of January. Then at dawn it was consecrated by the lord bishop don Diego Osorio. He consecrated the bell with the name of Jesús Nazareno. Also on the 1st day of February it was raised [to the belfry], on Sunday night at 6 o'clock. (–) In this same year a comet appeared during Lent, in March. Its tail faced upward.

In this same year of 1665 our ruler king Philip IV died, on the 17th of the month of September, Thursday, at 3 o'clock, early in the morning.[5] In this same year some Cholulans were hanged on Thursday, the 4th day of the month of November. One was named Gabriel, another Juan de Santiago, and the third Andrés Pochtli. [*f. 12*]

In this same year[6] the oath was taken,[7] on the 2nd day of the month of July, the feast day of Santa Isabel. A platform was set up in the marketplace. Very wonderfully was it done. All the [Spanish] gentlemen made an appearance.

---

[5]Philip IV reigned from 1661 to 1665.

[6]Here a mistake was made, for the account now actually speaks of events in 1666. Later the writer or someone else inserted "66" in the upper left-hand corner of the page.

[7]I.e., the oath of allegiance to the new monarch. Descriptions of that ceremony indicate that the governor of the indigenous cabildo held aloft a banner and participated in a manner parallel to that of the *alférez real* (royal ensign) of the Hispanic sector of the city. Leicht 1967, p.179.

y benabides yn omotlali yn totlatocatzin Don CaRloz II yn iquac ypan tablado omotlali niman oquitepeuhque tomin yhuan yn palasio yn alferes Omochiuh don fransisco fernãdes de salasar yn gobernador Don blas de galisia sã fran^co alcalde gaspar miguel regidor miguel de los s.tos

Sanno ypa xihuitl yc ome 2 tonali mani metztl agosto yn opeuhqui mosaca vigas[1] omotecata palasio asta santa calina[2] [*sic*] ypan calotli omotecato asta ycatenpan [*sic*] y señor Obispo asta yglesia mayor yn omotecac vigas sanno yquac yn omosacac ttumbulo[3] ynic huecapan quipia cenpuali yhuan nahui bara yc caxtoli ose 16 tonali mani metztli agosto ylhuitzin San Roque yn opeuhqui misa chiucnahui tonali yn omochiuh misa yn otlamito ypan ylhuitzin San bartolomen ypan martes oncan teotlac mochtin Oquisque yn ordenes yn omotlali yn Corona onpa palasio niman seseyaca Oquichiuhque Responso yn conbentoz teopixque San fran^co – San agustin – Santo domingo – San antonio – San ygnasio de Loyola – Sa Roque – Juan de dios[4] – niman opeuhqui prosesion Omoquixti yn Señor Obispo yhuan muchin yn ordenes yhuan colegiales[5] yn corona Oquihuicac yn Regidor don alonso dia auh yn setro Oquihuicac Don juan carmona depositario[6] auh y espada Oquihuicac don grabiel ansures auh yn imoztlatica omochiuh misa de pontifical ypan miercoles mochin yn Cabildotlaca [*f. 12v*] Oquihuilanque luto auh yn otlan misa niman nauhcanpa omotlalique yn itec tumbulo yn Canonigoz sesēyaca oquichiuhque rresponso satepan oquimochihuili yn señor Obispo auh yn yohuatzincopa sesen capilla oquichiuhque misas cantadas yn Conbentoz teopixque – San fran^co – Santo domingo – San agustin – San antonio San ygnasio de Loyola San Ju^o de dioz San rroque –mersenarioz — carmen teopixq̄

---

cali

1667   NiCan ypa xihuitl yn omochiuh tlatlasistli ypan cuaresma miec yc omomiquili — Sanno ypa xihuitl yn omoteochiuh monjas santa ynes[7] ipan sabado ycaxtoli yhuan yey 18 tonali ma [*sic*] metztli Junio (–) Sanno ypa xihuitl yn tlalolin ipan sabado ybisperas San ygnasio ypan matlactli ora yhuan tlaco yohuatzinco niman otlatlapan santa clara[8] (–) Oc sepa otlaloliln ypan bisperas S.^to domingo

---

[1]Gómez García et al. 2000 adds a sentence which clarifies the use of these wooden beams: they were painted black and used as barricades to define the procession route in a dramatic way. The additional text reads: "yhuan in tlatzaquali omochiuh mochi omotlileuh in cuiltl [?] in oq oquitlayahualoltique corona yhuan setro," "and the [back of the?] barricade that was made was all blackened while they paraded the crown and scepter."

[2]A Dominican convent for nuns, the first convent established in Puebla (Zerón Zapata, p. 91).

[3]Catafalques were elaborate wooden funerary constructions, often in the form of a church. They might be kept and reused each Easter, being moved in front of the main altar for the occasion.

When don Carlos II was installed as our ruler, the alcalde mayor don Estacio Coronel y Benavides took a place on the platform. Then they scattered money [from there], and at the palace. Don Francisco Fernández de Salazar was made ensign. The governor was don Blas de Galicia. The San Francisco alcalde was Gaspar Miguel, and the regidor was Miguel de los Santos.

In this same year, on the 2nd day of the month of August, began the carting of beams.[1] They were laid out from the palace as far as [the convent of] Santa Catalina.[2] They were laid on the street going along as far as the entry to the lord bishop's home, and the beams were laid as far as the cathedral. It was at the same time that they transported the catafalque,[3] which was 24 varas in height. On the 16th day of the month of August, the feast day of San Roque, masses began. For nine days masses were celebrated, ending on the feast day of San Bartolomé, on Tuesday. At that point, in the afternoon, all the orders of religious came out when the crown was put in place at the palace. Then each of the groups of religious from the various establishments—from San Francisco, San Agustín, Santo Domingo, San Antonio, San Ignacio de Loyola, [and the hospitals of] San Roque and [San] Juan de Dios[4]—said responsory prayers. Then the procession began. The lord bishop came out with all the orders of religious and the people of the colegios.[5] The regidor don Alonso Díaz carried the crown, and don Juan Carmona, depositary,[6] carried the scepter. Don Gabriel Anzures carried the sword. The next day, Wednesday, a pontifical mass was celebrated. All the members of the [Spanish] cabildo [*f. 12v*] wore mourning attire dragging on the ground. When the mass was over, the canons placed themselves in the four corners of the catafalque and each said responsory prayers; afterward the lord bishop also did it. Very early in the morning the religious of each of the establishments—San Francisco, Santo Domingo, San Agustín, San Antonio, San Ignacio de Loyola, San Juan de Dios, San Roque, the Mercedarians, the religious of Carmen—celebrated high masses in each of the chapels.

House

1667   Here in this year a cough broke out during Lent; many died of it. — In this same year the nuns of Santa Inés[7] were consecrated on Saturday the 18th day of the month of June. (–) In this same year there was an earthquake on Saturday, the eve of San Ignacio, at half past 10 o'clock in the morning. Then [the convent of] Santa Clara[8] cracked open in various places. (–) Again there was an earthquake

---

[4]San Juan de Dios was a hospital for the indigent (Zerón Zapata, pp. 98–102). On San Roque, see n. 6, p. 105. Each hospital housed its own group of religious.

[5]Perhaps here the author is making a distinction between the mendicant orders and the Jesuits, or he may be referring to students and other residents of the colegios.

[6]It is unclear whether this was a permanent office, or if the meaning is only that Carmona had been entrusted with keeping the sword and perhaps other items carried in the procession.

[7]A convent of Dominican nuns (Zerón Zapata, p. 92).

[8]A convent of Franciscan nuns (Zerón Zapata, p. 92).

yohuatzinCo ypan chicuey ora yhuā tlaco (–) Sanno ypan metzli yc matlactli onnahui tonali mani agosto yn omotocac simiento San juan dios ymaticatzinco yn Señor Obispo Oquimotoquili ypan domingo (–) Sāno ypa xihuitl yn oc sepa otlalolin ypā sabado yc yey 3 tonali mani metztli septtiembre ypan macuilli ora yhuan se cuarto teotlac (–) Sāno ypan ynic matlactli onnahui 14 tonali mani metztli septiembre yn otlalolin yohualtica hualathui miercoles Sāno ypan ynic sempuali ose 21 mani metztli ottubre ypā ylhuitzin Santa ursula ypan biernes ypan se ora yhuan tlaco yn otetecuicac[1] yn ilhuicatl (–) Sāno pa [sic] xihuitl ypan noche buena oc sepa Otlalolin ypan sabado yohualtica ypan Ome ora

——— [f. 13]

tochtli
———

———

1668   Nican ypan xihuitl yc matlactli Omey 13 tonali mani metztli febrero ypan ne-ahuiltilistli ypan lunes Oc sepa Otlalolin ypā chicuasen ora teotlac (–)
        Sāno ypa xihuitl ynic Senpuali yhuan chicnahui 29 tonali mani metztli febrero ypan martes yohualtica omomiquili alcalde mayor don diego estrada
        Sanno ypa xihuitl ynic nahui 4 tonali mani metztli março ypan domingo yn o-peuhqui yn iuhqui tonalmitl oquisticaya tonatiuh ycalaquian San yc Ontlayo-huaya niman monextiaya (–) Sāno pa [sic] xihuitl ynic ypan ylhuitzin y totlaço-mahuistatzin San josef ipan lunes omotocac simiento Sanctissima tRinidad[2] Oquimotoquili Sr Obisp [sic] (–) Sāno ypa xihuitl ynic matlactli 10 mani tonali metztli Mayo ypan asension del señor Otlalolin ypan chicuasen ora teotlac

———

acatl
———

———

1669   Nican ypa xihuitl yn otepouh Jues capitan don Fernando de silba Juares de san martin ypan febrero (–) Sāno ypa xihuitl yn oquimictique regidor don grabiel ansures[3] ypan martes yc caxtoli 15 tonali mani metztli febrero yn iquac oquimic-tique niman omotlalitihuetzq̄ soldadoz otlapiaya yglesia mayor caltenpan (–) Sanno ypa xihuitl oc sepa tlalolin yc caxtoli 15 tonali mani metztli Julio yohual-tica ypan martes ypan chicuasen ora (–) San ypa xihuitl yn omocanonisaro santa Rosa maria santo domingo ytlatecpantzin yn oquichihuilique ylhuitzin onpa yn iglesia mayor yc sepuali yhuan chicuasen 26 tonali mani metztli Agosto

———

tecpatl
———

1670
——— [f. 13v]

cali

———————————

[1]*Tetecuica* can also refer to buzzing, humming, whirring, reverberating, throbbing, etc.
[2]This was another Dominican convent for nuns (Zerón Zapata, p. 93). The reference is apparently to beginning the church that was consecrated in 1674 (see the entry for that year).

on the eve of Santo Domingo at half past 8 in the morning. (–) In this same month, on the 14th day of August, the foundation was laid for [the hospital of] San Juan de Dios, under the direction of the lord bishop. He laid it on Sunday. (–) In this same year there was another earthquake on Saturday, the 3rd day of the month of September, at a quarter past 5 o'clock in the afternoon. (–) At this same time, on the 14th day of the month of September, there was an earthquake in the night, Wednesday morning. At this same time, on Friday the 21st of the month of October, the feast day of Santa Ursula, at half past 1 o'clock, the heavens crackled.[1] (–) In this same year, on Christmas Eve, there was another earthquake. It was at night on Saturday, at 2 o'clock.

───────── [*f. 13*]

Rabbit

1668   Here in this year, on Monday the 13th day of the month of February, during the celebrations, again there was an earthquake, at 6 o'clock in the afternoon. (–)
In this same year, on Tuesday the 29th day of the month of February, during the night, the alcalde mayor, don Diego de Estrada, died.
In this same year, on Sunday the 4th day of the month of March, began something like a sunray. It came from the west; it would appear just as it grew dark. (–) In this same year, on a Monday, on the feast day of our precious revered father San José, the foundation of Santísima Trinidad[2] was laid. The lord bishop laid it. (–) In this same year, on the 10th day of the month of May, Ascensión del Señor, there was an earthquake at 6 o'clock in the afternoon.

─────────

Reed

1669   Here in this year a judge, captain don Fernando de Silva Juárez de San Martín, took a census, in February. (–) In this same year they killed the regidor don Gabriel Anzures,[3] on Tuesday the 15th day of the month of February. When they killed him, soldiers were quickly stationed who stood guard at the cathedral entrance. (–) In this same year there was another earthquake on Tuesday the 15th day of the month of July, at 6 o'clock at night. (–) In this same year Santa Rosa María, of the order of Santo Domingo, was canonized. They celebrated her feast day in the cathedral on the 26th day of the month of August.

─────────

Flint-knife

1670
───────── [*f. 13v*]

House

─────────────────────

[3]He was last seen here in a position of honor in the ceremonies of 1665. There is no indication in any other source I know of as to why he was killed.

1671 Nican ipa xihuitl yn opiloloque nahui tlacatl ypan yc senpuali onmatlactli 30 tonali mani metztli Enero ypan ybisperas san pedro nolasco se ytoca Ju⁰ pastelero – Oc Se Juan tzapa¹ – Oc Se sātiago chane – andres bauhtista san baltasar chane

tochtli

1672 Nican ypa xihuitl y mochiuh tore san fran^co Sanno ypan xihuitl yn omotzauc bobeda san Ju⁰ ycaltzin Jesus nasareno ypan yc caxtoli 15 tonali mani metztli agosto ypan lunes²

acatl

1673 Nican ypa xihuitl y omotocac simiento san christobal ypan [en]canasion sabado de rramos³ — Sanno ypa xihuitl yn omotlali pila san fran^co yhuā otlatemanaloc⁴ (–) Sanno ypa xihuitl yn omomiquili yn señor Obispo don diego osorio escobar y llamas ypa sabado 14 de otubre bisperas santa teresa de jesus teotlac auh in omotocac ypan ylhuitzin san lucas sāno ypa xihuitl yn ohuala biRey ynic nahui 4 tonali mani metztli nobiembre ohualtlamelauh san antonio ye quin domingo yn ocalac siudad ytoca don pedro colon de portugual y de castro conde de berahuas marques de gelbes y duque de Jamayca⁵ Sāno ypa xihuitl yn omomiquili birrey don pedro colon conde de beraguas ypan miercoles yc matlactli omey 13 tonali mani metztli disiembre

tecpatl

1674 Nicā ypa xihuitl yn omochiuh BiRey arsoobisp [sic] mexico san agustin teopixqui ytoca don Ju⁰ de payo⁶ Sāno ypa xihuitl yn omoteochiuh santissima trenidad teopan ipan sabado ipan ylhuitzin cōseipsion [sic] [f. 14]
Sanno ypa xihuitl yn opeuhqui yn icaltzin san ju⁰ baptista ca ynon yes macuilcan omoxelo⁷ yn opeuhqui ypan metztli Junio

cali

---

¹The second names are probably descriptors: *pastelero* is Spanish for "pastry-maker," and *tzapa* is Nahuatl for "dwarf."

²The barrio carefully housed a beloved figure of Jesús Nazareno in an elaborate niche. See the entries for 1690–1691.

³Gómez García et al. 2000 gives the word as "encanasion," making clear some connection with the word Encarnación in an earlier form. The day of the Annunciation, March 25, fell on the Saturday before Palm Sunday in 1673. Church literature does sometimes associate the incarnation with this day, though more often with Christmas. Moreover, Gómez García et al. 2000 gives the word "puriSsima" just before Sán Cristóbal.

1671   Here in this year four people were hanged, on the 30th day of the month of January, the eve of San Pedro Nolasco. One was named Juan Pastelero, another Juan Tzapa.[1] Another was from Santiago. Andrés Bautista was from San Baltasar.

Rabbit

1672   Here in this year the tower of San Francisco was built. In this same year the vault of the shrine of Jesús Nazareno at San Juan was completed, on Monday the 15th day of the month of August.[2]

Reed

1673   Here in this year the foundation of [the hospital of] San Cristóbal was laid on [Encarnación?], Palm Saturday.[3] (–) In this same year the font was set in place at [the convent of] San Francisco, and stonework was installed.[4] In this same year the lord bishop, don Diego Osorio Escobar y Llamas, died, on Saturday the 14th of October, on the eve of Santa Teresa de Jesús, in the afternoon, and he was buried on the feast day of San Lucas. In this same year the viceroy came, on the 4th day of the month of November. He came straight to San Antonio; later, on Sunday, he entered the city. His name was don Pedro Colón de Portugal y de Castro, conde de Veragua, marqués de Gelves and duque de Jamaica.[5] In this same year the viceroy don Pedro Colón, conde de Veragua, died, on Wednesday the 13th day of the month of December.

Flint-knife

1674   Here in this year the archbishop of Mexico, an Augustinian friar named don Juan de Payo,[6] became viceroy. In this same year the church of Santísima Trinidad was consecrated, on Saturday the feast day of Concepción. [*f. 14*]

    In this same year was begun [work on] the house of San Juan Bautista; that will be divided in five parts.[7] It was begun in the month of June.

House

---

[4]The reference may be to some sort of stone casing or platform, or paving around the font.

[5]Don Pedro Nuño Colón de Portugal, duque de Veragua, marqués de Jamaica, viceroy of New Spain (November–December, 1673).

[6]Don Payo Enríquez de Rivera, archbishop of Mexico (1670–81) and acting viceroy of New Spain (1673–80).

[7]The passage "ca ynon yes macuilcan omoxelo" is obscure. Conceivably the structure, not the work, was to be divided into five parts. The chapel of San Juan Bautista had been the Tlaxcalan community's focus of worship until they built the neighboring church of San Juan del Río at mid-century (see entries for 1616, 1633, and 1643). Now apparently it was in need of renovation.

1675   Nican ypa xihuitl yn omoteochiuh San Sebastian yc caxtoli yhuan ome 17 tonali
        mani metztli nobiembre

tochtli

1676   Nican ipā xihuitl yn omoteochiuh San marcoz ypan ylhuitzin Sauado (–) Sanno
        ypa xihuitl yn omoteochiuh sāta vera cruz ypan ssanctissima trinidad — Sāno
        ipa xihuitl yn opiloloc molato Otlachtec santo domingo teopan Oquimotlach-
        tequilili totlasomahuisnantzin de Rosario ytoca Josef yc chicuey 8 tonali mani
        metztli Otubre Sanno ypa xihuitl yn omocoronaro Rey ic matlactli Omey 13
        tonali mani metztli disiembre[1]

acatl

1677   Nican ypa xihuitl yn ohualmohuicac señor obispo ytocatzin D. manuel fernandes
        de Santa crus ypan ~~sanctissima~~ yc yey 3 tonali mani metztli Enero — Sano ypa
        xihuitl yn otepouh Jues ypan março ytoca don fran^co (–) Sano ypa xihuitl yn
        opiloloc çe tlacatl oychtequi chololan teopan ytoca domingo yc chicuey 8 tonali
        mani metztli julio (–) Sā pa xihuitl yno~~can posesion~~ yn otlalolin yc chicome 7
        tonali mani metztli agosto ypā sabado teotlac ypā ome ora – Sāno ypan xihuitl
        yn ocan posesion y Señor Obispo don manuel fernandes Santa crus ypā lunes yc
        chiucnahui 9 tonali mani metztli agosto auh ypan martes yn ocalac yglesia
        mayor niman onCan opeuhqui yn ilhuitl yn oquimochihuililique – Sanno ypa
        xihuitl yn oquitzatzaca y mochi yn yey altepetl alcaldes regidores alhuasil ma-
        yores pasados y muchin y huehuetque ypanpa ypan Otlatoque[2] yyn [sic] gover-
        nador don blas de galisia auh yehuatzin yn señor obispo oquinmoquixtili yn
        teylpilcalco [f. 14v] Omomiquili çe tlacatl ytoca catca juan geronimo Chane San
        Ju^o de Ryo

tecpatl

1678   Nican ypan xihuitl yn omoteochiuh yteopancaltzin sā lasaro yhuan y totlaso-
        mahuisnantzin de la misericordia yc matlactli onnahui 14 tonali mani metztli
        agosto ypan domingo ybisperas totlasonantzin assupsion yn prosesion ohualquis
        ycha toreno Ompa huey otlipan asta oncan san lasaro teopan auh yn ipā calotli
        huel otlaSencah [sic] otlapipiloloc

---

[1]Charles II had ascended when he was three years old and waited until now to be crowned.

[2]The expression *ipan tlatoa*, to speak about something, usually means to take care of or even
favor something. Here the indigenous officials opposed the governor, who was supported by the
Spanish alcalde mayor. A 1677 Spanish document mentions that the indigenous cabildo had expelled their leader don Blas Galicia (see Leicht 1967, p. 178). An alternative translation, however,

1675   Here in this year [the church of] San Sebastián was consecrated, on the 17th day of the month of November.

———

Rabbit

1676   Here in this year [the church of] San Marcos was consecrated on his feast day, a Saturday. (–) In this same year, [the church of] Santa Vera Cruz was consecrated, on [the day of] Santísima Trinidad. — In this same year a mulatto was hanged. He stole things in the church of Santo Domingo. He robbed our precious revered mother of Rosario. His name was Josef. It was on the 8th day of the month of October. In this same year the king was crowned, on the 13th day of the month of December.[1]

———

Reed

1677   Here in this year the lord bishop named don Manuel Fernández de Santa Cruz came, on the 3rd day of the month of January. — In this same year, in March, a judge named don Francisco took a census. (–) In this same year a person was hanged who had robbed a church in Cholula; his name was Domingo. It was on the 8th day of the month of July. (–) In this same year there was an earthquake, on Saturday the 7th day of the month of August, at 2 o'clock in the afternoon. – In this same year the lord bishop don Manuel Fernández de Santa Cruz took possession [of his office], on the 9th day of the month of August, and on Tuesday he entered the cathedral. Then at that point began the festivity which they celebrated for him. – In this same year they imprisoned all the past alcaldes, regidores and chief constables of the three altepetl, all the elders, because [the Spaniards favored?][2] the governor, don Blas de Galicia, but the lord bishop released them from jail. [*f. 14v*] [Of those who were held] an individual whose name was Juan Gerónimo, from San Juan del Río, died.

———

Flint-knife

1678   Here in this year was consecrated the church of San Lázaro and our precious revered mother of Misericordia on Sunday, the 14th day of the month of August, the eve of [the feast day of] our precious mother of Asunción. The procession came from Toreno's home on the main road as far as the church of San Lázaro. And along the street great preparations were made; festoons were hung.

———

might be that the cabildo members spoke about the governor in the sense of saying bad things about him. The governor and perhaps the event remained in the community's memory. Many years later, one of the keepers of this set of annals wrote on it "Sr D^n Blas de galisia Gobernador de la ciudad de los angeles, digo yo, francisco gomes," "Sr. don Blas de Galicia, governor of the Ciudad de los Angles; so say I, Francisco Gómez." The reason for this remark remains obscure, but it shows no hostility toward Galicia.

cali

1679   Nican ypa xihuitl yn ocanqui yn itequiuh don Josef de rribera yc chicome 7
        gobernador — Sanno ypa xihuitl yn oquimictique oncan san fran^co caltenpan yc
        ca hermita bañohueloz auh yn oquimicti sestudiante ypanpa oquixtetlatzini ypan
        yc se domingo de cuaresma – Sāno ypa xihuitl yn ocualoc yn tonatiuh ypā lunes
        ypan matlactli ose 11 ora ynic matlactli tonali mani metztli abril — San ypan
        xihuitl yn omoteochiuh yn san pedro yteopancaltzin yn prosesion asta yglesia
        mayor ohualquis asta oncan san pedro[1] ypan domingo yc chiucnahui 9 tonali
        mani metztli Julio

tochtli

1680   Nican ypan xihuitl yn omopopouh yn tianquistli ocalac arado ynic oquipo-
        poxoque yn tlalli ynic muchi yn quexquich xolal oquipopouh yn opeuhqui tla-
        popohualo ypan metztli ypan metztli [sic] março cuaresma [f. 15] muchin yn
        quexquich tlanamacaque oxixinca se [sic] oyaca san luis plashuela sequin yaque
        plashuela de peña sequi san xolalpan Otlanamacaya auh yn oCAlacohuac yn itic
        yn tianquistli yc sempuali omome 22 tonali mani metztli mayo muchin yn tla-
        namaCaque Oquixtlauhque tomin ynic Ocalaque yn tianquisco (–) Sanno ypa
        xihuitl yn oc sepa Ocalac arado yn tianquisco ypan metztli de septiembre yn
        otlamito ypan metztli de octubre huel muchi tlacatl yn otlalquixti ypampa yntcn-
        copa yn Justisia tlacatl alcalde mayor alcaldes regidores —
        Sāno ypa xihuitl yn otlallolin ypan lunes santo ypan chicuey ora yohuac niman
        nohuiyan otlaocolatzilin yn quexquich teopantli

virey   Sanno ycuac yn ohuala biRey ynic matlactli 10 tonali mani metztli octubre ypan
        juebes yn oasico yn ixtlahuacan ynic oquinamique ypan ome ora teotlac ypanpa
        oc oquiz yn ome cabildos yn señor obispo yhuan canonigos yhuan Justisia tlaca
        alcalde mayor alcaldes rregidores auh yn ohuasito ytec siudad ypan nahui ora
        teotlac auh yn itoca prrisipe birey Don thomas fran^co de la serda titulo de pare-
        des marques de laguna[2] nicā ocatca matlactli onnahui tonali huel nohuiyan
        quexquich teopantli nochi quimahuiso auh ypan lunes otlecoc San fran^co asta
        calbario yn birey san ycxipan yn isihuauh yca silla de manos oncan ynpan otzi-
        lin matlactli omome ora yn sepulco [sic] auh yn omocuep yca carroz

        Sanno ypa xihuitl yn opopocac sitlalin yn opeuhqui y popoca yc senpuali yhuā
        ome tonali mani metztli nobiembre auh yn omotlali yn sitlalin tonali yquisayan
        auh yn ipocyo Oytztoya tonali ycalaquian yn otlanqui yc popoca sanno ytlamian
        metztli nobiembre yn icuac quitoq̄ yn otla[l]polo chichimeca yancuic mexico

---

[1]The "asta" before "yglesia mayor" seems misplaced, though perhaps the sense is that the procession began as far back as the cathedral before coming on to San Pedro.

—————

House

1679   Here in this year don Josef de Ribera took up his post as seventh governor. — In
        this same year they killed him at the entry of the [convent of] San Francisco,
        where the shrine of Bañuelos is. The one who killed him was a student, because
        he gave him a blow in the face; it was on the first Sunday of Lent. – In this same
        year there was an eclipse of the sun on Monday, the 10th day of the month
        of April 10, at 11 o'clock. — In this same year the church of [the hospital of]
        San Pedro was consecrated. The procession came out of the cathedral and came
        as far as San Pedro.[1] This was on Sunday, the 9th day of the month of July .

—————

Rabbit

1680   Here in this year the marketplace was cleaned up. A plow came in and cleared
        off the land, cleaning up all the lots there were. The cleaning began in the month
        of March, during Lent. [*f. 15*] All the vendors there were dispersed; some went
        to the plazuela of San Luis, some to the plazuela of Peña, some just sold things
        on various lots. People entered inside the marketplace [again] on the 22nd day of
        the month of May. All the vendors paid money to enter the marketplace. (–) In
        this same year the plow entered the marketplace again, in the month of Septem-
        ber, and it was in the month of October that it ended. Absolutely everyone
        removed earth, because it was by order of the [Spanish] officers of the law, the
        alcalde mayor, alcaldes, and regidores. —
        In the same year there was an earthquake, on Monday of Holy Week, at 8
        o'clock at night. Then the bells tolled in sorrow at all the churches everywhere.

Viceroy At this same time a viceroy came, on the 10th day of the month of October. It
        was on Thursday that he reached the plain, where they met him at 2 o'clock in
        the afternoon. For that purpose first the two cabildos came out, [the cathedral
        chapter], the lord bishop and the canons, and [the secular officials], the law
        people, the alcalde mayor, the alcaldes, and the regidores. And it was at 4
        o'clock in the afternoon that he arrived inside the city. The name of the viceroy
        was Prince don Tomás Francisco de la Cerda, título de Paredes, marqués de
        Laguna.[2] He was here for 14 days. He admired all the churches absolutely
        everywhere. And on Monday he went up [the barrio of] San Francisco as far as
        the Calvario. The viceroy was just on foot; his wife was in a sedan chair. It rang
        12 o'clock when they were at the sepulcher. They returned in carriages.
        In this same year a comet appeared. It first appeared on the 22nd day of the
        month of November. The comet set in the east, its tail looking toward the west.
        When its appearance ended, it was at the end of November, at the same time that
        they said that the Chichimecs had laid waste to New Mexico and killed the

—————

[2]Don Tomás Antonio de la Cerda y Aragón, conde de Paredes, marqués de La Laguna, viceroy
of New Spain (1680–1686).

quinmicti san fran^{co} teopixque[1] [*f. 15v*]

oc sepa ypa se tonali mani metztli disiembre oc se motlali yuhquin tonaltemitl oquistoya tonatiuh ycalaquian auh yn icuitlapil ytztoya tlaxcalancopa huel temamauhti ayc yuhqui motta san yc omtlayohuaya motlaliyaya auh yn opoliuh yc caxtoli ose tonali mani metztli febrero

---

acatl

1681   Nican ypa xihuitl yn omixnaque[2] yn yey altepetl San pablo – Santiago – San fran^{co} ypanpa yn gobernasion quinequia san pablo tlaca quichihuasquia onpa quixquetzaya se tlacatl ytoca Ju^o agustin auh amo quineque San fran^{co} tlaca yhua santiago tlaca ypanpa ye huenhuentzin [*sic*] yhuan amo quipie ycaltzin[3] ynic huel miec neyxnamiquilistli omochiuh cabildo amo oquis gobernador auh ynic napa omochiuh cabildo yhcuac oquis gobernador yn D. Ju^o andres Santiago chane yc chicuey gobernador

Sanno ycuac yn ocāqui tenienteyotl[4] Ju^o bitanzos sāno ypa xihuitl yn oc sepa oquintzaca yn huehuetque yc mochi yey altepetl ipan yn tlacalaquili ynic opa oquintzaca[5] y miercoles ypan ylhuitzin San felipe de Jesus ynic macuili tonali m· [*sic*] metztli febrero

Sanno ypa xihuitl yn oquinhualhuicaque yepuali yhuan chicui yngleses ypan matlactli omome tonali mani metztli febrero auh nohuian oquinxexeloque yn-chachan tlatoque[6] tzauhcan tlaxcalChiuhcan onpa[7] oquinquixtique ypanpa amo quimoneltoquitia ȳ dioz chicotlaneltocaque yn oquimaxitico ypan biernes yc matlactli onnahui 14 tonali mani metztli febrero [*f. 16*]

Sanno ypan xihuitl yc sempua [*sic*] yhuan chiquasen tonali mani metztli mayo ypan yc omilhuitl pasqua del eSpitu [*sic*] Sancto ypan tonali lunes yn oquimicti-que alcalde pasado don nicolas de barSena[8] y san ycaltenpā oquipouhticatca se carta ypan matlactli ora yohuatzinco (–) Sanno ypan xihuitl yn omoteochiuh yn San Ju^o de Dioz teopancalli yc caxtoli 15 tonali mani metztli Junio ypan domin-go auh onpa yn catedral omoquixtitzino y sanctissimo sacramento yc mochi yn quexquich andas guiones rreligiosos canonigos regidores yn oquihualmohui-quilique yn prosesion yhuan yn San Ju^o de Dioz ynic omocalaquitzino yn ichantzinco auh yehuatzin yn Sr Obispo Don manuel fernande S.ta crus ymatica-tzinco oquimoteochilitzino [*sic*] auh yn omahuiltique yn caxtilteca yn oquimo-

---

[1] In August, the Pueblo Indians launched a major and successful revolt against the Spanish set-tlers of New Mexico and the Franciscans there.

[2] The intention was "omixnamique."   [3] And/or "did not maintain a household."

[4] Later entries make it clear that the office in question was that of deputy to the indigenous gov-ernor. Betanzos's surname and his lack of the don lead one to think that he was not functioning as an indigenous person, and indeed in 1684 he was one of those whom the indigenous cabildo tried to eject as non-indigenous.

[5] See the entry for1677.

[6] The word used is *tlatoque* (the plural of *tlatoani*, "ruler"), a form that in Nahuatl in general was quite often used for the entire membership of an indigenous cabildo, but here that usage is otherwise not seen. It thus seems more likely that the reference is to Spanish officeholders or prom-

Franciscan friars.[1] [*f. 15v*]

Again on the 1st day of the month of December another [comet] appeared, like a ray of the sun that issued from the west, and its tail looked toward Tlaxcala. It was really terrifying. Never had the like been seen. As soon as it was dark it would set. It disappeared on the 16th day of the month of February.

———

Reed

1681   Here in this year the three altepetl of San Pablo, Santiago, and San Francisco quarreled[2] over the governorship. The San Pablo people wanted to select a person named Juan Agustín. But the San Francisco and Santiago people didn't want it because he was already a feeble old man and didn't own a house.[3] Therefore a great deal of arguing took place in the cabildo. No governor emerged, but the fourth time that the cabildo met, don Juan Andrés from Santiago turned out as governor. He was the eighth governor.

At this same time Juan Betanzos assumed the position of deputy.[4] In this same year they again imprisoned the elders in all three altepetl over the tribute; it was the second time that they jailed them.[5] It was on Wednesday, the 5th day of the month of February, the feast day of San Felipe de Jesús.

In this same year they brought 68 Englishmen here, on the 12th day of the month of February. They distributed them all around the lords'[6] households and in obrajes and bakeries. They removed them from [where they were][7] because they do not believe in God; they are false believers [heretics]. They brought them here [to Puebla] on the 14th day of the month of February. [*f. 16*]

In this same year, on Monday the 26th day of the month of May, Pentecost, they killed former alcalde don Nicolás de Bárcena right at the entry of his house.[8] He was reading a letter, at 10 o'clock in the morning. (–) In this same year the church of [the hospital of] San Juan de Dios was consecrated, on Sunday, the 15th day of the month of June. The most holy Sacrament was brought out of the cathedral, with all the various litters and standards, and the religious, canons, and regidores, who went with the procession until it [the Sacrament] entered its home of San Juan de Dios. And the lord bishop don Manuel Fernández de Santa Cruz consecrated it with his own hands; and the Spaniards rejoiced as they celebrated the feast day in the marketplace. But it was not until the 25th of the

———

inent Spanish gentlemen in general, as in, among others, a passage in the entry for 1691 that refers to the Spanish regidores and other "tlatoque."

[7]The exact place of origin is not clear (the text says only "ompa," indicating a relatively distant "there"), but it was certainly somewhere in the Caribbean, as in the 1670s and early 80s that region had become a veritable war zone; English-backed buccaneers attacked Spanish islands and towns, and Spanish patrols tried to stem the tide by attacking impromptu settlements made by English people outside of the now-recognized colonies of Jamaica, St, Kitt's and Barbados. Many of those captured by the Spaniards were "buccaneer woodcutters" who would make temporary camp on isolated coasts in order to cut timber for sale elsewhere. See Lane 1998, pp. 124–26.

[8]Capitán don Nicolás de Jáuregui Bárcena is listed as an alcalde ordinario in the Spanish cabildo of Puebla in 1678 (Zerón Zapata, p. 72).

chihuililique ylhuitl onpa yn tianquisco ye quin yc senpuali yhuan macuili 25 tonali mani metztli Junio oc opanoc yn ilhuitzin San Ju⁰ baptista

San huel no ypan yvisperas San Ju⁰ baptista ynic senpuali omey 23 tonali mani metztli Junio ypan lunes omochiuh chicahuac tlalolinalistli ome credo omito ynic omania ypan macuili ora yhuan tlaco teotlac niman nohuiyan otlaocolatzilin ynic nohuiyan quexquich teopan huel temauhti yn omochiuh

San huel no ycuac yn ipa yc senpuali onchiucnahui 29 tonali mani metztli junio ypan domingo ylhuitzin San p⁰ y San pablo yn omopehualtitzino yn quimochi-huilitzino Sermon onpa yglesia mayor yn Señor Obispo yn yehuatzin Don manuel fernandes de santa cruz ~~tianquisco yhuan onpa palasio~~ auh y tiatinoz teopixque[1] oquimochihuilique oncan yn santa crus tianquisco yhuān ōpa [f. 16v] palasio muchi yn semana motemachtilique ynic mochi tlacatl moyolcuitisque mocencahuasque tlaselisque ynic tlanisque [sic] yn hui tlacnopilhuistli yn itoca Jubileo auh yn otlanqui yn se semana niman ypan domingo oyaqui yn prosesion onpa yn san Josef onpa muchin oyayaque yn la conpania teopixque quimochi-huilito sermon yhuan moteyolcuitilito[2] onpa tlaseliloc onpa no motlan Jubileo yhuan ypan on Semana no omochihuaya sermones yohualtica ypan calotli car-niseria yhuā yhuan ypan calotli tepozpitzcan yhuan ypan calotli santa bera Crus oyaya yn prosesion onpa yn sāta bera Crus ypan calotli muchihuaya sermōnes huel temamauhti yn omochiuh sa choquistli mania ayc yuhqui motta auh yn otlanqui y se semana san Josef niman ypan domingo omohuicac yn prosesion onpa yn sanctissima trenidad onpa no omochiuh sermones otlaseliloc onpa omotlan yn Jubileo ynic muchi se semana auh yn tlamito onpa ya la compania de Jesus ypanpa huel yehuantin yn onpa teopixque oquimolnamiquilique ynin tlacnopil-huilistli yn tomaquixitiloca yn ixpantzin [sic] yn ttoCuio [sic] Dios[3]

---

tecpatl

1682 Nican ypan xihuitl yn ocanqui gobernasion ytoca mateo xaen chino[4] nose mu-lato ocatca ytoca peña[5] yc chiucnahui gobernador

Sanno ypan xihuitl yn otlalolin huel chicahuac yey credo omito ynic ohuecahuac quaresma ypan ylhuitzin San Josef yc caxtolli onnahui tonali mani metztli marso

---

[1] An erroneous but common way of referring to the Jesuits.

[2] The Jesuits of this time were known in Puebla (and elsewhere) for their extraordinary fes-tivities on behalf of their patron saint and for what they called *misiones*, which rather resembled later fundamentalist revival campaigns. A 1681 document "Una Relación de lo que pasó en el solemne jubileo de las misones y doctrinas que celebraron y administraron los religiosos de la Compañía de Jesús en la Ciudad de Los Angeles," appears as an addendum in Zerón Zapata, pp. 194–208. The Jesuits were eager to demonstrate that their works affected Spaniards, indigenous, and blacks.

[3] This stock phrase would normally read *ixpantzinco yn totecuiyo dios* (*totecuiyo* was usually abbreviated as *tt⁰* or the like, and *ixpantzinco* was often *ixpan^{co}*). Throughout, the writer seems to pride himself on not abbreviating *totecuiyo*.

[4] The term *chino* seems originally to have referred to Filipinos, but it came to be applied to

month of June, and meanwhile the feast day of San Juan Bautista had passed.

Likewise right on the eve of San Juan Bautista, on Monday, the 23rd day of the month of June, there was a strong earthquake. It lasted for [the time it takes] to say two credos; it was at half past 5 o'clock in the afternoon. Then everywhere bells tolled in all the churches. What happened was really terrifying.

At this very same time, on Sunday the 29th day of the month of June, the feast day of San Pedro and San Pablo, the lord bishop don Manuel Fernández de Santa Cruz began preaching sermons in the cathedral, and the Theatine religious[1] delivered them at the Santa Cruz marketplace and at the [*f. 16v*] palace. They preached all week that everyone should confess, should prepare themselves, and take communion, in order to gain the great blessing called plenary indulgence. And when the week ended, on Sunday a procession went to [the church of] San José. All the religious of the Company [of Jesus] went there to preach sermons and hear people's confessions.[2] Communion was taken there, and also plenary indulgences granted. And in that week sermons were also preached at night on the street of the Carnecería [butchery], and on the street where the blacksmiths are, and on the street of Santa Vera Cruz; the procession went to Santa Vera Cruz, and sermons were delivered on the street. What was done was really frightening. Nothing but weeping prevailed. Never had the like been seen. And when a week ended at San José, then on Sunday a procession went to [the convent of] Santísima Trinidad. There also sermons were preached; communion was taken; plenary indulgences were gained, for a whole week. And when it came to its end [the activity] went to [the church] of the Company of Jesus because the religious there were the very ones who remembered this concession, our deliverance before our lord God.[3]

Flint-knife

1682   Here in this year one named Mateo Jaén, a *chino*,[4] assumed the governorship. [There was also?] a mulatto named Peña.[5] He was the ninth governor.

In this same year there was a really strong earthquake, lasting [the time it takes] to say three credos. It was during Lent, on the day of San Josef, Thursday, the

---

various types of mixture. In Puebla, it was generally used to describe a mulatto who had some indigenous ancestry (see Aguirre Beltrán 1972, p. 169). Note that Jaén is not accorded the don despite his position, showing perhaps the author's attitude toward him, perhaps that he was functioning as a person in the Spanish world, where the criteria for the use of the title were quite distinct.

[5]The phrase "mateo xaen chino nose mulato" in itself seems to say "Mateo Jaén, chino or mulatto." What follows, however, seems to assert that Peña was the mulatto; a passage under the year 1684 confirms that a mulatto named Peña was on the cabildo at that time. The Nahuatl as it stands might even mean that perhaps Peña was the governor, though he surely was not. Possibly the intention was "A person named Mateo Jaén, a chino or mulatto, assumed the governorship," and a statement about Peña being somehow associated with him once followed but was partially omitted, the copyist being thrown off by two appearances of "mulato" in close conjunction.

ipan Juebes ypan yey ora teotlac ypan ynon tonali oquimanque putos omona-
mictique [*f. 17*] onpa mexico y[*m*]pampa huel chicahuac o[*tlalolin*][1]

Sanno ypa xihuitl oc sepa otlalolin ypan [cax]toli ose 16 mani metztli mayo
ypan pascua [del] espiritu sancto domingo ypan yey ora yhuan tlaco teotlac (–)
Sanno ypan xihuitl yn opopocac sitlalin yn opeuhqui yc popoca ypan yc sempuali yonchicome 27 tonali mani metztli agosto ypan tonali Jueues ybisperas san
agustin auh yn omotlalica yn sitlalin tonali ycalaquian san yc ontlapoyahua o-
motlaliyaya (–) Sanno ypa xihuitl yn san oquinenpehualtique yn caxtilteca
oquitlasotilica yn tlaolli se peso ypatiuh oquitlalique yn tlaco Co cohuacali[2] auh
huel omotlamochiuhca [*sic*] yn icac [*sic*] on yuhqui tlaolli yuh trigo yn omo-
chiuhca yn oquimotemaquilaca [*sic*] yn dios auh sa oquinenpehualtica yn caxtilteca yn oquipehualtique quitlaçotilia ypan metztli agosto niman ticalaque metztli
de septiembre auh niman oncan omononotzque onpualli ommatlactli caxtilteca
ynin [*sic*] san yehuatin quichihuasq̃ yn pantzin[3] niman otlecoque yxpan alcalde
mayor ynic omobligaroque ynic san yehuantin quichihuasque pan ynic quitla-
cualtizque yn siudad de loz angeles auh niman yn justisia tlaca oquinnotzque yn
masehualtzitzintin ynic quinquixtilisque ȳ tlaxcalchihualistli oncan oquinpe-
natique ynic tonalli[4] oquimacaque termino ynic amo quichihuas yn pantzin san
oc yehuantin yn caxtilteca yn omixquesque quichihuasque auh amo huel oqui-
sustentaroque sann ica ome tonali ynic omochiuh yn itec siudad ynin ome tonali
ye ye [*sic*] oapismicoaya ypan tonali lunes yc sēpuali ose 21 tonali mani metztli
Septiembre [*f. 17v*] huel ypan ylhuitzin sā matheo lunes yhuan martes yn ohua-
pismicohuaya aocmo nesia ma pā ma tortillas yn tianquisco ma tienda auh yn
aquin ychtaca oquimochihuili yn se mita cacasoli yn conaxitiaya ȳ tianquisco
ma toltilla san ypan omomictiaya yn Caxtilteca manel huel momahuistilia aocan
quipoaya masehualtzintli yn aqui achtoa [*sic*] sa yehuatl quihuicaya yn tlaxcalli
Sa choquistli omania auh niman onca omacomanque ynic muchi tlacatl yuhqui
teopixque yuh Caxtilteca yuhqui masehualtzitzintin ynic mochi tlacatl ynpan
omomanque ymmasehualtzitzintin oquimacaque se amatl oquichiuhque masehualtzitzintin ymatica yn alcalde mayor yquac ye ontleco alcalde mayor ypalasio
niman muchin pipiltzitzintin yhuan sequintin huehuey tlaca oquitzatzilique o-

---

[1]This passage presents many challenges. It would even seem that possibly the verb "omona-
mictique" in this case might refer to contention rather than to marriage. The passage as it exists in
our text almost causes one to despair of a definite solution. The text of the cognate Gómez García
et al. 2000, however, offers help. Instead of our text's "ypampa," "because of it," we find "ympampa," "because of them," clearly in reference to the people who were arrested. Moreover, the
early eighteenth-century priest who translated that text into Spanish rendered this passage as:
"Cogieron a los someticos que se casaron. Por ellos tembló fuertemente." Accepting the provi-
dential *m* in "ympampa," I have followed the translation in the other text. In this version it is clear
that homosexuals were scapegoated in connection with the earthquake both as to the marrying and
as the supposed cause of the earthquake. Just what the content of the marriage or marriages was
remains a subject for speculation: whether they simply involved men who lived together, or there
was cross-dressing in order to indicate marriage partners, or a mock ceremony or ceremonies had
taken place, or some dissident priest had actually carried out the rites.

19th day of the month of March, at 3 o'clock in the afternoon. On that day they arrested the male homosexuals who had gotten married [*f. 17*] in Mexico City; because of them there was a very strong earthquake.[1]

In this same year there was another earthquake on Sunday the 16th of the month of May, Pentecost, at half past 3 o'clock in the afternoon. (–) In this same year a comet appeared. It began to appear on the 27th day of the month of August, on Thursday, the eve of San Agustín, and the comet set in the west. It would set just when night fell. (–) In this same year, without reason the Spaniards started raising the price of shelled maize. They set its price at 1 peso a half-basket.[2] At that time there had been a good yield; God had granted that maize as well as wheat had yielded abundantly. So without good reason the Spaniards began to raise prices in the month of August. Then the month of September came. At that point fifty Spaniards agreed that only they would make bread.[3] Then they went up before the alcalde mayor in order to obligate themselves that only they would make bread to feed the Ciudad de los Angeles [Puebla]. Then the [Spanish] law officials summoned the indigenous people [and told them] that they were going to take bread-making from them. They set a penalty on them, giving them a deadline of a day[4] not to make bread. Only those [particular] Spaniards were still authorized to make it. But they could not sustain it. For only two days was it done this way inside the city. In these two days there was already hunger. On Monday, the 21st day of the month of September, [*f. 17v*] right on the feast day of San Mateo, on Monday and Tuesday, there was hunger. No more did either wheat bread or tortillas appear in either marketplace or shop. When anyone secretly made half a carrying frame [full] and took it to the marketplace, even if it was tortillas, the Spaniards just fought over it. Even though it was someone very honored, the indigenous people no longer respected them; whoever was first took away the bread. Only weeping prevailed. And then everyone got worked up, priests, Spaniards and indigenous alike, so that everyone took the side of the indigenous people. The natives gave a letter with their own hands to the alcalde mayor. When they were going up to the palace of the alcalde mayor, all the small children and some adults shouted at him, saying to him, "Bread,

---

[2]The string "Co cohuacali" stems at least partly from inadvertent repetition. The first *co* seems to repeat the last syllable of the preceding word, *tlaco* (half). Then we are left with something that may be affected by the string of *co*'s but resembles *quauhacalli*, meaning a basket made of sticks or wood holding half a fanega, so that here the writer is giving the price for a quarter of a fanega. It will be seen that the copying in this whole passage leaves much to be desired.

[3]The loanword *pan* (*pantzin*) meant primarily wheat bread, but seems to be used here at times meaning any kind of bread, just as *tlaxcalli* is used not only for corn tortillas but for any bread, and *tlaxcalchiuhqui*, "maker of tlaxcalli," can mean baker in a general sense. At the same time, *pan* retains its sense of wheat bread, being used sometimes in distinction to *tortilla*, which exists here as a loanword from Spanish less ambiguous than *tlaxcalli*. The remainder of the paragraph makes it clear that the Spaniards were attempting to create a monopoly over both, and also that whatever the regulations about wheat bread, indigenous people were heavily engaged in producing and selling both. For some background see Loyde Cruz 1999.

[4]Perhaps the meaning is a deadline of a certain day instead of one day.

quilhuique pan pan pa señor capitan ye tapismiquisque ye tapismiquisque auh yn
iuh oquicac yn alcalde mayor yhuan oquipohuilique yn amatl yn iuhqui oquitotia
inic mochi polihuis yn itequipanolocatzin yn tohueytlatocatzin Rey yntla tech-
cahualtisque yn tooficio yn tlaxcalchihualistli ma yehuantin yn caxtilteca quichi-
huacan yn quexquich tlatequipanolistli yhuan yn tlacalaquili auh yn iuhqui oquicac yn alcalde mayor niman isiuhca otlanahuati mochihuas yn acto ynic niman
omotlastihuetz pregon ynic quichihuasque [f. 18] yn masehualtzitzin yn pantzin
auh yn caxtilteca otlatequiuhti quintzatzaquasque auh yn yehauntin niman ocho-
loque yn caxtilteca yn omixquetzca ytoca yn alcalde mayor D. astasio coronel y
benabides Sanno ycuac yn omochiuh puente ozpital de la bulas[1] yn maestro ytoca nicolas çamudio

---

cali

1683   Nica ypan xihuitl y [te]pouh Jues don fernando delgado huel oc telpochtl yn
otepouh ypan metztli abril quaresma (–) Sanno yquac ynic ypan macuili tonali
mani metztli abril ypan tonali lunes ye teotlac ypā orasion omochiuh chicahuac
yeyecatl san huel otlatlayohuac niman nohuiyan otlaocollatzilin yn teopan San
niman ymoztlayoc ypan tonali martes ynic chiquasen tonali mani metztli abril
yn otetCuicac ylhuicatl huel chicahuac ypan chicuey ora yhuan [tla]co yohuatzinco niman huel muchi tlacatl momauhti ynic nohuian (–) oc sepa ypan ynon
tonali martes yn ohualtlayohuac huel chicahuac otlapepetlacac tonatiuh yquisayan oc sepa nohuiyan yn quexquich teopan otlaocollatzilin temauhti yn omochiuh yn quac [sic] on oquisaco chicahuac tlatlasistli yc miec tlacatl momiqui-
lique

(–) yngleses (–)

Sanno ypan xihuitl ynic matlactli omey 13 tonali mani metztli mayo yn ohuasico
tlanahuatili amatl ypan tonali Jueues yn iuh quitotihuitz ye Oca Enemigos
yngleses yn beraCruz ye otlalpoloque[2] yn onpa tlaca Sequintin oquinmictīq
Sequin oquinhuicacque yuhqui teopixque yuhqui sa san quixtianotin auh yn
sihua huel ynca omahuiltique oquinmahuispoloque huel miec oquinmictique Sa
yca carreton quinsasaque ynic [f. 18v] Oquintocaque yhuan muchi yn quexquich
tlatquitl oquipiaya muchi oquinhuiquilique ypann on tonali Jueues San niman
oquihualsohutihuetzque yn estandarte de sangre yn onpa palasio ynn ayc quisani
yn ayc mosohuani yn niman omotlastihuetz pregones ynic muchin yn quexquich
Caxtiltecatl muchin moyaochichihuasque yn niman omacomanque ynic mochi
siudatlaca niman muchi yn quexquich banderas omaCoque

mulatos   auh yn imoztlayoc ypan tonali biernes yc matlactli onnahui 14 tonali mani metztli mayo OCaCoque yancuican bandera yn mulatoz auh yn oquis yn incapitan se

---

[1]In 1682 the alcalde mayor Coronel y Benavides inaugurated a hospital right by a bridge not far
from the Franciscan monastery (Zerón Zapata, p.43).

[2]The reference is to an attack on Veracruz orchestrated by eight buccaneer captains who first
met in the Gulf of Honduras to plan their operation. Of the eight captains, only two were actually

bread, bread, lord captain. We will starve! We will starve!" And when the alcalde mayor had heard it and they had read to him what the document said—that all our great ruler the king's service would be lost if we were deprived of our trade of breadmaking; let the Spaniards do whatever service there was and pay the tribute—when he heard that, the alcalde mayor quickly ordered that a decree be issued, so that a proclamation was hastily made that [*f. 18*] the indigenous people would make bread. And he ordered that the Spaniards be imprisoned. Then the Spaniards who had been authorized ran off. The alcalde mayor's name was don Estacio Coronel y Benavides. At this same time the Hospital de las Bulas was built at the bridge.[1] The master builder was named Nicolás Zamudio.

House

1683 Here in this year, the judge don Fernando Delgado took a census. He was still really just a youth. He counted people in the month of April, in Lent. (–) At this same time, on Monday, the 5th of April, in the afternoon, during prayers, there arose a strong wind. It grew very dark. Then everywhere in the churches the bells were tolled. The next day, on Tuesday, the 6th day of the month of April, the heavens crackled very loudly at half past 8 o'clock in the morning. Absolutely everyone, everywhere, was frightened. (–) Once again on that day, Tuesday, as night was coming on, there was a great sparkling in the east. Once again the bells tolled in all the churches everywhere. What happened was terrifying. At that time a bad cough broke out, of which many people died.

(–) Englishmen (–)

In this same year, on Thursday, the 13th day of the month of May, there arrived a dispatch saying that English enemies were in Veracruz; they had already laid waste to the land.[2] Some of the people there they killed, some they carried off with them, priests and ordinary Spaniards alike. And they amused themselves with the women; they dishonored them. They killed very many people; they just wheeled them off in carts in order [*f. 18v*] to bury them. They took from them all the goods that they had. On that Thursday, at the palace, they quickly unfurled the standard of blood, which had never come out before, which never before had been unfurled. Quickly proclamations were issued that all the Spaniards there were should outfit themselves for war. Then all the city people grew agitated. All the banners there were were raised.

Mulattoes The next day, Friday, the 14th day of the month of May, the mulattoes for the first time raised a banner, and their captain turned out to be a mulatto named

---

English, the others being French and Dutch, but it was the English who had aided and abetted pirates for many years. See Haring 1966 and for a detailed study of these events Marley 1993. A shocked visitor to the area, a Syrian Christian, the Reverend Elias al-Mûsili of the Chaldean church, wrote an account of the episode that is as colorful as this one (see Mûsili 2003).

mulato ytoca felipe monso y moJica chilero

negros   Niman ypan tonali sabado yc caxtoli 15 tonali mani metztli mayo yn ocacoque
bandera yn tliltique auh yn oquis yncapitan se tliltic ytoca lorenso de papia[1] yc
ymomeyxitin yancuicān ocacoque yc axcan

Nican ypā tonali omopetlauhtzino S obispo

San niman ypan ynon tonali sabado omocalaqui yn señor obispo yn onpa yn
ponttifical auh yn yquac ohualmoquixti sa ycxipetlauhtihuitz yhuan ye omopetlauhtzino quenami se soldado Oquihualmohuiquili se alfange huel huey auh
niman mochi luto omosouh yn itec yn pontifical auh yn icuac Oquimotelique
yuhcon sa mopetlahuiltitihuitz [f. 19] niman mochi tlacatl ochocac ynic ypanpa
ye mohuicas yn moyatilitiuh[2] yn onpa beracruz niman ysiuhca omochiuhtihuitz
pregon oncan yglesia mayor caltenpan ynic muchintin yn quexquich clerigos
moyaochichihuasque ynic muchintin quimohuiquilisque auh niman yn quexquich clerigos niman muchintin omoyaochichiuhque oquitlalique espada yhuan
daga carabinas[3] yn quexquich clerigos ynic omoyaochichiuhque ynic quimohuiquilisque yn yaotitihui auh yn omoquixti yncapitan yehuatzin y señor probisor
auh yn omoquixtisquia ypan tonali lunes niman yman isiuhca ohuasico yn tla-
nahuattili ynic aocmo mohuicas ypanpa ye otzinquisque yn enemigos ye atlan
cate ynic quitocayotica sacrifisio[4] ynic aocmo omohuicac auh niman yn ipan
ynic caxtoli omome 17 tonali mani metztli lunes yn opeuh quistimani yn soldados muchin oyaque beracrus auh muchi yn ipan on metztli mayo sa otlao-
coltlatzilintimania yhuan choquistli omania ynsihuahuan yn caxtilteca ypanpa
muchin yazquia yn intlahuicalhuan[5] yn yaotitihui yhuan aocac ypan caballo
onenemia ypanpa muchi quintecuiliyaya ma yaxca quixtiano ma aquī yaxca asta
axnotzitzin quintecuiliyaya sa mahuistli mania huel temamauhti yn omochiuh yn
aẏc Omottac yn ixquich cahuitl ohuala tlaneltoquilistli

ttapado

Sanno yquac ynic caxtoli onnahui 19 tonali mani metztli mayo pan [sic] tonali
mierColes yn ohuasiCo oquitotihuitz quilmach visitador[6] ynic quibisitaroz yn [f.
19v] nechichiuhtli yn quitocayotia yn caxtilteca armas ynic muchi yn quexquich
onca nican ytech yn siudad de loz angeles auh niman ysiuhca otlatequiuhti
omotlastihuetz pregon ynic quiteyxpanhuisque yn aquique quipia yn yaonechi-
chiuhtli yn pora yhuan balas yhuan tomin oquimacac yn alcalde mayor D.
astasio auh yn nican ocatca – Jueves – biernes – sauado – domingo yohuatzinco
yn omocuepaya yn onpa beracrus auh yn ye oquimomachiti yn biRey [on]pa

---

[1]Gómez García et al. 2000 has the name as "tapia" rather than "papia."

[2]In this writer's lexicon there clearly exists a word *yaoti*, to battle or to engage in war, though
this example lacks the *o*. A clearer example of what was intended occurs later in the paragraph.

[3]This word referred, as it still did as late as the American Civil War, to a light musket used by
cavalry. See *Dictionnaire de l'Académie Françoise*, first edition, 1694: carabine.

[4]The pirates went to Isla Sacrificios (originally named for the remains of sacrifices the Spaniards found there), just offshore, so that they would be safe from overland attack while they waited
to receive more booty in exchange for hostages. When they departed, they took with them hundreds

Felipe Monzón y Mujica, a chile-vendor.

Blacks   Then on Saturday, May 15, the blacks raised a banner, and a black named Lorenzo de Tapia[1] turned out to be their captain. Thus both of them now raised [banners] for the first time.

Here on this day the lord bishop disrobed

Right after that on that same day, Saturday, the lord bishop went in the chamber where his robes and ornaments are, and when he came back out, he just came barefoot and had already disrobed as a soldier. He came carrying a very large cutlass. Then mourning cloth was displayed inside the chamber of the ornaments. And when they saw him like that, coming disrobed, [*f. 19*] everyone wept about how he was now going to battle[2] in Veracruz. Then quickly a proclamation was made at the cathedral door that all the secular priests there were should outfit themselves for war, that all were to accompany him. Then all the secular priests armed themselves for war; they put on swords, daggers, and carbines.[3] All the secular priests thus armed themselves for war in order to accompany him into battle. And the lord vicar general turned out as their captain, and they were going to leave on Monday, but then at that moment there suddenly arrived a dispatch that they should no longer go, because the enemies had pulled back and were already at sea, at what they called Isla Sacrificios,[4] so that they didn't go after all. Then on Monday, the 17th day of the month, began the departure of the soldiers; they all went to Veracruz. And all that month of May there was nothing but tolling of bells and the weeping of the Spaniards' wives because all the men they were connected with[5] were going to fight. And no one went about on horseback any longer, because all [the horses] were taken away from people, whether they belonged to a Spaniard or to anyone else. They even took the poor little donkeys from them. There was only fear. What happened was really terrifying; never had it been seen ever since the arrival of the Faith.

The Covered One

At this same time, on Wednesday, the 19th day of the month of May, there arrived one who came saying he was supposedly an inspector[6] who had come to inspect [*f. 19v*] the equipment that the Spaniards call arms, all that were here in the Ciudad de los Angeles. And then quickly he saw to it that a proclamation was made that those who had war equipment—maces and bullets—should manifest it. And the alcalde mayor, don Estacio, gave him money. He was here Thursday, Friday, and Saturday. Sunday, early in the morning, he was going back to Veracruz. But when the viceroy who is in Mexico City learned of it, he

---

of black residents, slave and free, whom they sold in the Caribbean. See Marley 1993.

[5]Perhaps spouses specifically, perhaps all sorts of relatives and connections (*deudos*).

[6]Don Antonio de Benavides, sometimes styled marqués de San Vicente, arrived in Veracruz in May of 1683, probably with the pirates, and tried to pass himself off as a powerful inspector general. There really was an Antonio de Benavides in Santo Domingo who had personal ties to government officials there, and who seems to have gotten swept into the pirate cortege through contraband trade activities. See Utrera 1950.

moyetztica mexiCo niman ysiuhca oquihualmotitlanili yn yehuatzin don fruto[1]
ynic quimolpiliquiuh yn ipanpa sā nican omoculparo cuitlaxcoapan oquimitalhui
yn biRey yntla melahuac besitador tleyca yn amo nican oasico mexico ynic
nechmotelis aso san ymicniuh yn ingleses yn ocalaque beracrus ma xicmolpiliti
auh yn yehuatzin yn don fruto yn huel ysiuh[ca] yn oalmohuicac y nican cuitlaxcoapan ynic yollopachiuhtiquisaco cuix melahuac yn san nican Omocuep
auh yn oquimolhuili ca melahuac san niman omopanolti[2] quimotetemolita yn
aaltepepan auh yn oquimaxilito onpa la billa de Cordova ynJenio conde de
orisaban auh niman onpa oquimolpili oquimotzacuilili yn imahuan yca esposas
auh yn oquimaxitilico y Cuitlaxcoapan ypan yc se tonali mani metztli Junio ypā
tonali martes ypan chicuey ora yoatzinco niman oquimotlamelahualtili ychantzinco yn señor don Juan de abila ypā calotli [f. 20] Carniceria yc titleco santa
calina [sic] auh yn ye quimaxitilito yn caltenpa yquac ohualmoquixti yn don
~~juan de abila~~ fruto yn itec carrosa quimotilanilitiuh yca cadena de oro ynic
oquimocalaquili calitec niman ysiuhca oquintlali caltenpixque yhuan corredor
yhuan bentanas tlapixticatca auh yn imostlayoc yn ye quimoquixtilis ycuac con-
moteteposotili ytech ycxihuan ynic oquimohuiquili yn onpa mexico asta oc o-
motlatitlanili caxtillan ynic motta tleyn mochihuas auh yn oquitocayotica tapado
yn besitador

---

tochtli

1684   Nican ipan xihuitl yn ocanqui gobernasion y don felipe de Santiago yc matlactli
        10 gobernador
        Sanno ypan xihuitl yn ohualaque chicomenti teopixque San fran[co] teopixque
        onpa ohualmehuitique yn huey altepepan Roma yn oquimochihuilico misiones
        ypan ytlayohuilitzin yyn [sic] totecuio dios santa quaresma huel senca tema-
        mauhti yhuan tetequipacho yn oquimochihuilico oquimoquixtili prosesion mu-
        chin quexquich San fran[co] teopixque muchin oquisque yhuan muchtin oqui-
        tlalique mecatl ynquechtlantzinco yhuan huel miec otlamaseuhque ynic oyaque
        yn iglesia mayor yhuan ynic yn quexquich teopan nohuiyan oquimochihuilique
        sermones auh yn [yo]hoaltica ypan matlactli ose ora ypan tlaCo yohuac ypā se
        ora quimochihuiliyaya sermones yc nohuiyan cacalnacasco quinmoyecaniliti-
        nemia tronpeta yhuan canpanilla auh yn sequin oquimochihuilique sermo mexi-
        cacopa[3] auh yn yohuac ayocac yyolocacoochia [sic] auh yn bibiernes [sic] omo-
        tlecoltiyaya yn Santo calbario quimochihuilitihuitze sermon auh yn oquitlamiliq̄
        yn misiones ypan pasqua de resurecsion [f. 20v] Oquimoquixtili oc se prosesion
        de gloria oc sepa onpa omohuicaque yn iglesia mayor ynic oquimotomilique[4] yn

---

[1]The writer or copyists may or may not have realized it, but the reference is to doctor don
Frutos Delgado, judge of the Royal Audiencia, sent to the area as a special representative of the
viceroy. For more of the story see Schäfer 1947 (pp. 457, 461), Rivas Palacio 1870, Villas Flores
2008, and Núñez y Dominguez 1945.

quickly sent don Frutos[1] to come arrest him, wherefore he was accused [of wrongful behavior] here in Cuitlaxcohuapan. The viceroy said, "If he is an authentic inspector, why did he not come here to Mexico City to see me? Perhaps he is just a friend of the English who entered Veracruz. Go arrest him." And don Frutos came here to Cuitlaxcohuapan very quickly. He just came to appear here briefly to satisfy himself if [the inspector] was authentic. He returned and told him he was authentic, then he went away.[2] Altepetl to altepetl [don Frutos] went looking for him. And he caught him in the town of Córdoba, at the conde de Orizaba's [sugar] mill, and he arrested him there and restrained his hands with fetters. He brought him to Cuitlaxcohuapan on Tuesday, the first day of the month of June, at 8 o'clock in the morning. He brought him straight to the home of señor don Juan de Avila on the street of the [*f. 20*] Carnicería where one goes up to the convent of Santa Catalina. And when he brought him to the door, when don Fruto got out of the coach, he went dragging him with a golden chain to take him indoors. Then he quickly stationed guards at the entrance, and they were standing watch at the walkways and windows. And the next day when he was going to take him out he put irons on his feet to take him to Mexico City until word should be sent to Spain so that it could be known what was to be done. And they named the inspector "the covered one."

Rabbit

1684   Here in this year don Felipe de Santiago assumed the governorship. He was the tenth governor.

In this same year came seven friars, Franciscans who came from the great altepetl of Rome. They came to organize missions during our Lord's passion, during the holy Lenten season. What they came to do took people greatly aback and troubled them. They brought out a procession; all the Franciscan friars that there were came out, and all wore ropes about their necks, and they performed a great many acts of penance as they went to the cathedral. And they preached sermons everywhere in all the churches, and at night they preached sermons at half past 11 o'clock and 1 o'clock in the night at house corners everywhere. Trumpets and hand bells went ahead of them. And some preached sermons in Mexican.[3] At night no one wanted to go to sleep yet. And on Fridays they would go up to the holy Calvario to preach sermons. When they ended the missions on Easter Sunday, they [*f. 20v*] brought out another *procesión de gloria*. Again they went to the cathedral so that their priests could [let loose?][4]

---

[2]Here, with the pronouns left undefined, we must take it the writer means that the putative inspector returned to Puebla, assured the judge of his authenticity, and then left again. Since the judge immediately started a search for the inspector, the inconsistency is obvious.

[3]Note the use of the term *mexicacopa*, a Spanish-influenced innovation used for the Nahuatl language to this day, and not *nahuatlatolpan* or the like.

[4]The basic verb here seems to be *toma*, to let something loose, let the hair down, undo something, etc.

intemachtilitzin ynic muchi tlacatl oquimoyolalilique auh yn se teopixqui yn
iquac oquimochihuiliyaya sermon san huel omixtetlatlatziniaya san huel omomictiaya niman mosotlahualtiaya ytec yn pulpito huel se oratica omozcaliaya
auh yn icuac yohualmoscali niman quimitalhuiaya ye onihuia yn ixpantzinco yn
toteCuio dioz yn onpa ylhuicac ye onechmolhuilili ynic amechmotlapopolhuilis
yn amotlatlacol niman muchi tlacatl ochocaya omotequipachohuaya ya huel
miequintin omoyolcuepque auh se santo christo ymactzinco quimoquitzquiliaya
yhuan se miquitzontecomatl[1] ynic mochi tlacatl oqui[2] [sic] ynin teopixque ca
santome

ju⁰ de la motha

Sanno ypan xihuitl yn opiloloc se mulato ytoca ju⁰ de la mota delincuente
ocasique yhuan oc sequin caxtilteca se tlatohuani ytoca don tomas de marmol
huel tepilhuā cuitlaxcoapan auh yn opiloloc ypan tonali miercoles ypan yc
senpuali ose 21 tonali mani metztli Junio yhuan oquichiuh cuartos oquitlatlalique otli ypā ypanpa otlachteque tierra dentro ypan tlali huel miec teocuitlatl[3]
oquitecuilique auh yn oquimasic alcalde yehuatzin _____ [f. 21]

Sanno ypan xihuitl yn oquinquixttique yn molato ytoca peña yhuan mateo xaen
yhua bitancos[5] ynic aocmo calaquisque yn incabildo masehualtzitzintin ypanpa
ayoctle ypan oquimittaya yn teteachcahuan [ynsapadoz?][6] sa yehuantin te-
tlatahuilia yn cabildo auh niman oquinyolchicauh yn gobᵈᵒʳ ytoca don felipe de
santᵍᵒ ynic y altepetl otlatitlanque mexico ocanato se probision rreal ynic aocmo calaquisque cabildo ma quixtiano ma mestiso ma molato ma tliltic ma chino
sa mixcahuisque yn masehualtzitzintin auh yn huasico yn tlanahuatili domingo
yc chiucnahui tonali mani metztli Julio aun [sic] omopregonaro ypan Juebes yc
matlactli omey 13 tonali mani Julio[7]

aorca   San ypan xihuitl yn opiloloc ompa xico [sic] yn quitohuaya huey tlatohuani onpa
con el   castillan ytech motlamiaya yn tohueytlatocatzin Rey ypanpa oquito quilmach
tapado   bisitador general auh amo melahuac san oyztlacatia auh ypanpa on oquipiloque
yhuan oquitequilique yn itzontteco yhuan se yma auh yn ima oquitlalique onpa
mexico tepilolquahuitl auh yn itzonteco oquihualicaque nican cuitlaxcohuapan
quihualamelahualtique ychantzinco yn Señor alcalde oridinario [sic] carrillo[8]
ypan ynin siudā de loz angeles onpa oquitetzontzonque ytech cuauhquetzali

---

[1]Here we would expect *miccatzontecomatl*. The intention might have been *miquiztzontecomatl*,
"death skull," but it seems to me that the writer did in fact try to change the second *i* to an *a*.

[2]There is actually no verb present, most of it having been cut off. However, it is clear from the
rest of the sentence that the word would have been something like "believe" or "consider."

[3]*Teocuitlatl* meant silver as well as gold, and indeed by this time usually silver; the implication
here seems to be money in general. In the conquest period the term was often used for money, and
apparently that usage continues here. Otherwise bullion from mines would be meant.

[5]Jaén was a chino, governor in 1682, and Peña is mentioned in connection with him. In 1681
Juan de Betanzos was deputy governor.

their preaching to give solace to everyone. And one friar, as he was delivering the sermon, would give himself blows in the face; he was really beating himself up. Then he fainted in the pulpit. After a full hour he revived, and when he had come to he said, "I have gone before our lord God in heaven. He told me that He would pardon you your sins." Then everyone wept and was troubled; a great many were converted. And he grasped a Santo Cristo in his hands, and a dead person's skull.[1] Hence everyone [thought][2] that these friars were saints.

Juan de la Mota

In this same year a mulatto named Juan de la Mota, a criminal, was hanged. They captured him and others who were Spaniards and a gentleman named don Tomás de Mármol, who was of a very good family of Cuitlaxcohuapan. He [Mota] was hanged on Wednesday, the 21st day of the month of June. They quartered him and distributed [the parts] in various places along the road because they had committed robberies in the back country. They took a great deal of money[3] from people. The alcalde who captured them was _____. [*f. 21*]

In this same year they expelled the mulatto named Peña and Mateo Jaén and Betanzos[5] so that they would no longer enter the cabildo of the indigenous people, because they looked on the leading elders as if they were nothing [. . .?],[6] because they alone spoke for the cabildo. And then the governor, named don Felipe de Santiago, inspired the altepetl to send to Mexico City to get a royal decree that no Spaniard, mestizo, mulatto, black nor chino should enter the cabildo any more. The indigenous people exclusively should do it. The order arrived on Sunday the 9th day of the month of July, and it was proclaimed on Thursday the 13th day of July.[7]

To the In this same year, in Mexico City, was hanged one who they said was a great
gallows lord in Spain and was associated with our great ruler the king; he said he was
with the supposedly an inspector general, but it was not true. He just lied. And because
Covered of that they hanged him and cut off his head and an arm. And his arm they set on
One a gibbet in Mexico City. They brought his head here to Cuitlaxcohuapan. They brought it direct to the home of the alcalde ordinario Carrillo[8] here in the Ciudad de los Angeles. They hammered it to a long pole, then they went and stood

---

[6]Here the syllables *yn*, *pa*, and *doz* occur in that sequence, not suggesting any obvious interpretation to me. Above the line is the syllable *sa*, which could be for *ça* or *çan*, "just, only." If the whole is seen as "ynsapadoz," it might stand for *inçapatos*, "their shoes," tempting us to think that the outsiders considered the indigenous people as low as their shoes. But the expression for looking upon them as nothing is already complete, and the writer usually spells loanwords standardly. If an *r* were missing, it would be "yn sa pardoz," that only mulattoes were speaking for the cabildo.

[7]See related entries in 1681 and 1682. The viceregal government had issued many such decrees, both general and for specific municipalities. In nearby Tlaxcala in this same period, the indigenous cabildo was engaged in a similar struggle. In that case, they failed to circumvent the alcalde mayor successfully, even temporarily, as occurred here.

[8]Don Gabriel Carrillo de Aranda was alcalde ordinario in the Spanish cabildo in this period (Zerón Zapata, p. 72).

hueyac niman oquiquetzato ytech yn tepilolquahuitl tianquisco ynic muchi tlacatl quittas quitocayotia tapado auh yn ipan tonali oquipilo miercoles yc matlactli omome 12 tonali mani metztli Julio auh yn oasico yn itzontecō ypan
tonali sabado yc caxtolli 15 tonali mani metztli Julio auh yn oquimotocayotica
[*f. 21v*] don Antonio frotys de melo lusitano benabides marques Cabos de san
bisente de la crus Roxa caballero maestre de campo visitador geral[1] [*sic*] yehuatl yn tlacpac omoteneuh ypan oc se xihuitl huel se xiuhtica yn otzaucticatca –
tapado[2]

Sanno ypā xihuitl yn ocan tenienteyotl yn miguel de aparisio[3] ypan metztli 22 de
agosto ocanqui ypan tonali martes auh san nahui metztli yn oquipix niman oqui-
quixtilique

D. felipe   San huel no yquac yn ipan ytzonquisayan metztli agosto yn oquiquixttilique yn
ittopil yn don felip [*sic*] de santiago go^{or}. yhuan oquitzatzacca ypāpa oqui-
nacastec se tlacatl auh yn oquipix nin [*sic*] topilli se tlacatl ytoca melchor de loz
Reyes san matias chane auh yn oquicuepilique ye pan [*sic*] tlaco metztli de
nobiembre sa oquitlami xihuitl

Sanno ypa xihuitl ynic chicuey tonali mani metztli nobiembre ypan miercoles
yoac oquimaque [*sic*] garrote ytec y telpiloyan se ychtequi chololtecatl ytoca
Juan caretero[4] ypanpa oquimocuiti oquimicti chicuey tlacatl auh yn oalathuic
Juebes ynic chiucnahui tonali nobiembre oquihualpiloque ytech tepilolcuahuitl
auh yn ocasique ompa San Juan sentepec sa ytzcuintin quitzitzquique

Sāno yquac yn omomiquili alde mayor ytoca D. Jose de salaeta yc matlactli ose
11 tonali mani metztli nobiembre ypan tonali sabado ypan yey ora yhuā tlaco
teotlac amo omoyolcuiti sa oquitaque ye omic auh yn oc opeuhqui sā oqui-
cuahuique ypanpa ocasique yca sihuatl[5] [*f. 22*]

---

acatl

1685   Nican ypā xihuitl yn ocanqui gobernasion yn don miguel de loz santos san
fran^{co} chane ypan barrio san ju^o de Ryo yancuica otlecoc yn yn [*sic*] gobernasion barrio motenehua tlaxcaltecapan yc 11 go^{or}.

Sanno ycuac yn ocāqui tenienteyotl y don mateo jasinto sātiago chane

---

[1]The name as given is garbled (and in Gómez García et al. 2000 it is even worse). It seems that
in a previous version there may have been an interlinear remark giving an alternate explanation of
the imposter's identity, saying that he was really Frotis de Melo, a Portuguese. In the present copy
that remark was inserted right into the name. The hypothetical first name of the Portuguese may
have been affected by the doctor don Frutos Delgado so prominent in the story. If the insert is
ignored, the name corresponds to what is generally reported except that it would have been "marqués de Cabos de San Vicente, knight of the [order of the] Cruz Roja."

[2]This last phrase was added as an afterthought, stuck in prominently to catch the eye, probably
in order for a reader to tie this section easily to the story's fuller coverage in 1683.

[3]Miguel de Aparicio is a good name for an indigenous person, that being a saint's name, but the

it up next to the gibbet in the marketplace for all to see the so-called "covered one." It was on Wednesday, the 12th day of the month July, that he was hanged; his head arrived on Saturday, the 15th day of the month of July. They called him [*f. 21v*] don Antonio Frotis de Melo Lusitano Benavides, marqués de Cabos de San Vicente de la Cruz Roja, caballero, maestre de campo, inspector general.[1] He is the one mentioned above in another year; he was imprisoned for a full year. – The Covered One.[2]

In this same year Miguel de Aparicio assumed the office of deputy,[3] on Tuesday, the 22nd of the month of August. He held it only four months, then they took it from him.

Don Felipe At this very same time, at the end of August, they took governor don Felipe de Santiago's staff from him and imprisoned him because he cut someone's ears off. And a person named Melchor de los Reyes from San Matías took the staff. They returned it [to Santiago] half-way through the month of November. He just finished out the year [as governor].

In this same year, on Wednesday, the 8th day of the month of November, at night, they executed a robber, a Cholulan named Juan Carretero,[4] in the prison with the garrote, because he confessed that he had killed eight people. At dawn on Thursday, the 9th day of November, they came and hung him up on the gibbet. They captured him at San Juan Centepec. Just dogs seized him.

At this same time the alcalde mayor, named don José de Zalaeta, died, on Saturday, the 11th day of the month of November, at half past 3 o'clock in the afternoon. He made no confession. They just saw that he was already dead. It was when they were beginning to beat him with a stick because they caught him with a woman.[5] [*f. 22*]

———

Reed

1685   Here in this year don Miguel de los Santos assumed the governorship. He was a citizen of San Francisco in the barrio of San Juan del Río. For the first time this barrio, called Tlaxcaltecapan, rose to the governorship. He was the eleventh governor.

At this same time don Mateo Jacinto, citizen of Santiago, assumed the office of deputy.

————————

don is lacking, as with another holder of this office, Juan de Betanzos, and the latter was of mixed descent or Spanish. But after this most of the holders of the deputy governorship have don as well as typical names for indigenous people.

[4]The second name probably indicates his occupation, that he was a carter.

[5]Apparently this was an affair of honor among Spanish men. Gómez García et al. 2000 adds that they did not bury him until they received orders from Mexico City, and the eighteenth-century priest who copied that manuscript asserted that he was irresponsible in general and had purchased his office in the first place.

1   Sāno ypan xihuitl yn oylhuichiuh alcalde mayor ytoca D. ju⁰ ysidro pardiñas
     onpa tianquisco achtopa omahuiltique toroz niman oquisque galgos oquinto-
     tocaque totochtin ytic yn tianquistli yno yācuicā

2   yn imoztlayoc otlanahuati yn alcalde mayor quinechicozque mimistin quinte-
     quimaca tetepixque¹ yn ye oquintemacaque niman oquinquixtique tianquisco
     oquincalaquique ytec se pipa niman tla[co] tianquisco oquintlapoque ynic omo-
     tlatlaloque

3   niman oc se tonali otlnahuati [sic] ynic quinechicozque yn chichime oquinhuica-
     que yn tianquisco ompa oquinchichiuhque yca nochi bonbas oquinpetlasolqui-
     miloque ototoponque ynic omotlatlaloque tianquisco (+) [y]hua se tecuani oqui-
     tlasque yn ayc yuhqui mottac omochiuh ypā metztli julio oquimolhuichihuilili
     san ju⁰ baptizta²
     Sāno ypa xihuitl yn don miguel de loz santoz gobernador yn oquimotlallili yn
     santa cruz tetl yn onpa yncabildo masehualtzitzintin motenehua sā pablo oq[ui]-
     quixti y cuauhtzintli ocatca oquiquechili teopancaltenco s. pablo [f. 22v]

     Sāno ypa xihuitl ynic nahui tonali mani metztli agozto ipan biernes ypan ybis-
     peras santo domigo [sic] yn oquitlasque pregones yn iuh quito ynic muchin yn
     quexquich masehualtzitzitzin [sic] calanehui yn Caxtilteca muchin quisasque
     yasque ypan barrios auh san chicui tonali yn oquintlatlalilique ynic quisasque
     auh yn aquin amo tlatlacamatis niman mecatlayehualoltiloz ynic niman muchin
     oquisque yn itic siudad au yn caxtilteca o no quinpenatīq yn aquitlatis mase-
     hualtzintli quitlahuas [sic] pena macuilpuali pesoz yhuan totocoz senpuali leguas
     auh niman ynic matlactli onnahui 14 tonali mani metztli agosto ypan ybisperas
     yn totlasonantzin asunpsion ypan tonali martes oc sepa oquitlasque pregones
     ynic quintlalmacasque auh amo oneltic san hui³ omocauh oc sepa omocuepque
     yn canpa calanehuia yhuan oquitlacahualti yn gobernador yn alcalde mayor
     ypanpa yn tlacalaquili ye muchi opolihuia yn itoca yn alcalde mayor D. juan
     ysidro pardiñas auh yn gᵒʳ D. miguel de loz santoz

     Sanno ypan xihuitl ynic caxtolli onnahui 19 tonali mani metztli agosto pan [sic]
     domingo yn ohuasico tlanahuatili ynic ye oquintlanā yn onpa canpech yn enemi-
     goz auh niman oquitlasque pregon ynic monechicozque soldadoz omotecati-
     huetz banderas Caxtilteca yhuan mulatoz huel pena niman omonechicoque auh
     niman oquinnahualnotzā yn alcalde mayor yc muchin niman oquintzauc telpi-
     loyan auh ynic senpualli yhuan chicuy 28 tonali mani metztli de agosto ypan
     martes ylhuitzin san agostin huel yohuatzinco yn oquīquixtīq mulatoz yn oquin-
     titlan yn onpa beracrus auh nimā ye ypan matlactli ora tlaca oquinquixtique yn

---

¹The usual plural of *tepixqui*, a minor official in charge of handling people almost like an usher
or beadle, was *tepixque*. The "tete" here is probably inadvertent repetition rather than conscious
reduplication to form a plural. The Spaniards said *tepisque* in the singular, *tepisques* in the plural.

1 In this same year the alcalde mayor, named don Juan Isidro Pardiñas, celebrated [his] feast day in the market place. First they amused themselves with bulls, and then greyhounds came out; they chased rabbits in the marketplace; that was the first time.

2 The next day the alcalde mayor ordered that cats be rounded up. He assigned the task to the *tepixque*.[1] When they had gotten them, they brought them out in the marketplace and put them in a cask. Then in the middle of the marketplace they opened it so that they ran here and there.

3 Then on the next day he ordered that dogs be rounded up. They took them to the marketplace. There they outfitted them with firecrackers that they wrapped in old mats. They exploded, so that they ran around in the marketplace. (+) And they let loose a wild beast. Never had the like been seen. It was done in July, in celebration of the feast day of San Juan Bautista. [2]

In this same year don Miguel de los Santos, governor, set up a holy cross of stone at the cabildo of the indigenous people [in the district] called San Pablo. He removed the former wooden one and set it up at the entrance to the church of San Pablo. [*f. 22v*]

In this same year, on Friday, the 4th day of the month of August, the eve of Santo Domingo, proclamations were made saying that all the indigenous people who rented houses from the Spaniards were to leave and go to the barrios, and they gave them only a week to leave, and that whoever would not obey was immediately to be marched about [the streets] being whipped, so that they all left the interior of the city right away. And the Spaniards also imposed a punishment on anyone who would conceal an indigenous person: he was to pay a fine of 100 pesos and be banished twenty leagues [from the city]. And then on Tuesday the 14th day of the month of August, on the eve of our precious mother Asunción, they issued proclamations again, that they would give them land. But it was not carried out; things remained as they were.[3] Once again they returned to where they rented houses. And the governor made the alcalde mayor stop because the tribute was all being lost. The alcalde mayor's name was don Juan Isidro Pardiñas, and the governor was don Miguel de los Santos.

In this same year, on Sunday the 19th day of the month of August, there arrived a dispatch that the enemy had defeated [the people] in Campeche, and then they issued a proclamation that soldiers were to be raised. Flags were soon unfurled; Spaniards and mulattoes were gathered together under severe penalty. Then the alcalde mayor summoned them by trickery, for then he shut them all up in the jail. On Tuesday the 28th day of the month of August, the feast day of San Agustín, very early in the morning, he released the mulattoes and sent them to Veracruz. Then at 10 o'clock in the day he released the Spaniards and sent them

---

[2] The feast day of San Juan Bautista is in June, and is given as in June elsewhere here. The error, presuming it is one, is shared by Gómez García et al. 2000.

[3] The intention of "san hui" is apparently "san iuh, saniuh," standard *çaniuh*, meaning "unchanged, as it was."

Caxtilteca in oquintitlan san chicahua[*f. 23*]listica oyaque ma namique macanos-
omo sa san oyaque sa choquistli mania yn innamichuan yn inpilhuan yc oquico-
colique yn alcalde mayor pardiñas auh yn ohualmocuepque ye ypan yc matlactli
onnahui 14 de octubre ypan domingo ybisperas santa teresa huel miyec momiquilito yhuan hualmococotihualaque

———————

tecpatl

———————

1686 NiCan ypa xihuitl oc sepa ytlacauh yn gobernasion ypanpa yn alcalde mayor
oquinequia quitlalis mestiso ytoca don Ju^o de galisia^1 auh ynic muchi yn yey
altepetl amo oquiselique huel yc oquixnamicque yn alcalde mayor auh opa
omochiuh cabildo auh yopayxti omochiuh elecsion yn achtopa omochiuh oquis
g^{or}: yn don felipe de s.tiago auh amo oquiseli yn alcalde mayor ypanpa otenacas-
tec^2 yhuan huel miec oquitlalilique ynic otlatlaco auh ynic opa omochiuh yn
elecsion oquisqui g^{or} yn do mateo Jasinto auh amo no oquiseli yn alcalde mayor
auh niman otlatitlantihuetzque yn masehualtzitzintin mexico auh yn alcalde mayor yhuan yn mestiso no otlatitlanque mexico ypanpa ypan momanaya sequitin
huehuetque – se ytoca Ju^o agustin – oc se ytoca gregorio oc se ytoca diego luis –
oc se ytoca don gaspar y [*sic*] yhuan oc sequintin ypanpa quintlacualti oquin-
tlahuanti auh ypanpa o huel ypan omomaya [*sic*] auh niman ohuasico y tlanahuatili ynn iuh quitotihuitz yn amo tonahuac mocalaquis ma quixtiano ma mulato ma mestiso ma tliltic ma chino amo oncan tlatozque ynnahuac yn masehual-
tzitzintin^3 auh niman yn alcalde mayor oc sepa mochihuas cabildo san yecyotica
oquititlan Josef moscoso alhuasil de la guera^4 yhua se escriuano ytoca abiles
ynic ymixpan mochihuas yn elecçion ypanpa amo onyes [*f. 23v*] neyxnamictli
niman ocalaque en cabildo omononotzque oc sepa oquichiuhque elecçion oquisqui oc se~~pa~~ g^{or} ytoca don miguel de la crus santiago chane yc yexpa omochiuh
elecçion niman oquimacato yn amatl yn alcalde mayor ocantehuac yn amatl
oquihuicac mexico auh yn masehualtzintzintin oc çepa oyaque no mexico auh
yn yancuic xihuitl muchin in metztli Enero amo ocatca g^{or} san yxquich se ente-
rino oquitlalitehuac yn alcalde mayor ytoca don melchor ycpan [*sic*] hualmo-
cuepas mexico otlanqui metztli Enero ni^5 otoncalaque febrero auh ypan yc
caxtolli oçe 16 tonali mani metztli febrero yn ohuasico yn alcalde mayor nimā
oquitotasico amo nananquinequi [*sic*] yes g^{or} yn don Ju^o de galisia nictlalis yes
cobrador yehuatl cololoz yn tlacalaquili niman oquicauh opanoc macuilli tonali
ynic omochiuh 21 de febrero yn oquimacac yn topilli yni cobrador^6 ypan tonali

———————

^{1}Most likely a relative, even a son, of the don Blas de Galicia who had been governor previously. The author is disingenuous in simply calling don Juan a mestizo when he had illustrious antecedents on the local cabildo, and the name Galicia had been distinguished in Tlaxcala, in the Tizatla
subaltepetl, since its first holder, the governor of Tlaxcala Pablo de Galicia. Don Juan was in an
entirely different category than such a person as the chino Mateo Jaén, for example.

^{2}Don Felipe had been governor previously and got into trouble for this very offense. See the
entry for 1684.

^{3}See the virtually identical decree asked for and received during the year of 1684.

off. They went by force; [*f. 23*] whether they were married or not they just went anyway. Nothing but weeping prevailed; their wives and children hated alcalde mayor Pardiñas for this. And when they came back on Sunday the 14th of October, the eve of Santa Teresa, very many had already died or came back sick.

———————

Flint-knife

1686   Here in this year the position of governor went wrong again, because the alcalde mayor wanted to install a mestizo named don Juan de Galicia,[1] and none of the three altepetl would accept him; they greatly resisted the alcalde mayor over it. The cabildo met twice; both times an election was held. The first time it was done, don Felipe de Santiago turned out as governor, but the alcalde mayor did not accept him because he had cut someone's ears off,[2] and they gave many examples of things he had done wrong. And the second time an election was held, don Mateo Jacinto came out as governor, but the alcalde mayor wouldn't accept him either. Then the indigenous people quickly sent messages to Mexico City, and the alcalde mayor and the mestizo also sent messages to Mexico City, for some of the elders took his side. One [of these] was named Juan Agustín; another was named Gregorio; another was named Diego Luis; another was named don Gaspar; and there were others, because he fed them and got them drunk. Because of that they really took his side. Then the order arrived saying that no Spaniard, mulatto, mestizo, black, or chino was to enter among us; they were not to have a voice among the indigenous people.[3] Then the alcalde mayor [said that] a cabildo meeting was to be held again without dispute; he sent Josef Moscoso, as *alguacil de la guerra*,[4] with a notary named Avilés, so that the election might be held before them and there would be no [*f. 23v*] contention. Then they went into the cabildo and consulted among themselves. Again they held an election. The third time an election was held, another person turned out as governor, don Miguel de la Cruz of Santiago. Then they went to give the [election] document to the alcalde mayor. He took the document and went away, taking it to Mexico City. And the indigenous people also went to Mexico City again. And in the new year, all of the month of January, there was no governor; there was only an acting [governor] named don Melchor whom the alcalde mayor had installed on leaving until he should return from Mexico City. The month of January ended; then[5] February came, and on the 16th day of the month of February the alcalde mayor arrived. On arrival he said, "You don't want don Juan de Galicia to be governor; I will install him to be [tribute] collector; he will gather the tribute." Then he dropped [the matter]. Five days passed; on Thursday the 21st of February he gave him the staff [of office] as tribute collector.[6] And

---

[4]This could be translated as war constable.

[5]In the Nahuatl "ni" is for *niman*. The intention of "ycpan" a few words before is not so clear.

[6]The string "yni cobrador" seems to be for *inic cobrador*.

Juebes auh yn don miguel de la crus yn oquitzqui[1] ynic g^{or}. oc çepa otlatitlan
mexico auh ypan yc 8 de Julio yn oasico yn tlanahuatili ynic quimacasque yn
topili san niman ypan on tonali yc a 8 de julio quiseli ynic gobernador auh amo
yehuatl ocololo yn yn [*sic*] tlacalaquili san yuh otlan auh yn teniente oquis onpa
san pablo chane ytoca don lucas Sano ynman oquiseli topilli yn ipan metztli
julio yc matlactli omome 12 g^{or}.

Sanno ypan xihuitl yn opiloloc çe tlacatl ytoca ju^o nicolas ychtequi yhuan sa
oquimitlani ynic piloloz ypan yc 20 mani metztli mayo ypan lunes [*f. 24*]
Sanno ypan xihuitl ynic 4 de Julio ypan tonali lunes hualtlay[*ohu*]ac ypan chicome ora yn ohuetzqui se tletolontli yn ohualehuac totomihuacanpa auh yn ohue-
tzito onpa yn cuauhtla ytech y matlalcueyetzin huel temamauhti niman omito ye
ynman ye tipolihuisq̄ auh ytetzauh omochiuh san niman opeuhqui chiCahuac
tlatlasistli huel miec yc omomiquilique yuhqui masehualtzitzintin yuhqui caxtilteca yuhqui sa san muchi tlacatl auh yn motocaya se tonali yn espital san
pedro matlactli tlacatl nos [*sic*] chicuey tlacatl oc ye yn ipa varioz huel temauhti
yn omochiuh san niman opeuhqui yc nohuiyan yn teopan otlatlatlauhtiloc yc
nohuiyan omochiuh misas auh yn oseuhqui ypan metztli de septienbre auh yn
oquitocayotica yn tlatlasistli medias de la yndia yhuan tanburito[2]
Sanno ypan xihuitl ynic 16 de otubre yn ohuala biRey yn ocalac ypan tonali
miercoles auh yn ocatca nican caxtolli tonali huel otlamahuisotehuac yn quexquich teopantli oquibisitaro auh yn itoca yn biRey D. melchor fernandes poerto-
carrero laso de la bega conde moclona[3] [*sic*] auh mancotzin quitoque mano de
plata
Sanno ypan xihuitl yn oquixitinique yn teopantli San Ju^o de rrio ynic oquihue-
capanoque yn sinburrio ypan tonali domingo ypan yc 10 mani metztli nobiembre
yhuan otzinquisasquia[4] ye omotocaca yn simiento miman [*sic*] ohuala yn justisia
oquintzatzacuasqui yn huehuetque oquinequia tomin ypanpa o niman omocauh
auh yn teopixqui bicario ytoca gaspar tamayo[5] auh satepan oc sepa ochicauh D.
miguel de los sātoz ynic oyaqui yXpā Justisia oquitlanito lisēsia ynic tzinquisas
ȳ teopā nimā hualecoc ȳ Justisia ynic oquitaco yn teopantli nimā oquitemacac
lisēsia ynic otzinquis [*f. 24v*]

_____

calli

_____

_____

[1]There is a verb *quitzquia*, to grasp or take, which occurs elsewhere in the text. The writer
apparently failed to copy one *qui* syllable, intending "oquiquitzqui."

[2] Experts do not recognize the name "tamburito," but in 1686 an epidemic of *tabardillo*, or
typhus, raged in the vicinity of Puebla. See Malvido 1973. Probably someone misheard or mis-
copied the Spanish word. One symptom of typhus is a rash on the arms and legs, hence (perhaps)
the nickname, which might be read as "Stockings of the Indies."

[3]Don Melchor Portocarrero Laso de la Vega, conde de la Monclova, viceroy of New Spain
(1686–1688).

don Miguel de la Cruz took office[1] as governor. Once again there was sending of messages to Mexico City, and on the 8th of July an order arrived that they should give him the staff. On that same day, the 8th of July, [the alcalde mayor] accepted him as governor, but he was not the one who gathered the tribute. And so it ended. And the deputy [governor] turned out to be a citizen of San Pablo named don Lucas; he likewise received the staff then, in the month of July. [This was] the twelfth governor.

In this same year a person named Juan Nicolás, a thief, was hanged. He just asked to be hanged. It was on Monday, the 20th of the month of May. [*f. 24*]

In this same year, on Monday, the 4th of July, as dark was coming on, at 7 o'clock, a fireball fell. It came from the direction of Totimehuacan, and it fell in the forest on Matlalcueye. It was really terrifying. Then it was said, "Now is the time that we shall perish. Its omen has occurred." Then began a bad cough. Very many died of it, indigenous people as well as Spaniards and all kinds of people. At the hospital of San Pedro, they would bury eight or ten people a day, plus more in the barrios. What happened was really terrifying. Immediately in the churches praying began everywhere there; everywhere masses were said. It abated in the month of September. They called the cough *medias de la india* and *tamborito*.[2]

In this same year a viceroy came, on October 16. He entered [the city] on a Wednesday and was here for two weeks. Before leaving he really beheld and admired everything; he inspected all the churches there were. The viceroy's name was don Melchor Fernández Portocarrero Laso de la Vega, conde de Monclova.[3] He was missing a hand; they called him "silver hand."

In this same year, on Sunday the 10th of the month of November, they [partly] demolished the church of San Juan del Río in order to heighten the dome. [It was about to be brought down];[4] they had already opened the foundation. Then an officer of the law came in order to imprison the elders [cabildo members]. He wanted money. Because of that it was stopped. But the vicar, a priest named Gaspar Tamayo,[5] and later another time don Miguel de los Santos took courage, went before the law to obtain a license for the church to be torn down. Then the judge arrived to see the church. Then he issued a license for it to be torn down. [*f. 24v*]

House

---

[4]Since it was already said that the church was demolished, it is hard to understand how it was still only about to be brought down, but the rest of the passage leads to that conclusion. Also, in view of the content of some future entries, it may be that here *tzinquiçaz* means only for the height of some walls to be reduced and not for the church to be fully destroyed or demolished, which is the implication of the verb *xitinia* that was used first.

[5]This order of the clauses seems awkward. In Gómez García et al. 2000, the writer pauses at this point to list all the public posts involved in the controversy and the names of the people who filled them before proceeding with his story. Don Miguel is given even higher praise than here.

1687   NiCan ypan xihuitl ocanqui gobernasion yn dō Josef lasaro San miguel chane auh çan tlaco xihuitl oquipix yn bara niman omiqui çan oquitelicçac mula ynic omiqui niman ocanqui yn ipiltzin[1] y gobernasion oquitlami yn oc tlaco xihuitl sano ytoca D. josef lasaro huel oc telpochtli yc matlactli omey 13 gobernador

Sanno ypan xihuitl ynic 22 mani meztli de septtiembre ypan tonali lunes yn opiloloc se mestiso ytoca felipe pullero ocatca auh ychtequi omocueph [*sic*] auh otetzacuilique oncan atoyatenpan auh yn oqui[*n*]tzacuilique omentin caxtilteca yn se oquimictique auh yn oc se huel omomicti ynnahuac yn ichteque niman oquimasique yhuan se teopixqui agustino de misa no ychtequi catca auh niman oquihuicaque mexico auh sa ysel opiloloc yn felipe yhuan oquichiuhque cuartoz oquitlatlalique ypan otli auh in itzontecon onpa oquitlalito yn canpa otemictique

Sanno ypan xihuitl ynic 13 mani meztli de otubre ypan tonali lunes yohuac ypan ome ora omochiuh chicahuac tlalolinalistli hualtlathui martes auh nimā omocalaqui y señor obispo yn yglesia mayor niman oquitlatlapoque yn puertas ynic omotlatlatlauhtilique yhuan otlatzilin ynic nohuiyan teopan opanoc martes semilhuitl yn otlayohuac ypan chicuey ora oc sepa otlalolin oc sepa nohuiyan otlatzilin yn quexquich teopan niman ypan tlaco yohuac oc sepa otlalolin chicahuac auh yn canpana yglesia mayor otzilin ome campanada ysel ayac oquitzilini ynic chicahuac tlalolin niman oc sepa tlaocolatzilin ynic nohuiyan teopan huel temamauhti yn omochiuh auh yn canpana otzilin ynoma yehuatl ytoca doña maria hualathui miercoles ypan ylhuitzin santa teresa de jesus ynic yepa caxtoli 15 tonali otubre [*f. 25*]

Sanno ypan xihuitl ynicquipan nahui tonali mani meztli de nobienbre yn opiloloque nahuintin ypā tonalli martes ypanpa quitohque yehuantin yn otlachteque oncan san agustin calcuitlapan calnacasco yhuan oquimictique yn caxtiltecatl chane ypā biernes santo yohuac hualtlathui sabado y mochiuhque auh yn se ytoca Ju⁰ de santiago yn oc çe ytoca bernabel de santiago oc se ytoca Juan antonio ȳ oc se ytoca Ju⁰ pedro auh yn itoca Ju⁰ de s.tiago oquitequilique yn itzontecon onpa oquitlalito yn calnacasco san agustin calcuitlapan yn canpa otlachteque ypāpa yhuatl [*sic*] tlatlacole auh yn oc çequintin amo yntlatlacol san yntech oquitlamique auh yn itzontecon amo ohuecauh martes oquitlalique teotlac niman miercoles oquiquixtique ypanpa amo oquihiyohuique yn San agustin teopixque

Sanno ypan xihuitl yn ipan 25 tonali mani meztli de nobiembre huel ypan ylhuitzin santa carina [*sic*] ypan tonali martes yn huel achtopa tetl oquitlalique ynic oquipehualtique yn portada san Ju⁰ de rrio yn maestro omochiuh yehuatl ytoca diego luis

---

[1]In traditional Nahuatl usage *-piltzin* was someone's child of either gender, so that in texts of Stage 2 "child" is the normal translation. By the eighteenth century in some areas the word was

1687   Here in this year don Josef Lázaro from San Miguel assumed the governorship, but he held the staff for only half a year, then he died. A mule kicked him so that he died. Then his son[1] took the governorship and finished the remaining half-year. His name is likewise don Josef Lázaro. He was still very young. He [the father] was the thirteenth governor.

In this same year, on Monday the 22nd of the month of September, a mestizo named Felipe was hanged. He had been a poulterer but turned into a thief. They intercepted people on the banks of the Atoyac. When they intercepted two Spaniards, they killed one of the two, but the other really fought with the thieves, and then they caught them. Among them was an ordained Augustinian friar, who was also a thief. Then they took them to Mexico City. Felipe was the only one who was hanged. And they quartered him and placed [the parts] at various places on the road. They went to place his head where they had killed people.

In this same year, the 13th of the month of October, Monday night at 2 o'clock, before dawn on Tuesday, there was a strong earthquake. Then the lord bishop went into the cathedral and they opened the doors for prayer, and the bells were rung everywhere in the churches. The whole day of Tuesday passed. After dark, at 8 o'clock, there was another earthquake. Again the bells rang in all the churches everywhere. Then at midnight there was another strong earthquake, and a cathedral bell rang two peals unattended; no one rang it, so violently did the earth shake. Then again bells were tolled everywhere in the churches. What happened was really terrifying. And the bell called doña María rang of its own accord [again] in the night before Wednesday, the feast day of Santa Teresa de Jesús. It was the third time. This was on the 15th day of October. [*f. 25*]

In this same year, on Tuesday the 4th day of the month of November, four people were hanged because it was said that they were the ones who committed robbery at the rear of [the monastery of] San Agustín, at the corner of the building, and they killed a Spanish householder, on Good Friday, at night. In the night before Saturday was when they did it. One was named Juan de Santiago; another was named Bernabé de Santiago; another was named Juan Antonio; the other was named Juan Pedro. And they cut off the head of the one named Juan de Santiago. They placed it at the corner of San Agustín, behind the building, where they commited robbery, because he was the one at fault, and it was not the fault of the others, they just blamed them for it. But his head was not there long. They placed it there on Tuesday afternoon; then on Wednesday they removed it because the Augustinian friars couldn't bear it.

In this same year, on Tuesday the 25th day of the month of November, right on the feast day of Santa Catarina, for the very first time they set in place the stones with which they began the portal of [the church of] San Juan del Río. The master artisan was named Diego Luis.

---

veering toward the meaning "son" in certain contexts, and perhaps it has already attained that sense in this case.

Sanno ypan xihuitl yn ohuala alcalde mayor caxtillan otlatocatico nican cuitlaxcohuapan auh yn ocanqui posesion ypan yc senpuhualli yonchicui 28 tonali
mani metztli nobiembre yn ocalac yn palasio auh yn itoca D. Gabriel del Castillo
Sanno ypan xihuitl yn omoteochiuh yn iteopanCaltzin yn totlasomahuisnantzin
purissima la linpia consepsion ypan yc 8 mani metztli disiēbre ypan tonali lunes
yn ohuetz yn ilhuitzin auh ynon lunes onpa oquimochihuililique yn ilhuitzin [*f.
25v*] yN iglesia mayor ye quin teotlac yn oquihualmohuiquilique yn ichantzinco
auh ynic oquihualmohuiquilique muchi yn quexquich Religiones yhuan cofra-
dias oquihualmoyecanilique niman yehuatzin Sanctissimo cramento [*sic*] ye
quin martes yn oquimochihuililique yn ilhuitzin huel otlapipiloloc yn ipa calotli
huel mamahuistic altares oquintlatlalique

---

tochtli

1688   NiCan ypan xihuitl yn ocanqui gobernasion D. Ju^o de galisia mestiso yc matlactli onnahui 14 g^{or}: auh yn teniente oquis y don pascual _____ santiago chane

Sanno ypan xihuitl yn icpan [*sic*] chicome 7 tonali mani metztli abril ypan
miercoles yn opiloloque yeyntin caxtilteca ychteque ypanpa oquitzacuilique
Recua yca tlapactli onpa yn quitocayotia mal pays ypanpa ynon oquinpiloque
yhuan oquinchiuh cuartos sequi onpa oquihuicaque yn canpa oychteque onpa
oquitlalito auh yn oc sequi yn nohuiyan yn ipan otli oquintlatlalique yhuan nican
chaneque cuitlaxcohuapan yn se ytoca Ju^o pacheco achto opiloloc niman fran^{co}
domingues satepan Josef domingues ome hermanoz^1 ypan cuaresma semana de
ramoz
Sanno ypan xihuitl yn oquicuilique yn don miguel de loz santoz gobernador pasado ynic obrero^2 oCatca san Juan de rio yey bobedas oquintzacuh yn ome
cruseroz yhuan altar mayor asta ypan sotabanca cuali oquisqui auh niman oquimacaque oc çe tlacatl lasaro matias ynic obrero yesquia^3 auh yn alcalde Ju^o de
la crus alhuasil ~~mayor~~ menor [*f. 26*] felipe de santiago – fiscal marcos de
S.tiago auh y amantecatl ytoca Josef fran^{co} auh ymac yn oytlacauh yn media
naranja ye oquitzaca yn bobeda niman nochi otzatzayacac aocmo quali niman
oquinotzque se maestro caxtiltecatl oquitaco san yc oquitac nimā oquito hualas
cahuitl actihuetzis huel monequi oc sepa xitinis yc nochi sotabanca amo quipia
oc se ypatica^4 niman nochi tlacatl huel omotequipacho ypanpa huel miec tomin-
tzin opoliuh auh niman oc sepa ypan yc senpuali omome 22 tonali mani metztli

---

^{1}This is a remarkable expression from the point of view of traditional Nahuatl, in which all
kinship terms bore a possessive prefix, all sibling words made age distinctions, and there were no
inclusive collective words like brothers or sisters. See the further discussion of the point above on
p. 50.

^{2}The word meant a person in charge of orchestrating major construction and repair projects.
The post of obrero mayor had existed on the Spanish cabildo of Puebla from the sixteenth century.
Espinosa 1997, p. 80.

^{3}The church underwent major renovations in this period. The date on the façade, "20 de enero

In this same year an alcalde mayor came from Spain to rule here in Cuitlaxco-huapan. He took possession [of the office] on the 28th day of the month of November when he entered the palace. His name was don Gabriel del Castillo.

In this same year the church of our precious revered purest mother of the Limpia Concepción was consecrated on Monday the 8th of the month of December, the day on which her feast day fell. On that Monday they celebrated her feast day [*f. 25v*] in the cathedral. Later, in the afternoon, they brought her to her home, and as they brought her, all the religious orders and cofradías came ahead of her. Then later, on Tuesday, they celebrated the feast day of the most holy Sacrament; everything was greatly festooned, and they set up very magnificent altars here and there on the streets.

Rabbit

1688   Here in this year don Juan de Galicia, mestizo, assumed the governorship. He was the fourteenth governor. And don Pascual _____, a citizen of Santiago, turned out to be deputy [governor].

In this same year, on Wednesday the 7th day of the month of April, three Spanish thieves were hanged because they intercepted pack trains with fulled woolen cloth in what they call the badlands. For that they hanged and quartered them. Some of the quarters they took to where they had committed the robberies and placed them there. The rest they put in various places everywhere along the road. And they were from here in Cuitlaxcohuapan. One was named Juan Pacheco. He was hanged first. Then Francisco Domínguez, followed by Josef Domínguez, two brothers.[1] This was in Lent, in the week of palms.

In this same year they took from don Miguel de los Santos, former governor, the position of *obrero* he had held.[2] He completed the three vaults at [the church of] San Juan del Río. The two transepts and the main altar as far as the pediment of the arch over the cornice came out well. Then they gave [the position] to another person, Lázaro Matías, so that he would be the obrero.[3] The alcalde was Juan de la Cruz, the alguacil menor [*f. 26*] Felipe de Santiago, the fiscal Marcos de Santiago. The artisan was named Josef Francisco. But at his hands the dome went wrong. When he had closed the vault, everything cracked in various places; it was no longer good. Then they summoned a Spanish master craftsman. He came to see it; he no sooner saw it than he said, "In time it will collapse. It is very necessary that everything, including the pediment of the arch over the cornice, be demolished. There is no other remedy."[4] Then everyone was much concerned, because a great deal of money had been spent. Then on the 22nd day

---

de 1687," was visible until the twentieth century. The structure was known for its impressive vaulted archways and elaborate decorations in relief. Toussaint 1954, pp. 202–03.

   [4]One might expect "amo quipiya patli," and indeed, that is what Gómez García et al. 2000 has at this point. Possibly "ypatica" is a rare possessed abstract noun from an intransitive verb, in this case the related *pati*, "to be remedied."

marso oquipehualtique yn quixitinia san oc yehuatl yn media na naranja [*sic*]
asta ytech sotabanca niman oc sepa oquīnotzque omentin maestroz se ytoca Ju⁰
de la puebla yn oc çe ytoca andres rrodrigues niman nohuiyan oquitaque yn itic
yhuan oquiyahualoque yn teopantli niman quitoque amo monequi xitinis yn
sotabanca san ypan oc sepa quipehualtisque cualtitica yn tlatzintlan amo huelitis
huetzis nimā ypan oquipehualtique auh yn oc sepa oquitzaque yn bobeda huel
ypan yn itlecahuilitzin y tonali Juebes ypan chicome ora ye yohuac ypan yc
sempuali omchicome 27 tonali mani metztli de mayo niman oquicuilique yn
lasaro matias ynic obrero oquimacaque oc se tlacatl ytoca fran^co de la crus ynic
obrero yesqui auh yn regidor mayor ytoca Ju⁰ miguel alhuasil mayor fran^co
sanches fiscal andres martin cuechiuhqui

Sanno yquac yn omochiuh chicahuac yeyecatl San huel otlatlayohuac yhuan
miec xacali oquecatocti ypan tonali lunes ypan macuili ora teotlac yc caxtolli
omome 17 tonali mani metztli mayo huel temauhti yn omochiuh nohiuyan otla-
coltlatzilin [*sic*]
Sanno ypā xihuitl yn ohuala birey yn ocalac yc caxtoli ose 16 otubre pan [*sic*]
sabado yuh yalhua catca ylhuitzin santa teresa huel nohuiyan otlamahuistehuac
yn cuitlaxcoapan auh yn itoca yn birrey D. gaspar de silba y mēdosa de la serda
conde de oropesa¹ [*f. 26v*]

---

acatl

1689   NiCan ypan xihuitl ypan domingo yc senpuali yonnahui 24 mani metztli de Julio
       ypan bisperas yn apostol santiago ypan nahui ora teotlac omochiuh chicahuac
       quiahuitl yhuan tesihuitl yca ehecacoatl san huel otlatlayohuac auh oquicolo yn
       beleta yn icpac ca yn torre catedral yhuan tore san Ju⁰ sentepec niman oqui-
       ma[*ya*]uh sāno yhuan yn beleta samctissima trenidad yhuā se ermita ipan barrio
       San Ju⁰ de rio no oquihuicac yn crus amo ones yn canpa oquihuicac yquac on
       oquitoque tlamisquia semanahuac huel senca temamauhti yn omochiuh

       Sanno ypan xihuitl yc senpualli onnahui 24 tonali mani metztli agosto ypan
       miercoles ylhuitzin san bartome [*sic*] apostol yn omopilo çe teopixqui clerigo
       ytoca ocatca pedro prieto santa ynes caltitlan yn omochiuh yn señor obispo huel
       omotequipacho omotocac san pedro
       Sanno ypan xihuitl yc yey 3 tonali mani metztli otubre yn opiloloque yn omentin
       ypan ybisperas san fran^co ypan lunes quintocayotiaya leones oquinchiuhque
       quartoz çe ytoca Ju⁰ de leon yn oc çe ytoca diego enamorado²
       Sanno ypan yc 19 de otubre yn omotemahmacac amatl ynic timotlapaloz³ yn

¹Don Gaspar de la Cerda y Sandoval Silva y Mendoza, conde de Galve, viceroy of New Spain
(1688–1696).
²Gómez García et al. 2000 adds two interesting sentences regarding this event: "tetex auh amo
quimasilique causas inic oquinpiloque," "He [Diego Enamorado] was the brother-in-law. They did

of the month of March they began to demolish again just the dome as far down as the pediment of the arch over the cornice. Then again they summoned two master craftsmen, one named Juan de la Puebla and the other named Andrés Rodríguez. They looked everywhere inside and went all around the church. Then they said, "It is not necessary to demolish the pediment of the arch over the cornice; rather they are to begin on it again. What is below is fine. It cannot fall." Then they began on it. Again they closed the vault right on the Ascension of [our Lord], on Thursday, the 27th day of the month of May, at 7 o'clock at night. Then they took the position of obrero from Lázaro Matías and gave it to another person named Francisco de la Cruz so that he would be obrero. The regidor mayor was named Juan Miguel. The alguacil mayor was Francisco Sánchez, and the fiscal was Andrés Martín, skirtmaker.

At this same time a great wind arose. It grew very dark and many thatch huts were blown away by the wind. It was at 5 o'clock in the afternoon, Monday the 17th day of the month May. What happened was really terrifying. Everywhere there was tolling of bells.

In this same year a viceroy came. He entered on Saturday the 16th of October, the day after the feast day of Santa Teresa. He beheld and admired things absolutely all over Cuitlaxcohuapan before leaving. The viceroy's name was don Gaspar de Silva y Mendoza de la Cerda, conde de Oropesa.[1] [*f. 26v*]

Reed

1689   Here in this year, on Sunday the 24th of the month of July, on the eve of Santiago Apóstol, at 4 o'clock in the afternoon, there was a great rainstorm with hail and a whirlwind. It grew very dark. And it bent the weathervanes on top of the cathedral tower and the tower of [the church of] San Juan at Centepec. It likewise knocked down the weathervanes of the [convent of] Santísima Trinidad and of a shrine in the barrio of San Juan del Río. Also it carried off the cross; where it took it was not discovered. At that time they said the world would come to an end. What happened was really very frightening.

In this same year, on Wednesday the 24th day of the month of August, on the feast day of San Bartolomé Apóstol, a secular priest hanged himself. His name was Pedro Prieto. It happened near the buildings of [the convent of] Santa Inés. The lord bishop was much distressed. He was buried at San Pedro.

In this same year, on Monday the 3rd day of the month of October, the eve of San Francisco, two people whom they called the Leóns were hanged and quartered. One was named Juan de León; the other was named Diego Enamorado.[2]

In this same year, on October 19, papers were distributed telling how we are to

not specify reasons why they hanged them."

   [3]The context makes it clear that with "timotlapaloz" the intention is "timotlapalozque," using *mo* for the first person plural reflexive prefix. As the reader will see, the greetings are given in Spanish in the Nahuatl text.

tiquitozque Aue maria auh yn tlananquililistli quitoz sin pecados consebida yn omotemacac yn amatl ypan miercoles

Sanno yquac ypan metztli de nobiembre yn ohualmohuicac çe obispo onpa ohualmehualti ynahuac Jerusalen ypanpa oquimonechicalhuico huentzintli oquimitlanilico limozna ypanpa oquitlanilique ome altepetl yn iyaohuan oquinmotlacauhtique [f. 27] yc mochin yn imaçehualhuan huel miyec tomin oquitlatlanilique ynic quinquixtis ypanpa ynon yc nican ohualmohuicac yhuan nohuiyan omonemiti yn nican cuitlaxcoapan miec tomin oquimohuiquili[2]

Sanno ypan xihuitl ypan yc chicuey 8 tonali mani metztli de disiembre omotlali çe cometa yuhqui tonalmitl oquistihcaya oncan ytlamelauhca yn tepexochotzin achi ytechhuic yn iquiçayā yn tonatiuh ypan yey ora tlanestihuitz Çan oc tepiton auh yn tzilinis nahui ora ye nochi oquis huel huey huel tlanextiaya auh yn icuitlapil yc tlacpac oyatoya auh yn opoliuh ytlamian pascua[3]

Sanno ypan xihuitl yn omotlali lanternilla[4] yn icpac ca yn media naranja yn teopantli san Ju[o] de rio yhuan inic omotlali yn açulexo yn icpac lanterna yn icpac ca yn media naranxa yn omomacac[5] yn ipatiuh matlactli omome pesos yhua chiquasen tomin oquicouh altepetl auh yn rretetoton[6] yn icaticate sanno ompa tlacpac ynon oquicouh yn diego de leon ycuac oalcaldetic oquimacac chicuaçen pesos san yxquich auh ynon tomin yc oquinechico sera ypatiuh omonequisquia quaresma ypan lunes santo yhuan no yquac yn onenen corniJa inic omocoronaro yn teopantli ynic tlayahualotoc yhuan yquac omochiuh yn escaleras yc titleco tlapanco no yquac y mochiuh ynn acocali[7] fiscal blas de los s.toz

---

tecpatl

1690   NiCan ypan xihuitl yn ipan yc çepuali yhuan chicnahui tonali mani metztli Enero ypan domingo yn omononotz yn icolateraltzin yn totlasotatzin San Juan baptista auh yn oquimononochilique yehuatzin yn bicario gaspar tamayo yhuan yn don miguel de loz Santoz g[or]: pasado – yhuan diego de leon alcalde pasado [f. 27v] yhuan fiscal blas de loz santoz yhuan Regidor mayor marcoz de santiago – yhuan alhuasil mayor felipe de sātiago – yhua fran[co] de la crus alcalde pasado auh ynic oquimononochilique yn omomacac chicopa mamacuilpuali pesos auh

---

[1]The Nahuatl of this expression is discussed in n. 3, p. 145.

[2]In 1683, a Syrian-born Christian who was a member of the Chaldean church in Baghdad had visited Puebla. The reverend Elias al-Mûsili first begged for funds for the beleaguered churches of his city from the pope, who referred him to the Spanish monarch, who gave him permission to go and beg in the Indies. He traveled through colonial Spanish America from 1675 to 1683. He met with interest and sympathy and received many contributions to his cause; his description of Puebla is especially warm and full of praise. Upon his return, he met with the pope and gave a full account of his trip, then when he returned home he wrote of it. Whether this entry is placed in the wrong year, or whether al-Mûsili's success inspired another traveler, I do not know. See Farah 2003.

[3]The reference might be to Christmas as the closest major holiday, or Easter, or even another holiday: the word *pascua* was used for any religious festival lasting more than two days.

greet each other.[1] What we are to say is "Ave María." And the answer is to be "Conceived without sin." The papers were given out on a Wednesday.

At this same time, in the month of November, a bishop came who was from near Jerusalem. He came to collect offerings and request alms. He requested them because two altepetl, all of whose subjects their enemies had enslaved, requested them. [*f. 27*] They kept requesting very much money in order to free them. Because of that he came here; he went everywhere here in Cuitlaxcohuapan and took much money away with him.[2]

In this same year, on the 8th day of the month of December, a comet appeared; it would come out like a ray of sunshine in a straight line toward Mount Tepexochotzin, somewhat toward the east. It came shining at 3 o'clock, still small, but when it rang 4 o'clock, the whole thing came out, very big. It shone brightly; its tail went pointing up. It disappeared at the end of the holiday season.[3]

In this same year the *linternilla*[4] that is on top of the dome of the church of San Juan del Río was set in place. And when the glazed tiles were placed on the top of the linternilla that is on top of the dome, 12 pesos and 6 reales were given for their price.[5] The altepetl bought them. And the little [guards, stops?][6] that also stand up above were bought by don Diego de León when he served as alcalde. He gave only 6 pesos for them. And that money he gathered as the price of the wax candles that were going to be used in Lent on Monday of Holy Week. And also at that time was made the cornice with which the church was crowned, so that it goes all around. And at that time the stairs were built by which one goes up to the roof. Also at that time the structure on the roof was made.[7] The fiscal was Blas de los Santos.

––––––––

Flint-knife

––––––––

1690   Here in this year, on Sunday, the 29th day of the month of January, there was a consultation about our precious father San Juan Bautista's side altarpiece, and those who consulted were the vicar Gaspar Tamayo, don Miguel de los Santos former governor, Diego de León former alcalde, [*27v*] the fiscal Blas de los Santos, the regidor mayor Marcos de Santiago, the alguacil mayor Felipe de Santiago, and Francisco de la Cruz former alcalde, and what they talked about was that on seven occasions, 100 pesos each time were given for it. The one

––––––––

[4]An ornate form of a skylight, a tiny tower set atop a dome which was open at the sides to let in light.

[5]Usually the verb *maca* has both a direct and an indirect object. Here and in another instance just below, an indirect object seems to be missing. In both cases the indirect object seems to be replaced by the price and the connection to be more like the applicative.

[6]I am not sure, but it seems to me that the loanword in "rretetoton" may be *retén*.

[7]Molina defines *acocalli* as *sobrado de casa*. In architecture, the term could mean a small roofed (but not necessarily walled) area constructed on top of a building to cover something like an open stairway or a water tank. However, *acocalli* was used in Nahuatl for the second story of any building or for any structure built on a roof terrace.

yn oquimochihuili ytocatzin diego de loz santoz onpa chane san miguel

Sanno yquac ynic matlactli 10 tonali mani metztli abril yn opeuhqui ynic mochi-
pahua yn teopantli yn san Juan de rio ypan tonali lunes yhuā mochi omotlali
tlamachtli[1] yn tlacpac yn itech yn bobedas yhuan otlacuiloloc

Sanno ypan xihuitl yn omoteochiuh yn icapillatzin yn totlasomahuisnantzin Rosario[2] onpa santo domingo yn oquimoquixtilique ypan tonali Juebes yc matlactli
onnahui 14 tonali mani metztli abril niman Oquimohuiquilique ompa sāta carina
[*sic*] ompa omocochiti niman vienes [*sic*] oquimohuiquilique ompa sanctissima
trenidad ompa omocochiti auh yn sabado yohuatzinco yn oquimohuiquilique yn
Cathedral auh niman teotlac yn ohualmohuiCatzino ychantzinco huel miec tla-
mahuiçoli omochiuh ocatca comedias ypan calotli auh yn Juebes teotlac yhcuac
oquimoquixtilique yn ichantzinco huel chicahuac Ehecatl omochiuh aocmo huel
aca onenen ynic chicahuac ehecatl mochiuh aocmo monexitiyaya ynic oquimohuiquilique niman y biernes yn opeuhqui yn Ehecatl ypan matli [*sic*] omome ora
yhuan tlaco huel temamauhti yn omochiuh niman nohuiyan otlatzilin [*f. 28*]

Sanno yquac yn oquimopehualtilique yn Jesus nasareno yn ometzticatca yn santa crus tianquisco ynic quimoquixtilique yc mochin tepamitl ypan metztli abril
yn oquimotemohuilique ypan yc yey 3 tonali de Junio ypan sabado oquimotlali-
lique ypan matlactli ca carretillas [*sic*] muchi quincuitlaxquimiloque san yohuatzincopa auh amo miec oquimonenemitilique ypanpa opachiuhtihuetz yn tlate-
mantli yn ithualco auh ye quin lunes yn oquimocalaquilique cathedral auh san
yuhqui yn quenamicatzin metzticatca ytech yn tepanitl [*sic*] yuhqui oquimocalaquilique oquihuepalquiquimiloque huel miyec nentlamachilistli oquimochili
[*sic*] yn maestro mayor auh yn achtopa oquimocopinilicah yn maestroz yn tla-
pallaCuiloque pintores amo yuhcatzintli omoquixti yn itlaÇoxayacatzin

Sanno ypan xihuitl ynic caxtoli omome 18[3] tonali mani metztli junio yn oqui-
mopehualtili miçiones yn quichiuhque teopixque tiatinos yn oquichiuhque achtopa catedral asta ypan san Ju⁰ auh yn otlanqui catedral niman oyaque ypan
tonali domingo yn calbario oquichiuhque yey tonali sermones auh niman oyaque
onpa yn parroquia otlaçeliloc yhuan sermones ocatca [*f. 28v*]

Sanno ypan xihuitl ynic çēpuhuali ose 21 tonali mani metztli Junio yn opiloloc
çe tlacatl ytoca Juachin peres ypanpa ytech oquitlamique ychtecayotl auh amo
melahuac oquitoque oquimahuispolo çe xinola ychpochtli yhuan yn tenan yhuan
oquimicti çe tlacatl ytoca anton de la noch[4] onpa ypan bario de loz rremedioz

Sanno ypan xihuitl ypan yc çenpuali omome 22 tonalli çeptiembre ypan ylhuitzin san mauriÇio yn oquitlatique Çe mulato huel tlilihqui ypanpa puto ytoca
ocatca domingo onpa oquihualhuicaque amillpan[5] cuauhco yn oquihualhuicac
yehuatl don fran^co albares onpa Santiago Calyecac[6] yn oquitlatique auh ynic

---

[1]*Tlamachtli* often means cloth embroidery, but it can refer to any elaborate decoration, here
apparently to arabesque stucco designs (*yesería*) such as were often placed on church walls.

[2]The most splendid chapel in the Dominican complex (Zerón Zapata, pp. 83–84).

[3]The Nahuatl words for "seventeen" are followed by the Arabic numeral "18."

who did it is named Diego de los Santos, citizen of San Miguel.

At this same time, on Monday the 10th day of the month of April, cleaning [renovating] the church of San Juan del Río began. Lacework[1] was placed all over up high on the vaults, and it was painted.

In this same year the chapel of our precious revered mother of Rosario[2] at [the convent of] Santo Domingo was dedicated. They brought her out on Thursday the 14th day of the month of April. Then they took her to [the convent of] Santa Catarina; there she slept. Then on Friday they took her to [the convent of] Santísima Trinidad; there she slept. And early on Saturday morning they took her to the cathedral, and then in the afternoon she came back to her home. A great many marvels were performed. There were plays in the streets. On Thursday afternoon, when they brought her out of her home, a very great wind rose. No one went about any longer, so strong was the wind. As they carried her, she could no longer be seen. Then on Friday the wind began at half past 12 o'clock. What happened was really terrifying. Then the bells rang everywhere. [*f. 28*]

In this same year they began [work] on the Jesús Nazareno which was in the Santa Cruz marketplace, so that in the month of April they removed him together with the whole wall. On Saturday, the 3rd day of June, they lowered him and placed him on ten little carts that they wrapped all in hides. It was toward early morning. But they didn't get far with him because the courtyard pavement collapsed. It wasn't until Monday that they brought him into the cathedral. He was just the same as he had been before on the wall. They brought him in that way, covered with planks. It caused much grief to the chief master artisan. The first time the master artisans, the painters, had made a copy of him, his precious face did not come out as a good likeness.

In this same year, on the 17th[3] day of the month of June, the Theatine religious began carrying out missions. They carried them out first from the cathedral as far as San Juan, and they ended [back] at the cathedral. Then on Sunday they went to the Calvario; for three days they delivered sermons. Then they went to the parochial church. There communion was received, and there were sermons. [*f. 28v*]

In this same year, on the 21st day of the month of June, a person named Joaquín Pérez was hanged because he was accused of theft, but it was not true. They said he dishonored a Spanish woman, a maiden, and the mother, and he killed a person named Antón [de la Noche?][4] in the barrio of Los Remedios.

In this same year, on the 22nd day of the month of September, the feast day of San Mauricio, they burned a very dark mulatto because he was a homosexual. His name was Domingo. They brought him from Amilpan[5] in a cage; don Francisco Alvarez was the one who brought him. It was at Santiago, in front,[6]

---

[4]The name "de la noch" seems peculiar, but the incident is not recorded in any other annals, so we have no way of knowing what it might have been.

[5]Or from the low-lying, well irrigated lands off to the south.

[6]The word "Calyecac" seems to mean in front of a building, probably the church.

oquitlaquentique quiltic bayeta yn imontera no quiltic niman se crus chichiltic yxquac yCuitlan [*sic*] no chichiltic ome estandarte oquiyecan Çe quiltic Çe chichiltic[1] auh yn tlapitzalli[2] amo yuh yn iquac pillolo yc quipitza çan yuhqui yn iquac tlalhuiquixtia niman oc çe mulato san oquiyecan oquimecahuitectiāq̃ no oquitlalilique ymontera quiltic no çe crus yxquac no chichiltic amo oquitlatique oc çepa oquihualhuicaque telpilloyan auh yn oquiquixtique yn telpiloyan ypan chicuey ora yohuatzinco yn omic çe ypan chiucnahui ora huel semilhuitl yn otlatlac ypan tonali biernes auh yn oquitocaque ynexo onpa yn san matias ynic huel yancuicā nican otlatlac puto yn cuitlaxcohuapan[3]

Sanno ypan xihuitl ynic 11 disiembre ypan tonali lunes yn oquicalaquique capilla[4] Çe telpochtli quixtiano ynic quipilozque ypanpa oquixtlatzini ytatzin auh niman yn itepantlatocahuan conde de santiago no otlatitlātihuetzque mexico ynic ypan tlatohua ynic amo piloloz ypan tonali martes yn oquis coreo y[*f. 29*]pan matlactli ose ora tlaco niman ypan miercoles tlanestihuitz oc çepa ohuasico y correo yn ohuala tlanahuatili ynic tlapopolhuilo aocmo piloloz Ça yas china

---

calli

1691 NiCan ypan xihuitl yn ocanqui gobernacion yn don diego de leon San Ju⁰ de Ryo chane auh amo oquinechico yehuatl yn itlacalaquiltzin yn tohueytlatoncatzī Rey yehuatl yn don ju⁰ galisia oquinechico auh yn teniente san ye ye [*sic*] mateo Çacatero[5] ynic 15 go⁰ᵉʳ?

Sanno ypan xihuitl yc 28 de marÇo y tlecoc yn Canpana San agustin ypan miercoles ipa yey ora teotlac auh yn otlanqui ynic oquipiloque ypan chicome ora yohuac niman huel oquitzilinique

Sanno ynic macuili 5 tonali abril yn açico yn tlanahuatili ynic mocanonisaroz yn San Ju⁰ de Dioz ypan tonali Juebes niman huel nohuiyan otlatzilin yn quexquich teopan

Sanno yquac ynic çenpuali ose 21 abril ypan tonali sabado yn oc çe otlatlac puto sanno mulato chipahuac ytoca ocatca manuel yn oquitemacaya polboz ynic ynca omocacayahua pipiltoton sanno onpa yn santiago calyecac[6]

---

[1]Experts do not recognize the significance of the colors red and green as they are used in this context. Tertullian does connect "stains of red and green" with fornication (Roberts et al. 1994, "On Modesty," Ch. 20). Research continues.

[2]The instrument could be a flute, trumpet, or some other wind instrument.

[3]Gómez García et al. 2000 gives a much shorter version of these events. However, it adds one interesting sentence: "otlatlac se puto mulato prietto inahuac Se Sihuatl in oquichiuh in itlacol [*sic*]." The first part means "a male homosexual, a dark mulatto, was burned." With the rest I can come to no definitive interpretation. One possibility is: "it was at the house of a woman that he committed his sin." Another might be "he committed his sin with a woman," either that she was implicated, or that the two committed acts together, which would seem to call for another definition

that they burned him. And they dressed him in green flannel; his cap was also green. Then there was a red cross on his forehead [and another one], also red, on his back. Two standards preceded him, one green, one red.[1] And the trumpet[2] was not blown as it is when someone is hanged, but as when a feast day is celebrated. Another mulatto went ahead of him; they went along whipping him. They put a green cap on him too, and also a cross on his forehead, also red. They did not burn him; they brought him back to the jail. And they removed them from jail at 8 o'clock, early in the morning, and one of them died at 9 o'clock. The whole day Friday he burned, and they buried his ashes at San Matías. Thus for the very first time a male homosexual was burned here in Cuitlaxcohuapan.[3]

In this same year, on Monday, December 11, they put a Spanish youth in a chapel[4] because they were to hang him for striking his father in the face. Then his intercessors, including the conde de Santiago, quickly sent to Mexico City to advocate that he not be hanged. On Tuesday a courier left at [*f. 29*] half past 11. Then on Wednesday, as daylight came, the courier got back again; [with him] came an order that [the youth] was pardoned. He would no longer be hanged, but would be sent to China [the Philippines].

_____

House

1691　　Here in this year don Diego de León assumed the governorship. He was a citizen of San Juan del Río. But he did not collect the tribute of our great ruler the king; don Juan de Galicia collected it. The deputy [governor] was Mateo Zacatero.[5] [Don Diego de León] was the fifteenth governor.

In this same year, on Wednesday the 28th of March, the bell was raised at [the convent of]] San Agustín at 3 o'clock in the afternoon. They finished hanging it at 7 o'clock at night. Then they really rang it.

At this same [time], on Thursday the 5th day of April, news came that San Juan de Dios was to be canonized. Then the bells rang absolutely everywhere in all the churches.

At this same time, on Saturday the 21st of April, another male homosexual was burned. He was also a mulatto, light-colored; his name was Manuel. He gave out powders by means of which he took advantage of small children. It was likewise at Santiago in front of the building [church].[6]

_____

and not be likely. Grammatically the passage seems open to the interpretation that the man was burned "next to a woman who committed his [or her] sin," in other words that she was burned for something similar, but that would have been nearly sui generis and surely would have drawn a report from our present author.

[4] Although the text is not explicit, the youth was apparently seeking asylum in the chapel.

[5] The name also doubtless refers to Mateo's occupation as gatherer and seller of dried grass or hay.

[6] See n. 6, p. 149.

Sanno ypan xihuitl ynic ypan chicome tonali abril ypan sabado de ramoz yn omotlapo yn icapillatzin ȳ Jesus nazareno yn tianquis [*sic*] omoyetzticata [*sic*] yn tlacpac omoteneuh ynic muchi tepamitl oquimoquixtilica yhuan ye oquimocalaquilica tepā[1] auh 19 de abril yn oquimotlaliliyaya ypan altar auh amo quixt[e]caque[2] oquihualmotepexihuilique nimā oxixitin auh yn axcan moyetztica yancuican oquimicuilhuilique oc çepa huel miyec tomin opopoliuh çe cachopopin[3] y[n] quimoquixtilia ytoca diego de la siera [*f. 29v*]

Sanno yquac ypan ytlamian metztli abril quin quinhualicaque [*sic*] matlactli omome Çihuame ynglesas yca ynpipilhuā quintzitzquique onpa san [*sic*] domingo caracas[4] auh huel miyeque yn ohualaya auh ȳ muchin yn oquichtin onpa oquīmictique sa ye yn sihua oquinhualhuicaque auh yn nican san amo onesqui canpa oquincauhque

Sanno ypan yc chiquasen 6 tonali mani metztli mayo yn omoteochiuh yn iRetablotzin s. x͞pobal yn catedral metztica ypan domingo yn ipan bisperas huel otlatlatique ytech yn torre

Sanno ypan xihuitl yc ypan matlactli omome 12 mani metz [*sic*] mayo yn ohuala tlanahuatili ynic omonamicti yn tohueytlatocatzin Rey caxtillan ypan tonali çabado auh niman yn rregidores yc muchin oc sequin tlatoque oquichiuhque cabil [*sic*] ynic omononotzque cuix mochihuas yn tlatocaylhuitl cuix no amo niman oquitoque macamo mochihua yn ilhuitl man [*sic*] çan mochihuili [*sic*] misa de grasia auh niman yn Señor obispo sanno yuhqui oquimitalhui ma yuhqui mochihua oc achi huel cuali yesqui niman ypan tonali lunes omotlas pregon ynic nohuiyan tlatlatlatiloz nipan Calotli yhuan yn quexquich teopantli niman ypan tonali martes huallayohua huel mahuistic ynic otlatlatlac niman hualtlathui miercoles yn omochiuh yn misa de grasia huel miec tlatzotzonali tlapitzalli huel no miec xinmatlatl[5] yhuan yc muchi conbentoz muchi hualaque yn teopixque yhuan huel [*f. 30*] nohuiyan otlatzilin huel omoçenchiuh onpa yn catedral ypan miercoles

~~Sanno yquac ypan yc çempuali on nahui 24 tonali mani metztli mayo yn opeuhqui chicahuac~~

Sanno ypan xihuitl ypan domingo yc mahtlactli ttonali mani metztli Junio huel ypan Sanctissima TRENidad yn opeuhqui yn quiahuitl yn otlapalnalti[6] momoztla quiyahuiya çeçenyohualtica anmonma mocahuaya[7] auh niman ypan Juebes yc matlactli onnahui tonali Junio corpus cristi amo omoquixttitzino yn Sanctissimo Sacramento yn ipan calotli yn quimotoquili yn ÇeÇe xihuitl san oncan calitic omotlayehualhuitzino niman ypan domingo sanno yuhqui amo no omoquixtitzino ypanpa chicahuac quiahuiya auh çanno ypan cahuitl yn omocueçoque mexico tla[8] yn oquitlatique palasio quimictisnequia yn viRey[9] auh yn

[1]Although other theories can be devised, it seems most likely that "tepan" was intended as "teopan," "into the church." See the entry on this topic under 1690.

[2]Despite an obscure letter, the verb in question must be *ixteca* (to level or plane a surface).

[3]The form "cachopopin" seems unorthodox but is priceless as a seventeenth-century attestation of the word in an authentic Nahuatl text.

[4]There is no such place. Possibly the meaning is Santo Domingo on Hispaniola plus Caracas.

In this same year, on the 7th day of April, Palm Saturday, the chapel of the Jesús Nazareno who used to be in the marketplace was opened. It has been told above how they had removed the whole wall and brought it into the church.[1] On the 19th of April they were placing [the statue] on the altar, but they didn't get it level;[2] they dropped it and it came apart. They painted anew the one that is there now. Again a very great deal of money was spent. It was a gachupín[3] named Diego de la Sierra who did the likeness. [*f. 29v*]

At the same time, at the end of April, they brought here twelve English women with their children. They seized them at Santo Domingo Caracas.[4] A great many were coming, but they killed all the men there and brought only the women. Here it has not been found out at all where they left them [i.e., the men?].

In this same [year], on the 6th day of the month of May, the altarpiece of San Cristóbal that is in the cathedral was consecrated, on Sunday at vespers. They had really big fires on the tower [in celebration].

In this same year, on Saturday the 12th of the month of May, news came that our great ruler the king of Spain had married. Then the regidores and all the rest of the [Spanish] gentlemen held a cabildo meeting, at which they discussed whether or not a holiday for the king should be celebrated. Then they said, "Let a holiday not be made of it; let only a mass of thanksgiving be celebrated." Then the lord bishop said the same thing, "Let it be done that way; it will be much better." Then on Monday a proclamation was issued that there were to be bonfires in the streets everywhere and at all the churches. Then on Tuesday, as dark was coming, the burning was very marvelous. At dawn on Wednesday a mass of thanksgiving was said. There was much drumming and blowing of wind instruments; there was also a great deal of [blue-green netting].[5] And from all the monasteries all the friars came to the cathedral, and [*f. 30*] absolutely everywhere the bells rang all at the same time on Wednesday.

~~At this same time, on the 24th day of the month of June, right on [the feast day of] Santísima Trinidad, there began a strong . . . .~~

In this same year, on Sunday the 10th day of the month of June, right on [the feast day of] Santísima Trinidad, the rains began which rotted[6] things. It rained every day, every night. It never stopped at all.[7] Then on Thursday, the 14th day of June, Corpus Christi day, the most holy Sacrament was not brought out in the streets that it follows every year. It only went around inside the building. Then likewise neither did it come out on Sunday, because it was raining hard. And at this same time the people[8] in Mexico City rioted, when they burned the palace and wanted to kill the viceroy.[9] And it rained here until Thursday the

---

[5]Presumably a decorative item.

[6]The intention is "otlapalanalti" from *palanaltia* (to cause something to rot).

[7]The string "anmonma mocahuaya" should probably be read as *amo ma mocahuaya*.

[8]I take it that "tla" here is for "tlaca."

[9]Perhaps "were on the point of killing the viceroy." The famous insurrection of 1692 is chronologically misplaced here, coming before the eclipse of 1691 (see below).

oquiahuiya asta nican ypan tonali Jueues auh yc matlactli oçe 11 tonali mani metztli Julio yn ye tlachipahuatiuh yhuan nimā opeuhqui tlaçoti tlacualtzintli ypatiuh chicuaçē yhuan medio yn tlaoli

Sanno ypan xihuitl ynic ypan Jueues yc çenpuali yhuan yey tonali mani metztli agosto ybisperatzin yn tlaçomahuistic santo San bartolome yn omito huel ypan chicome ora huel opeuhqui cualo yn itonatiuhtzin yn çemanahuac tlatoani dioz yn huel ypan chicuey ora huel tlaCotian Ohuasic ynic qualotica yn melahuac yn itlatenehual yn tlamatini yn itlatlalil OaÇic yn chiucnahui hora niman Oçentla-yuhtimoman [*sic*] Oquinenehuili yn chicome hora yohuac auh huel çe quarta ora ynic huecahuac yn otlayohuatimania auh y tototzitzintin yn cacalome yn tzotzo-pilo[me] [*f. 30v*] niman muchin tlalpan huetzque ça papatlacatinemia huel otlao-coltzatzatzique auh yn tetepeh yuhquin costic tlemiyahuatl ynpan motecaya yn popocatzin yuhqui yn tlepoctli yn ipan catca auh yn tlatlaca niman Çan yuhqui yn omotlapoltique teopan çequintin omotlaloque Çequintin omauhcahuehuetz-que auh Çan yey yn niman omomiquilique yn iquac ça choquis [*sic*] omania aocmo omiximatia yn tlatlaca[1] auh niman nohuiyan otlaocoltlatzilin yn quex-quich teopan çan yxquich yn catedral yhuan s. fran^co amo otlatzilin ypāpa amo oquimonequilti yn s.^r obispo ypanpa huel miyec tlacatl miquisquia[2] auh huel ypan mahtlactli ora yn otlachipahuac auh yn tleyn oquitzaucticatca yn tonali ça çe tliltic yn iquac oquitlalcahuitia huel muchi tlacatl quittac yn quenami quitlal-cahuitia yc huetztia ytech matlalcueyetzin yn quenami nestica tlayXpan yn punto N.[3] onpa ohetztia [*sic*] yn tleyn quitzaucticatca yn tonatiuh auh yn omen-tin sisitlaltin quiyacanaya yn tonali yc mottas ynin punto P. auh yn çe qui-hualycan [*sic*] tonatiuh yn tonali mottas yca ynin punto O. ca huel iuh mottaya hueyhueyntin ca huel tlanextiaya auh yn tzocotzitzin amo san tlapualtin ca huel quinenehuilia yn ticatla auh yn Çemilhuitl yeyecapitzactli oquistoya ca huel çeçec auh ypan yey ora asta ypan nahui ora teotlac oquiahuhticaya temamauhti yn oquimochihuili ȳ tloque nahuaque totecuiyo Dioz ypan on teotlactli Jueues[4]

---

[1]Spanish chroniclers left similar descriptions of panic in the churches, engendered by the utter darkness, with the stars clearly visible and bird noises distinctly audible. Carrión 1970, p. 29.

[2]Spanish chroniclers (as mentioned in Carrión) also felt the priests who rang the bells con-tributed needlessly to panic and raised the death count, presumably creating stampeding or crush conditions.

11th day of the month of July, when it began to clear. Then food began to get more expensive; the price of shelled corn was 6½ reales [per fanega].

In this same year, on Thursday the 23rd day of the month of August, the eve of our precious revered holy San Bartolomé, it was said that right at 7 o'clock began an eclipse of God the universal ruler's sun. Right at 8 o'clock it reached fully half an eclipse. The prediction and decree of the scholar [astronomer?] was true. When 9 o'clock arrived, it got completely dark; it resembled 7 o'clock in the evening, and for a good quarter of an hour darkness lingered, and the little birds, the crows, the buzzards, [*f. 30v*] all fell on the ground and went about fluttering and making very mournful cries. And something like yellow tassels of flame spread over Popocatepetl. Something like the smoke of flames was on it. Then it was as if people lost their senses; some ran to church; some kept falling in their terror; but only three died right then. At that time nothing but weeping reigned. People no longer recognized each other.[1] And then everywhere the bells tolled in all the churches. Only at the cathedral and [the convent of] San Francisco did the bells not ring, because the lord bishop did not wish it, because many people would die.[2] Right at 10 o'clock it got light. What was blocking the sun was just a black [person?]. When he abandoned it, absolutely everyone saw how he abandoned it and went falling on Matlalcueye, how what was blocking the sun appeared facing the north[3] point of the compass. And [during the eclipse] the two stars that were preceding the sun could be seen at the west point. And the one that the sun preceded could be seen by the east point. The big [stars] looked just as usual; they shone brightly. And the very small ones were without number. It was exactly like midnight. All day light winds blew, which were very cold. From 3 until 4 o'clock in the afternoon it was raining. What the lord of the near and the nigh, our lord God, did on that Thursday afternoon was terrifying.[4]

---

[3] I am assuming that N stands for *norte*, P for *poniente* and O for *oriente*.

[4] Why the events of the afternoon are so described when what happened in the morning was so much more frightening remains a mystery. The whole preceding passage presents many translation problems. This segment does not appear in Gómez Garcia et al. 2000, leading me to wonder if it may have been added by a copyist and not have originated with our main author.

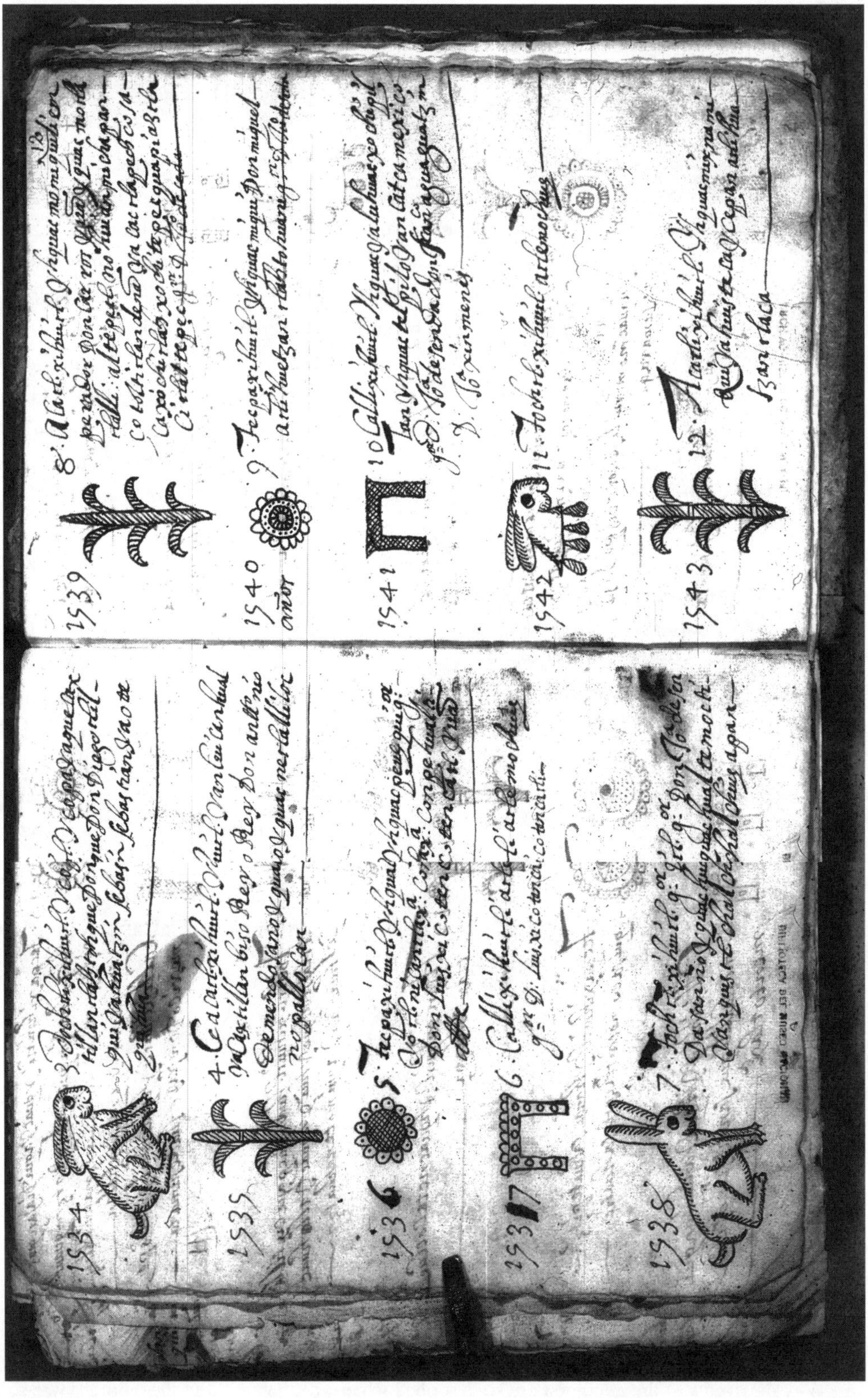

FIGURE 2. Annals of Tlaxcala, ff. 11v–12, 1534–1543. Biblioteca Nacional de Antropología e Historia, Colección Antigua 872. Courtesy of the Instituto Nacional de Antropología e Historia.

Annals of Tlaxcala

17022[1]

17023

17024

151[2]   Acatli xihuitli huala Don hernando Cortes y nican quitlaniCo tlalli ypan nueba
espania de las ynDias

1705

152   decpaxihuitli [*f. 8*]

150_3   Calli xihuitli

150_4   dochtli xihuitli

1519[3]

150_5   Acatli xihuitli nicann ipan hualmohuicaque yn teopixque matlactli homomentin
quihualhuiCaque iteoyoztzin yn tt^o Dios nican motocayotia = fray martin maldonado De balencia CosDoDio guardian = fray fran^co xinmenes 2 = fray toripio
motolinia 3 = fray pitebas[4] 4 = fray fran^co De soto 5 = fray luys buēsareta 6 =
fray antt^Onio De ciudad lodrigo 7 = fray garcia De sisnero 8 = fray martin De la
Corinan 9 = fray Suares 10 = fray juā de balon quatesotzin[5] 11 = fray Andres
de gorDova quatesontzin 12 = Ca yehuātin quihualmohuiquilique y tlaneltoquilistli = Sancto Euagelio

150_6   decp~axihuitli~ [*f. 8v*]

150_7   calli xihuitli

150_8   Dochtli xihuitli

150_9   acaxihuitli

1510   decpaxihuitli ycquac huala preciDente yaCuican tlatocatico mexiCo[6] sanno ypan
xihuitli monextitzinno totlaçonantzin De hualalope quimonextili maçehualtzintli
ytoca Ju^o Diego[7] [*f. 9*]

1511   Calli xihuitli

1512   dochtli xihuitli

1513   acaxihuitli yn omotlalli altepetli Cuitlaxcolapan[8] [*sic*] quitlalique tlaxcaltecac
[*sic*]

1514   decpaxihuitli [*f. 9v*]

---

[1]Another author worked on the end of this set of annals, and these early eighteenth century
dates were apparently added by him. That author was in the habit of writing out strings of years
with blank spaces and then gradually filling them in, and he seems to have planned to save paper by
using the partly blank early pages to continue the work, though he never wrote the entries.

[2]This date is clearly in error, based on an early misunderstanding of the Spanish calendar. The
same mistake was copied more than once by annalists working in the Tlaxcala region. See Frances
Krug, "The Nahuatl Annals of the Tlaxcala-Puebla Region," unfinished doctoral dissertation,
Department of History, UCLA, under the direction of James Lockhart. Indeed, it seems someone
copied this material from one of the other erroneous versions and added it here long after the main
author began his work. The main author begins in 1519; there the pictures begin, and there the
handwriting shifts noticeably. For more detail on these points see the introduction, pp. 23–25.

[3]This was inserted later by someone who was not satisfied to leave the error above without
comment. It is in another hand and another ink.

1722[1]

1723

1724

1501[2]   Reed year. Don Hernando Cortés came, he who came here to win the land in New Spain of the Indies.

1705

1502   Flint-knife year. [*f. 8*]

1503   House year.

1504   Rabbit year.

1519[3]

1505   Reed year. Here in this year the twelve friars came here. They brought the holy things [sacraments] of our Lord God. Here they are named: fray Martín Maldonado de Valencia, custodian and guardian; fray Francisco Jiménez, the second; fray Toribio Motolinia, the third; fray [Juan de Ribas],[4] the fourth; fray Francisco de Soto, the fifth; fray Luis de Fuensalida, the sixth; fray Antonio de Ciudad Rodrigo, the seventh; fray García de Cisneros, the eighth; fray Martín de la Coruna, the ninth; fray [Juan] Suárez, the tenth; fray Juan de Palos, a lay brother,[5] the eleventh; fray Andrés de Córdoba, a lay brother, the twelfth. They were the ones who brought the faith, the Holy Gospel.

1506   Flint-knife year. [*f. 8v*]

1507   House year.

1508   Rabbit year.

1509   Reed year.

1510   Flint-knife year. At this time, the president [of the Audiencia] came to rule in Mexico City for the first time.[6] In this same year our precious mother of Guadalupe appeared: she showed herself to a poor commoner named Juan Diego.[7] [*f. 9*]

1511   House year.

1512   Rabbit year.

1513   Reed year. The altepetl of Cuitlaxcohuapan[8] was founded. The Tlaxcalans founded it.

1514   Flint-knife year. [*f. 9v*]

---

[4]"Pitebas" must surely have represented a misunderstanding of an early annals entry attempting to represent the friar whose name was Juan de Ribas.

[5]*Quateçontzin* literally means "a person with a tonsure," but it was used to refer to lay brothers.

[6]Don Sebastián Ramírez de Fuenleal was president of the Second Audiencia from 1530 to 1535. The dates in this sequence are all nineteen or twenty years off (see n. 2, p. 158).

[7]This reference dates the writing of this section to no earlier than 1649. For a discussion of the retroactive creation of the Juan Diego story, see Sousa, Poole, and Lockhart 1998.

[8]The usual indigenous name for Puebla (de los Angeles). See introduction, p. 41. This text also makes considerable use of the original form Cuetlaxcohuapan.

1515   Cali xihuitli

1516   Dochtli xihuitli

1517   acatli xihuitli huala BiRei Don Antonio De mentosa[1]

1518   decpaxihuitli [*f. 10*]

priCipiel años de 1519

1519 años 1 çe ACatli xihuitli yhquac açico marques nican tlaxcallan Don hernanto gor-
        des yn capitan viernes sanctos san esteban tisatla oncan yanCuica quichiuh misa
        Ju⁰ dias clerigos yuā oncā micqui ce solDados onca toctoc san estevan yn solta-
        dos itoca esteuan

1520   2 Tecpatli xihuitli yhquac quisaco huey çahuatli[2] mochi tlacatl çahuatic

1521   3 Calli xihuitli yhquac poliuhque Mexica yhquac tlalpolo marques oquimoma-
        tlanili yn Senor SanDiago yhuan tlaxcalteca huel yehuan omomictique tlaxcal-
        teca omomictique ynahuac motesoma ytlacahuan

1522   4 Tochtli xihuitli atle mochiuh [*f. 10v*]

1523   5. Acatl. xihuitl. yhquac açico Deopixque niman icquac tlatlacatecollo ycal xi-
        xitin

1524   6. Tecpaxihuitl. atle mochiuh

1525   7. Calli xihuitl. yhQuac cohuatlan yallohuac tlalpoloto tiyanquistlahtohuatzin

1526   8. Tochtli xihuitl. yhQuac yalohuac quauhtemalan yaoquixohuac ycquac motla-
        tlalo mixpantli ytech ylhuiCatli

1527   9. ACatli xihuitli yquac piloloque tlahtoque guauhtotohua denamasCuiCuiltzin
        dexotecatl altontzin[3] Çano yquac yaque temachtique yhuan yhquac motlalique
        teopixque tlax.ᵃ yhuā hualya Obispo Don fray Juliano[4] [*f. 11*]

1528   10. Tecpaxihuitli yquac yaqui Dianquistlahtohuatzin quetzalcoyotzin quauhpil-
        tzintli ÇitlalinyCuetz mahuitlatotzi yanCuicann oyaque Caxtillan[5]

1529   11. Calli xihuitl. yhquac hualya Obispo mexico Don fray Jua de Sumara[6] [*sic*]

1530 años 12. Tochtli xihuitl. hualmocuepque caxtillā lā [*sic*] tlahtohque yhuā yhquac
        yallohuac ColhuacCan yaqui motenehuatzin[7]

1531   13. Acatl. xihuitl. yhquac neteCoc Cuetlaxcohuapa

1532   1. Tecpaxihuitl. yhquac sahuatepitzin quisaco[8] mochi tlacatl sahuatic

1533   2. Calli. xihuitl. yhqua yanCuican quimotlallilique sanctissimo saCramento tlax.ᵃ
        [*f. 11v*]

---

[1]Don Antonio de Mendoza, conde de Tendillas, viceroy of New Spain (1535–1550).

[2]They actually called the disease "the great pox," but it is customary to use the English word "smallpox" in translations.

[3]Don Juan Zapata, the premier annalist of seventeenth-century Tlaxcala, gives different variants of the names: "tlaltotzin. quauhtotohuā. tenamazcuicuiltzin topYāco. acxotecatli atlihuetziā. oc çe acxotecatli tzōpātzinco." See Zapata, pp. 136–37.

[4]Don fray Julián Garcés, first bishop of Tlaxcala (1529–42).

1515   House year.

1516   Rabbit year.

1517   Reed year. Viceroy don Antonio de Mendoza came.[1]

1518   Flint-knife year. [*f. 10*]

The year 1519 begins.

1519   1 Reed year. At this time, the marqués don Hernando Cortés, the Captain, ar-
        rived here in Tlaxcala. The secular priest Juan Díaz celebrated mass for the first
        time on Good Friday at San Esteban Tizatla. And a soldier died there. The
        soldier, whose name was Esteban, lies buried at San Esteban.

1520   2 Flint-knife year. At this time smallpox[2] broke out. Everyone got the pox.

1521   3 House year. At this time the Mexica were defeated. At this time the Marqués
        conquered the land. The lord Santiago, together with the Tlaxcalans, defeated
        them by his hand. The Tlaxcalans really fought hard; they fought with Mo-
        teucçoma's vassals.

1522   4 Rabbit year. Nothing happened. [*f. 10v*]

1523   5 Reed year. At this time the friars arrived. Then was the time that the devils'
        houses were demolished.

1524   6 Flint-knife year. Nothing happened.

1525   7 House year. At this time a [war] party went to Coatlan. Tianquiztlatoatzin
        went to conquer the land.

1526   8 Rabbit year. At this time a party went to Guatemala to war. At this time large
        clouds kept racing across the sky.

1527   9 Reed year. At this time the rulers Quauhtotohua, Tenamazcuicuiltzin, Texo-
        tecatl, and Altontzin were hanged.[3] It was also at this time that preachers went
        out, and friars established themselves in Tlaxcala, and bishop don fray Julián[4]
        came. [*f. 11*]

1528   10 Flint-knife year. At this time Tianquiztlatoatzin, Quetzalcoatzin, Quauh-
        piltzintli, Citlalinicuetzin, and Mahuitlatotzin went to Spain for the first time.[5]

1529   11 House year. At this time the bishop of Mexico, don fray Juan de Zumárraga,
        came.[6]

1530   12 Rabbit year. The rulers returned from Spain. And it was at this time that a
        party went to Culhuacan. Motenehuatzin went.[7]

1531   13 Reed year. At this time settlement took place in Cuitlaxcohuapan.

1532   1 Flint-knife year. At this time the little pox broke out.[8] Everyone got the pox.

1533   2 House year. At this time they first put in place the most holy Sacrament in
        Tlaxcala. [*f. 11v*]

---

[5]Zapata gives the same names in this case.

[6]Fray Juan de Zumárraga, first bishop of Mexico (1527–47). Our annalist seems to have re-
versed the year of his entry into office with that of the first bishop of Tlaxcala (see n. 4 here).

[7]This no doubt refers to present Culiacan rather than Culhuacan in the Valley of Mexico. The
Tlaxcalans provided aid to the Nuño de Guzman expedition to Nueva Galicia. Motenehuatzin is
known to have gone, and to have died at Culiacan. See Gibson 1967, p. 93.

[8]This could mean chickenpox or more probably measles.

1534   3. dochtli xihuitl. yc opa yaque caxtillan tlahtohque Don Diego tlilquiyahuatzin
        Sebastian yaottequihua

1535   4. Ce acatl. xihuitl.[1] yanCuican hualya Caxtillan bisoRey Don antt^{o}nio de men-
        dosa[2] no yquac netlalliloc nopallocan

1536   5. Tecpaxihuitl. yhquac peuhqui g$^{or}_o$yotl nican tlax^a_o conpehualti Don Luis xico-
        tencatl yuā al̶de

1537   6. Calli xihuitli atle mochiuh g$^{or}_o$ D luis xicotencatli

1538   7. tochtli xihuitl. g$^{or}_o$ Don Jo^a desenDa[3] sanno yquac hualtemoc tiyanquistl chal-
        chiuhapan[4] [f. 12]

1539   8. ACatl. xihuitl. yhquac momiquili emperador Don Carros[5] yuā yquac motla-
        tlalli: altepetl nohuian michapan çotoltitlan denāyacac tlapechco sacaxochitlah
        xochitepec quapiaztla citlaltepec[6] g$^{or}_o$ D ju^o deseda

1540 años   9. Tecpaxihuitl. yhquac miqui Don Miguel atlihuetzan tlahtohuani[7] g$^{or}_o$ D
        ju^o deseda

1541   10. Calli xihuitl. Yhquac yaluhuac xochipillan[8] yhquac telpiloyan catca mexico
        g$^{or}_o$ d: jo^a desenda don fran^{co} aguaguatzin D: jo^a xinmenis[9]

1542   11. Tochtli xihuitl. atle mochiuh

1543   12. Acatli xihuitli Yhquac mixnami Quiyahuisteca[10] ycepan atlihuetzan tlaca [f.
        12v]

1544   13. decpaxihuitli yhquac miqui xicotenCatly yuā xochimayanaloc[11] nican tlax^a_o

1545   1. Calli xihuitl. yhquac yanCuican motlalli gonRegidor[12] yhuā huei cocolis [sic]
        quisaco yhuan yanCuican homanqui posescion yc nochi nahui cabeçerra
        omoyehualo oyhuidor oquitemacaco

1546   2. Tochtli xihuitl. yquac hualaque yauquisque xochipillan

1547   3. acatl. xihuitl.Yhquac miqui Don hernādo Cordes

1548   4. decpaxihuitl. yhquac gonregidor catca Sr D. Diego Ramires ypan mochiuh

---

[1]The writer actually put "4 One-reed year."

[2]This entry repeats information given above, but this section is more accurate than the first (see
n. 1, p. 160).

[3]We cannot be absolutely certain that the man was named Tejeda. The name takes a different
form a year later in 1539 ("deseda" vs. "desenDa"). Indeed, it takes a variety of forms in different
Tlaxcalan annals. Krug, "Nahuatl Annals," finds it in different sets of annals in the same time
period as "de^{te}Xeda," "deteSeta," "deSeta," "delaSonda," and "deJeda."

[4]The sentence could be translated in two different ways: that the market was brought either "to"
or "from" Chalchiuhapan, but Zapata puts the matter in such a way as to leave no doubt, though he
places the event a year later (pp. 144–45).

[5]Don Carlos really died in 1558, and news of it reached Mexico in 1559, so the annals are again
20 years off (see n. 2, p. 158.)

[6]The governmental reorganization of the indigenous entities in the area does date to the 1530s.
But if the text is still twenty years off, then it may be referring to the congregations planned, though
not always carried out, in the late 1550s. See TA, p. 59.

1534   3 Rabbit year. For a second time rulers went to Spain, don Diego Tlilquiyahuatzin and Sebastián Yaotequihua.

1535   4 Reed year.[1] For the first time a viceroy came from Spain, don Antonio de
Mendoza.[2] Also at this time there was settlement at Nopalocan.

1536   5 Flint-knife year. At this time the governorship began here in Tlaxcala. Don
Luis Xicotencatl began it, along with the alcaldes.

1537   6 House year. Nothing happened. The governor was don Luis Xicotencatl.

1538   7 Rabbit year. The governor was don Juan Tejeda.[3] It was also at this time that
the market was brought down to Chalchiuhapan.[4] [*f. 12*]

1539   8 Reed year. At this time the Emperor don Carlos died.[5] And at this time altepetl
were established everywhere—Michapan, Çotoltitlan, Tenanyacac, Tlapechco,
Çacaxochitla, Xochitepec, Quappiaztla, and Citlaltepec.[6] The governor was don
Juan Tejeda.

1540   9 Flint-knife year. At this time don Miguel, ruler in Atlihuetzan, died.[7] The
governor was don Juan Tejeda.

1541   10 House year. At this time a party went to Xochipillan.[8] At this time governor
don Juan Tejeda, don Francisco Ahuahuatzin, and don Juan Jiménez were in jail
in Mexico City.[9]

1542   11 Rabbit year. Nothing happened.

1543   12 Reed year. At this time the people of Quiyahuiztlan were disputing[10] with the
people of Atlihuetzan. [*f. 12v*]

1544   13 Flint-knife year. At this time Xicotencatl died, and there was a great famine[11]
here in Tlaxcala.

1545   1 House year. At this time a corregidor was installed for the first time,[12] and an
epidemic broke out. And for the first time it was formally established that [the
governorship] rotated through all four cabeceras. An oidor [Audiencia judge]
came to issue the arrangement.

1546   2 Rabbit year. At this time the warriors came back from Xochipillan.

1547   3 Reed year. At this time don Hernando Cortés died.

1548   4 Flint-knife year. At this time the corregidor was señor don Diego Ramírez. In

---

[7]In a confusing passage Zapata seems to say that the tlatoani was stoned to death in a land
dispute (pp. 144–45).

[8]In other words, they went to fight in the so-called Mixton War. Ida Altman is currently
engaged in a study of this conflict; see Altman forthcoming.

[9]Indigenous cabildo officers were often jailed when their entities failed to meet tax levies. This
is a central theme of the so-called "Anales de Juan Bautista" from sixteenth-century Mexico City:
Reyes García 2001. In his lifetime, the Juan Jiménez mentioned here actually lacked the title don.

[10]The writer seems to have meant "mixnamiquiya quiyahuisteca" and easily forgot to put
(probably to copy) the second *quiya*.

[11]*Mayanaloc* means "there was famine." The thrust of the prefixed *xochi-*, literally "flower," is
not certain, but it appears to act as an intensifier. The term in this form appears in the Historia
Tolteca-Chichimeca, and there, too, translators have struggled with it.

[12]There had been Spanish governors, but the title *corregidor* was employed for the first time in
1545. See Gibson 1967, p. 215.

atzontli[1] tianquisco quichiuh fran^co de las nāvas yhquac momiquili senor Obispo D: Ju^o de sumaraga

1549   5. Calli xihuitl. Yhquac mochiuh tienta[2] Tlax^a [f. 13]

1550 año. 6. Tochtl. xihuitl. yhquac mochiuh temamatlah deopan g^or? D: Lucas Garcia[3] ohualya BiRey D: Luis de velasco[4]

1551   7. Acatli xihuitl. g^or? D: Lucas Garcia hualya bisoRey D: Luis de belasco[5]

1552   8. decpaxihuitl. g^or? don domingo de ancolo yhquac detzahuitl[6] quisaco yhquac yecatococ deocali tepeticpac

1553   9. Calli xiuitl. yhquac quixixini deocalli senor fran^co berdogo[7]

1554   10. Tochtli xihuitli g^or? Don Diego de palledes yhquac acico arsobispo no yquac miqui Don Diego de cosman D: fran^co damian yuā yhquac motlalique teopixque deopoyanco[8] [f. 13v]

1555   ii. Acatli xihuitl. yhquac motlalli Sanctissimo SaCramento atlihuetzyan yuā hualya topoyanco alcalte mayor Don fran^co berdogo

1556   12. decpaxihuitl. g^or? D: Martin de ballenÇia

1557   13. Calli xiuitl. g^or? D: martin de ballenÇia sesepotzin yhquac yāCuican quimiCuiloque masehualtin tlax^a yhquac huitza Rey[9] D: Luis de belasco yuā miqui D: Andres quauhsaoltzin

1558   1. dochtl. Xihuitl. quicauh ydequih D: Jua martin yquac ticeCualoque ypan espiri pasqua[10] [f. 14]

1559   2. Acaxiuitl. g^or? D: Domingo de ancolo yhquac vitza ViRey yquac yaque yaoquisque la prorida ypan tlahtolnahuac xochimayaloc nican motlayecoltique bino pan tlaca[11]

1560 año 3. decpaxivitl. g^or? D: Domingo de ancolo no yhquac tlachiyalloCo co albares. oc sepa yaque yauhquizque la prorida: aytic yuā yāCuican motlalli Reros

[1]*Atzontli* is interpreted as "fountain" because the Tlaxcalan Actas record that the corregidor Ramírez organized the construction of a better central fountain in May of 1548 (TA, p. 39). He was not really called don. The annals writer or some predecessor has, as so often in this text, used the standards of a later time, when any Spanish chief magistrate of Tlaxcala would have borne the title.

[2]The Tlaxcalan Actas in April of 1549 record the construction of arcades in the marketplace, meant to beautify the city, shelter people who sold things, and provide sites for shops (TA, p. 41).

[3]According to the Tlaxcalan Actas, he did not bear the title of don in his lifetime. As with corregidor Ramírez, the standards of a later time are applied here.

[4]Don Luis de Velasco, conde de Santiago, viceroy of New Spain (1550–1564).

[5]He did not really come twice. He arrived in 1550 and passed through Tlaxcala, causing a flurry of arrangements to be made.

[6]The word *tetzahuitl* could mean a bad omen, but sometimes it covered anything unexpected, amazing or especially noteworthy, a prodigy.

[7]Verdugo was the first Spanish magistrate of Tlaxcala with the title alcalde mayor. He lacked the title don, as in this entry (below he appears as don). The Tlaxcalan Actas for December of 1553

his time the fountain was made in the marketplace.[1] Francisco de las Navas made it. At this time the lord bishop don Juan de Zumárraga died.

1549   5 House year. At this time shops[2] were built in Tlaxcala. [*f. 13*]

1550   6 Rabbit year. At this time the church at Temamatla was built. The governor was don Lucas García.[3] The viceroy don Luis de Velasco came.[4]

1551   7 Reed year. The governor was don Lucas García. The viceroy don Luis de Velasco came.[5]

1552   8 Flint-knife year. The governor was don Domingo de Angulo. At this time there was a frightening, inexplicable event[6] when the church at Tepeticpac was carried off by the wind.

1553   9 House year. At this time señor Francisco Verdugo demolished some churches.[7]

1554   10 Rabbit year. The governor was don Diego de Paredes. At this time the archbishop arrived. Also at this time don Diego de Guzmán and don Francisco Damián died. At this time friars were established at Topoyanco.[8] [*f. 13v*]

1555   11 Reed year. At this time the most holy Sacrament was placed in Atlihuetzan, and the alcalde mayor don Francisco Verdugo came to Topoyanco.

1556   12 Flint-knife year. The governor was don Martín de Valencia.

1557   13 House year. The governor was don Martín de Valencia Cecepotzin. At this time they registered the indigenous people of Tlaxcala for the first time. At this time viceroy[9] don Luis de Velasco came [for a visit], and don Andrés Quauh-çayoltzin died.

1558   1 Rabbit year. Don Juan Martín gave up his post [as governor]. At this time it froze at Pentecost.[10] [*f. 14*]

1559   2 Reed year. The governor was don Domingo de Angulo. At this time the viceroy came. At this time warriors went to Florida, about which they had been [urged?]. There was a great famine. The wine and wheat bread people [made a good living?] here.[11]

1560   3 Flint-knife year. The governor was don Domingo de Angulo. Also at this time [the viceroy?] came to look around. Once again warriors went to Florida, across

---

tell us (TA, p. 54) that certain churches were suppressed because they were too close to others and therefore burdening to the population.

[8]The Franciscan monastery was indeed founded in that year. See Gibson 1967, p. 46.

[9]The term actually used is *rey*, "king," but in some Nahuatl usage that word referred to the viceroy as well.

[10]In "Espiri pasqua" the first word is truncated from *Espíritu*, as in *pascua del Espíritu Santo* (Pentecost or Whitsunday).

[11]The translation of this paragraph is not certain. *Ipan tlatolnahuac* does not correspond to any known phrase. *Ipan tlatoa* is to urge, expedite, or take care of a matter, thus the sense that I have taken, and recruitment did occur in this year (Carrión 1970, p. 18). "Xochimayaloc" lacks a syllable to make *xochimayanaloc*, but that word is itself problematic. (See p. 163, n. 11.) "Bino pan tlaca" is literally "wine bread people," not a common phrase to my knowledge, and *motlayecoltia* means "to do business" or "make a living"; thus I have concluded that the "wine and bread people" were sellers, possibly importers. The word "here" might mean either "here in Tlaxcala" or "at this point." There is no clue about this matter in other annals or in the Actas.

Tlax[al]

1561   4. Calli xivitli g^{or}.. D: pablo de balenÇia[2] no yquacq ualla Rey ychpoch nican
monamicti Tlax[a] no nican quihualnamicta Rey D: Luys de belasco[3]

1562   5. Tochtli xivitli g^{or}.. d: pablo de balençia yquac yaque Caxtillan tlahtoque D:n
Lucas carçia D:n alonso gomes D: antt^{o}nio del pedroso[4] yuā yquac miqui D: Jo[a]
maxixcatzin sa quitzonquixtili ytequiuh Cordes[5] [f. 14v]

1563   6. acaxihuitli g^{or}.. D: Hernando de salasal[6] yhquac huala visidador Castillan
yquac miqui D: fran^{co} de mendoza[7]

1564   7. decpaxivitli g^{or}.. d: Hernando de salasal yquac hualmocuepque tlahtoque Castillan yuā miqui D: Jo[a] xicotencatli

1565   8. Calli xiuitli g^{or}.. D: antt^{o}nio frores oquitlami ytequiuh sa maCuilli mestli qui-
pix sa ye quitzonquixtili D: Jo[a] martin no yq̄c miqui D: Luis de belasco Rey
piloloque otomime[8]

1566   9. dochtl. xiuitli no yq̄c motlalli Sanctissimo saCramento quamanco bisoRey
Don Caston de perarta[9]

1567   10. Acaxiuitl. g^{or}.. D// buenapentora quauhtlaocellotzin[10] sa naui mestica momiquili yquac oquintitlanque[11] Castillan Marq̄:z ypan[12] yquac huallaque Castillann
ovitores hobispo alcalde de corde Jues biscal alhuaCil mayor [f. 15]

---

[1]The passage "tlachiyalloCo co albares" at the beginning of the entry appears to be corrupt,
somewhere along the chain copied wrongly and without comprehension. *Tlachialoco* would convey
that a group came to look around; inadvertent repetition at some point would account for the extra
co. "albares," possibly for Alvarez, seems to come out of the blue. If we consult Zapata (pp. 160–
61), we find that he reports a viceroy's visit and an expedition to Florida for 1559 as here, but not
for 1560 (though he does mention the new clock in that year). Some predecessor of the present
writer may have absentmindedly repeated the expedition and the viceroy's visit of 1559 for 1560.
Our writer now takes this for a second Florida expedition and seems to have given up trying to
understand about the visit. Possibly at the root of "alvares" was something like "el virey," the verb
was *tlachiaco*, and the sense "the viceroy came to look at things, look around."

[2]Actually Pablo de Galicia (not don); see Zapata (pp. 160–61).

[3]The Tlaxcalan Actas (TA, p. 61) confirm that the young woman came from Spain to join her
father and that he came to receive her in Tlaxcala.

[4]Actually none of the three bore the don at that time (Zapata, pp. 162–63).

[5]Don Juan Maxixcatzin had been ruler of the cabecera of Ocotelolco since 1546. His daughter
wished to succeed him but was barred from doing so. The seat remained vacant until don Francisco
Pimental obtained it in 1591. See Gibson 1967, pp. 220–22. "Cordes" would have referred to
Baltasar Cortés, who became acting governor on April 20 of that year. (The governor, Pablo de
Galicia, went to Spain to represent the city before the king.)

[6]Hernando de Salazar had lacked the don up to this point in his life, and Zapata still withholds
it on this occasion (pp. 162–63), but in the Tlaxcalan Actas he indeed acquires it on becoming
governor (TA, p. 63).

the sea. And for the first time a clock was set in place in Tlaxcala.[1]

1561   4 House year. The governor was don Pablo de Valencia.[2] Also at this time the viceroy's daughter came. She was met here in Tlaxcala and the viceroy don Luis de Velasco came here to meet her.[3]

1562   5 Rabbit year. The governor was don Pablo de Valencia. At this time the rulers don Lucas García, don Alonso Gómez, and don Antonio del Pedroso[4] went to Spain. And at this time don Juan Maxixcatzin died. Cortés just finished his term of office for him.[5] [*f. 14v*]

1563   6 Reed year. The governor was don Hernando de Salazar.[6] At this time an inspector general came from Spain. At this time don Francisco de Mendoza died.[7]

1564   7 Flint-knife year. The governor was don Hernando de Salazar. At this time the rulers came back from Spain, and don Juan Xicotencatl died.

1565   8 House year. The governor was don Antonio Flores. He ended his term of office [early]; he held office for only five months. Don Juan Martín just finished [his term] for him. Also at this time viceroy don Luis de Velasco died, and some Otomis were hanged.[8]

1566   9 Rabbit year. Also at this time the Most Holy Sacrament was set in place at Quamanco. The viceroy was don Gastón de Peralta.[9]

1567   10 Reed year. The governor was don Buenaventura Quauhtlaocelotzin;[10] after only four months he died. At this time they sent the Marqués [and another or others][11] to Spain, for which reason[12] at this time there came from Spain oidores [civil judges of the Audiencia], a bishop, an alcalde de corte [criminal judge], a juez fiscal [prosecuting attorney], and an alguacil mayor [chief constable]. [*f. 15*]

---

[7]Mendoza was tlatoani for Tepeticpac and indeed died in 1563 (TA, p. 136–37).

[8]Velasco died in 1564, but it is possible that news of it did not reach Tlaxcala until 1565. Zapata mentions that Otomis were hanged on a Friday in May at 4 o'clock, but he gives no reason (pp. 164–65).

[9]Don Gastón de Peralta, marqués de Falces, viceroy of New Spain (1566–1568). The Audiencia had been governing for two years, following the sudden death of don Luis de Velasco, during which time plots and counterplots had surfaced.

[10]Called by Zapata Buenaventura Oñate without don, as in fact he had been known for many years (pp. 166–67). The Nahuatl second name is probably authentic even though it had been submerged in the written records of the time.

[11]The legitimate son and heir of Hernando Cortés, don Martín Cortés, had been involved in some sort of a conspiracy against the Audiencia (see n. 9 just above). The matter probably had not gone beyond the stage of talking and vague planning, but he was arrested, and when the new viceroy arrived, he was sent back to Spain. Guilty by association were his two half-brothers. One of them, also named don Martín Cortés, was the son of doña Marina. He stayed behind in Mexico, but the third brother traveled with the marqués. This would explain the plural object used with the verb, although the text does not identify the others who were exiled. I doubt that the plural prefix was included unintentionally, as at least two other indigenous annalists also described the Cortés brothers in the plural in their treatment of this incident. See Reyes García 2001, p. 149. See also Celestino Solís and Reyes García 1992, p. 53. It was well known to all New Spain that multiple sons of Cortés were involved.

[12]The intention of "ypan" is presumably "ypanpa."

1568   11. decpaxihuitl. g^{or}: D: Jo^a sitlalCuetzin^1 yhq̄c hualla bisoRey D: Martin
           eriques^2

1569   12. Calli xiuitli g^{or}: D: buenaventoran osurio^3 yhQuac tlayxnamique nopallucan
           tlaca : oquittecaco tepantli Jues Juachi selo^4

1570 año   13. dochtli xiuitl. yc ome xiuitl g^{or}: D: buenabentoran osurio moyanCuillico
           tepantli. atlihuetzyan tlax^a yuā tlallolin chiquacepa yhuā huala BirRey D: luis de
           velasco^5

1571   1. Acaxihuitl. g^{or}: D: Diego delles yquac conpehualtique yneteylhuil hotonpā^6
           tlaca [*marginal note:* tlalpilli Marques]^7

1572   2. decpaxihuitl. g^{or}: D: Diego delles yhquac macoque possecion otonpan tlaca
           yxpan a̶l̶de mayor Jusdandino^8 [*f. 15v*]

1573   3. Calli xiuitl. g^{or} D: Juliano de silbah yquac peuhqui Cohuatequitl. atlixco^9

1574   4. dochtl. xihuitli D: Juliano de silbah yquac miq̄. D: buenabentoran osurio

1575   5. Acaxiuitl. g^{or} Don Andres tlachmatzin^{10}

1576   6. decpaxiuitli g^{or}: d: Andres tlachmatzin no yquac gedencia^{11} quinCuilique o-
           tonpan tlaca yuan mochiuh huey cocolistli

1577   7. calli xiuitli g^{or} D: penebantora de pas^{12} yquac popocaya Citlalin ome mestiCa
           a̶l̶de mayor D: fran^{co} bertogo^{13} yquac omotlali ofiçio cabirdo yaxca

1578   8. dochtli xiuitl. g^{or} D: pe^{ra} de pas yquach [*sic*] peuhqui Canpanario mochi-
           huasquiya visorei D: Martin enriq^Z [*f. 16*]

1579   9. ACaxiuitl. g^{or} D: matheo de pallio yhquac huey atli quiquis tlax^a atlihuetzyā
           peuhqui cocolistli ypan mayanalistli.

---

[1]This could hardly be the same Citlalinicuetzin in the entry for 1528. In Zapata (pp. 166–69),
Juan Citlalcuetzin (though Zapata has a wrong form of the name), without don, took over as governor for Buenaventura Oñate on his death in 1567. As governor in 1568 Zapata calls him don Juan
de Avalos (see also TA, p. 134).

[2]Don Martín Enríquez de Almansa, viceroy of New Spain (1568–1580).

[3]In Zapata (168–69), Blas Osorio, without don.

[4]This may be a reference to an action taken by indigenous people in Iztacmaxtitlan and Nopalocan to stop an intrusion into their lands on the part of some Spanish cattle ranchers. Jorge Ce-
rón Carvajal was alcalde mayor of Tlaxcala in 1569–71. See Gibson 1967, p. 83.

[5]Krug, "Nahuatl Annals," found a reference in another set of annals to a dispute between some
residents of Atlancatepec and Tlaxcala over the placement of a church. This might be the dispute
mentioned regarding Atlihuetzan. Velasco could not have visited, as he was dead, but Zapata (pp.
168–69) mentions that in 1568 the new viceroy, don Martín Enriquez, did indeed visit. He even
dined in Topoyanco.

[6]*Otompan* could be a place name, but I find no mention of it in the exhaustive compilation of

1568   11 Flint-knife year. The governor was don Juan Citlalcuetzin.[1] At this time the
        viceroy don Martín Enríquez came.[2]

1569   12 House year. The governor was don Buenaventura Osorio.[3] At this time the
        people of Nopalocan had a dispute. The judge Joaquín Cerón came to place the
        boundary.[4]

1570   13 Rabbit year. Don Buenaventura Osorio was governor for the second year.
        The border was renewed between Atlihuetzan and Tlaxcala, and there were
        earthquakes six times, and viceroy don Luis de Velasco came.[5]

1571   1 Reed year. The governor was don Diego Téllez. At this time the people of the
        Otomi country[6] began their lawsuit. [*marginal note*: 52 years since the Marqués
        came][7]

1572   2 Flint-knife year. The governor was don Diego Téllez. At this time the people
        of the Otomi country were given possession before the alcalde mayor Constan-
        tino as judge.[8] [*f. 15v*]

1573   3 House year. The governor was don Julián de Silva. At this time draft rotary
        labor [the repartimiento] began at Atlixco.[9]

1574   4 Rabbit year. [The governor was] don Julián de Silva. At this time don Buena-
        ventura Osorio died.

1575   5 Reed year. The governor was don Andrés Tlachmatzin.[10]

1576   6 Flint-knife year. The governor was don Andrés Tlachmatzin. Also at this time
        they carried out a general review of the conduct of the people of the Otomi
        country,[11] and an epidemic occurred.

1577   7 House year. The governor was don Buenaventura de Paz.[12] At this time a
        comet could be seen for two months. The alcalde mayor was don Francisco
        Verdugo.[13] At this time an office belonging to the cabildo was set up.

1578   8 Rabbit year. The governor was don Buenaventura de Paz. At this time began a
        bell tower that was going to be built. The viceroy was don Martín Enríquez. [*f.
        16*]

1579   9 Reed year. The governor was don Mateo de Barrios. At this time there was
        flooding in Tlaxcala and Atlihuetzan. An epidemic began in the time of famine.

---

known place names in Trautmann 1980. Nor does Zapata mention such a place, though he includes
several hundred place names in the course of his manuscript.

[7]This set of annals faithfully records the completion of the traditional 52-year bundles, beginning with the arrival of Cortés in 1519.

[8]Constantino Bravo de Lagunas was alcalde mayor from 1571 to 1574. Here the name is left
incomplete and what must have originally been *juez Constantino* has been amalgamated.

[9]Atlixco was known for its Spanish farmers producing the Spanish crop wheat.

[10]According to Gibson 1967, p.226, the name is Tlachinatzin. Zapata (pp. 171–72) gives the
governor as Andrés de Herrera, without don.

[11]The translation cannot be certain. "Gedencia" is most probably an indigenous interpretation
of *residencia*, and the verb *cui* corresponds to the *tomar*, "take," that would be used with that word
in Spanish; thus the sense in which I take the passage. First syllables were sometimes omitted, and
s and *g* sometimes replaced each other, along with *x* and *j*, as all were used at times to represent the
sound heard as [sh].

[12]Zapata (pp. 172–73) gives the name without don.

[13]As seen under the year 1553, Francisco Verdugo did not bear the don.

1580 años 10. decpaxihuitl. g$^{or}_{:}$ D: matheo de palio no yquac hualla bisoRey Castillan cōDe de coruna[1]

1581   11. CAlli xiuitli g$^{or}_{:}$ D: sacarias[2] yqua mayanaloc: a~~lde~~ D: Ju^o pauh$^{ta}_{:}$ Guauhmantlah[3]

1582   12. dochtl. xiuitl. g$^{or}_{:}$ D: sacarias a~~lde~~ D: Diego de topal

1583   13. ACaxihuitli g$^{or}_{:}$ D: antt^{o}nio mocallio[4] yquac yaoquisque haJabana sando domingo yuā momiquili Rey D: Lurenso [f. 16v]

1584   1. decpaxihuitli g$^{or}_{:}$ D: antt^{o}nio mocallio yq^{a}c tlahtoque yaque Castillan Don antt^{o}nio delles de quebara don p^o de torres Diego delles Dō sacarias de Santiago Diego mayor ypiltzin Don Diego delles[5]

1585   2. Calli xiuitl. g$^{or}_{:}$ D: p^o de calicia[6] yquac hualyaque tlahtoque huiya Caxtillan

1586   3 dochtl. xiuitl. g$^{or}_{:}$ D: p^o de callician yuā tlacequaloc no yquac mochiuh cocollistli

1587   4 Acaxiuitl. g$^{or}_{:}$ D: Diego monos[7] yuā mayanalistli

1588   5 decpaxiuitli g$^{or}_{:}$ Don Diego monos yuā motlalli yanCuica Reros tlax^a [f. 17]

1589   6 CAlli xivitli g$^{or}_{:}$ D: Sacarias de sanctiago yh [sic] Mochiuh alco tlanipa[8] ~~yhuan huala Biso Rey D: Luis de Velasco~~

1590 años 7 Tochtli xivitli g$^{or}_{:}$ D: sacarias de S$^n_{:}$tiago yhuan huala BirRey D: Luis de velasco ycc opa[9]

1591   8 Acaxivitli g$^{or}_{:}$ D: alvero de morande a~~lde~~ D: Diego mexia D: Jo^a de pas. D: agostin de las casas. D: ypolito de s$^n_{:}$ simo[10] yuā yalohuac chichimecapan yaque Tlax^{a}deca sentzontli tlacatli mamaCuilpohuali çeçencabeçera oquizqui capitan omochiuhta D: Lucas de motealegre nahui Caro oyaqui [marginal note: chichimecapan]

1592   9 decpaxivitli g$^{or}_{:}$ D: Jo^a de pas yuā poliohuato chichimecapan

---

[1]Don Lorenzo Suárez de Mendoza, conde de la Coruña, viceroy of New Spain (1580–1583).

[2]Zapata (pp. 172–73) gives us the full name.

[3]This is the first time that this set of annals has taken the perspective of Huamantla (a provincial entity in the Tizatla sector), though it occurs again much later, for 1626, for example.

[4]Called don Antonio Mocallio de Guevara in Gibson 1967, p. 225. In Zapata (pp. 174–75) he appears his first year as Antonio de Guevara without don, and the second year with it.

[5]It seems from Zapata (pp. 174–75) that the first of the envoys was the governor himself. The list is the same in Zapata except that the first name is don Antonio de Guevara, the same name given to the governor there, and the Diego Téllez in the list bears the don, making it clear that the Diego mentioned last is that person's child. The present writer uses the Spanish mayor, "eldest," which was highly unusual in Nahuatl in that sense at this time; the normal word for eldest child was the Nahuatl yacapantli. Actually, it turns out that Zapata employs the same words, "Diego mayor. Ypiltzin D. diego. deles." In that better expounded context, the indicated translation is "Diego Mayor, child of don Diego Téllez," and the editors of the Zapata edition have so rendered it. Even though Mayor is rare as the second name of a Nahua, it has been sighted at times in the eastern region of Nahuatl speech, and therefore I have chosen to interpret the word in that fashion here.

1580 10 Flint-knife year. The governor was don Mateo de Barrios. Also at this time a viceroy, the conde de Coruña, [1] came from Spain.

1581 11 House year. The governor was don Zacarías [de Santiago].[2] At this time there was a famine. Don Juan Bautista was alcalde for Huamantla.[3]

1582 12 Rabbit year. The governor was don Zacarías. Don Diego de Tovar was alcalde.

1583 13 Reed year. The governor was don Antonio Mocallio.[4] At this time they went to war at Havana and Santo Domingo, and viceroy don Lorenzo died. [f. 16v]

1584 1 Flint-knife year. The governor was don Antonio Mocallio. At this time the rulers went to Spain: don Antonio Téllez de Guevara; don Pedro de Torres; Diego Téllez; don Zacarías de Santiago; and Diego Mayor, child of don Diego Téllez. [5]

1585 2 House year. The governor was don Pedro de Galicia.[6] At this time the rulers who had gone to Spain came back.

1586 3 Rabbit year. The governor was don Pedro de Galicia, and the plants froze. Also at this time there was an epidemic.

1587 4 Reed year. The governor was don Diego Muñoz,[7] and there was a famine.

1588 5 Flint-knife year. The governor was don Diego Muñoz, and a new clock was put in place in Tlaxcala. [f. 17]

1589 6 House year. The governor was don Zacarías de Santiago. At this time the arches were built below [the belfry].[8]

1590 7 Rabbit year. The governor was don Zacarías de Santiago. And viceroy don Luis de Velasco came. It was the second time [a viceroy of that name came].[9]

1591 8 Reed year. The governor was don Alvaro de Morante; the alcaldes were don Diego Mejía, don Juan de Paz, don Agustín de las Casas, and don Hipólito de San Simón.[10] And a party went to Chichimeca country. Four hundred Tlaxcalans went, one hundred from each cabecera. Don Lucas de Montealegre emerged as the one made captain. Four carts went. [*marginal note:* Chichimeca country.]

1592 9 Flint-knife year. The governor was don Juan de Paz. And a group of people perished in Chichimeca country.

---

[6]Zapata (pp. 174–75) also gives don Pedro de Galicia. The editors there take it that the intention was Pablo de Galicia, who was governor before (and might meanwhile have attained the don). I have no further evidence, but after the passage of so much time, this might be not Pablo but a son.

[7]This is almost certainly a cousin of the historian Diego Múñoz Camargo, who was the mestizo son of a Spanish conquistador and a Tlaxcalan noblewoman. See Gibson 1950. Note that the governor bore the don, while the historian, belonging to the Hispanic world, did not.

[8]The writer started a new entry after this word, then scratched it out, but never finished this sentence. The mystery is resolved by Zapata, for in the entry for 1588 (pp. 176–77), we find the following: "Yhuã yquac mochiuhque. Arcos: coyolcaltitlan." "At this time arches were made next to the bell house." They were probably the arches that still stand below the Franciscan belfry.

[9]This don Luis de Velasco was the son of the first viceroy of that name. This one assumed office in 1589. It may be that the present writer did not make a distinction between the two.

[10]There was no need to spell out which subaltepetl each of the four represented: such listings follow the normal postconquest order of Ocotelolco, Tizatla, Quiyahuiztlan and Tepeticpac.

1593   10 CAlli xivitl. g^{or} D: Diego monos yanCuican mochiuh nanahui tomi tlax^a

1594   11 dochtli xivitli g^{or} SaCarias de S^n:tiago [*f. 17v*]

1595   12 ACaxivitli g^{or} D: Jo^a lipas yquac mochiuh Sarapio sahuatli yuā hualya bisoRey Don GasBar Conde[1]

1596   13 decpaxihuitl. g^{or} D: leonalto xicotencatli

1597   1 Calli xivitli g^{or} D: Diego monos yuā tonatiuh Cualoc yuā hehecatli mochiuh yehCatotoc hanahuactli no yhquac momiquillito deopixque xapon

1598   2 dochtli xivitli g^{or} D: Diego de lloss ageless

1599   3 Acaxivitli g^{or} D: Doripio[2] yanCuican maCoc panteras[3]

1600 año 4 decpaxivitli g^{or} D: Jo^a liuas huicoque mexico tlahtoque[4] [*f. 18*]

1601   5 CAlli xivitli g^{or} D: Jo^a liuas yuān oncan moteneuh ye nauhtzontli xihuitli motlacatili yn Dios ypiltzin auh y huehue tlapohualli 13 decpaxihuitli: oncan monamique yxiuhtlapohualtzin yn Dios yuā cenpohualli xihuitl.[5] yuā mochiuh arco tlax^a mochiuh cocolistli

1602   6 dochtli xivitli g^{or} D: Jo^a Liuas yhuā yhquac piloloque Tlahtoque ypanpa yei mil pesos[6]

1603   7 Acaxivitli g^{or} D: Jo^a Liuas mochiuh gonGregacion[7] yhuā huala BirRey marques de montesclaros[8]

1604   8 decpaxivitli g^{or} D: Jo^a Liuas yquac mochiuh zentesahuatli

1605   9 CAlli xivitli g^{or} D: Jo^a Liuas mochiuh cocolistli yalohuac acolhuancan[9]

1606   10 dochtli xihuitli g^{or} D: Jo^a Liuas obispo Dō Diego Roman mochiuh gonGrecacion ConGrecador D: alōso Comes a~~l~~de mayor [*f. 18v*]

1607   11 ACaxivitli g^{or} D: Jo^a de parcas yc opa bisoRey. D: Luys de belas [*sic*] yuā yquac atica poliohuac mexico huehuetocan yalohuac atzaCualoto

1608   12 decpaxivitli g^{or} D: Diego monos gamarco[10] yhcuac: acico atli nican tlax^{a}lan

---

[1]Don Gaspar de Zúñiga y Acevedo, conde de Monterrey, viceroy of New Spain (1595–1603).

[2]Zapata tells us this was don Toribio González of Ocotelolco.

[3]In connection with the death of Philip II (1598). See also 1621, when Philip III died.

[4]Literally rulers; see the introductory matter, pp. 60–61. Zapata gives details concerning this event, when noblemen of the cabildo were held responsible for the people's failure to perform their "duty." These would have been the same "rulers" (that is, cabildo members) who are said to have been hanged in 1602 "because of three thousand pesos."

[5]This was important to the writer because 1600, four sets of 400, was an especially round number in the Nahua counting system, at least equivalent to a millennium break in the western calendar.

[6]Zapata (pp. 196–97) agrees that 3,000 pesos were involved but asserts that after a year and a half of imprisonment the officials were released.

1593   10 House year. The governor was don Diego Muñoz. For the first time 4 reales were raised from each [tribute payer] in Tlaxcala.

1594   11 Rabbit year. The governor was don Zacarías de Santiago. [*f. 17v*]

1595   12 Reed year. The governor was don Juan de Ribas. At this time measles broke out. And viceroy don Gaspar, a count, came.[1]

1596   13 Flint-knife year. The governor was don Leonardo Xicotencatl.

1597   1 House year. The governor was don Diego Muñoz. And there was an eclipse of the sun, and winds developed; the coast lands were lashed by gales. And also at this time some friars died in Japan.

1598   2 Rabbit year. The governor was don Diego de los Angeles.

1599   3 Reed year. The governor was don Toribio [González].[2] For the first time the banner [of the king] was given to him [for ceremonial parading].[3]

1600   4 Flint-knife year. The governor was don Juan de Ribas. Some cabildo members[4] were taken to Mexico City. [*f. 18*]

1601   5 House year. The governor was don Juan de Ribas. And it was said that at that time it had been 1600 years since the child of God was born, in the old count the year of 13 Flint-knife. There met God's year-count and the 20-year counts.[5] And arches were built in Tlaxcala. There was an epidemic.

1602   6 Rabbit year. The governor was don Juan de Ribas. And at this time the cabildo members were hanged because of 3,000 pesos.[6]

1603   7 Reed year. The governor was don Juan de Ribas. A congregation was carried out[7] and viceroy marqués de Montesclaros came.[8]

1604   8 Flint-knife year. The governor was don Juan de Ribas. At this time a pox broke out.

1605   9 House year. The governor was don Juan de Ribas. An epidemic occurred. A party went to Acolhuacan.[9]

1606   10 Rabbit year. The governor was don Juan de Ribas. The bishop was don Diego Romano. A congregation was carried out. The congregator was the alcalde mayor don Alonso Gómez. [*f. 18v*]

1607   11 Reed year. The governor was don Juan de Vargas. Don Luis de Velasco was viceroy for the second time. And at this time people perished by water in Mexico City; a party went to Huehuetocan to dam up the water.

1608   12 Flint-knife year. The governor was don Diego Muñoz Camargo.[10] At this

---

[7]The Spaniards repeatedly tried to make the dwindling and dispersed indigenous population move to more densely populated centers, primarily so that the tribute in labor and goods could be more tightly controlled.

[8]Don Juan de Mendoza y Luna, marqués de Montesclaros, viceroy of New Spain (1603–1607).

[9]Zapata (pp. 202–05) tells us that the workers served for four weeks each on a dike or dam. It could have involved plans related to the first *desagüe* (draining) of the central valley. See Zapata's entry for 1607 as well as the one here for that year.

[10]This was the son of the first Diego Múñoz Camargo the historian (see also the entry for 1587 and the note there), who was himself the mestizo son of a Spanish conquistador and an indigenous noblewoman, and is known to us today for his account (in Spanish) of Tlaxcala's history. This son married doña Francisca Maxixcatzin, heiress of the rulership of Ocotelolco, thereby insuring his acceptance in the indigenous community.

ymac Señor x̄poual de sanctiago oc cepa BiRey mochiuh D: Luis De Velasco

1609 13 Calli xihuitli g̃ọ̃r D: Diego monos camarco yc opa huicoque mexico tlahtohque sanno ypā xihui [*sic*] yn momiquilito totlatocatzin Rey pelipeh terçero[1]

1610 año 1 dochtli xihuitl. g̃ọ̃r d: Diego monos camarco yquac mochiuh yeyecatli yuā
cehzepayahuitli mochi huetzqui quahuitli yuā yolcame motolinique

1611 2 Acaxivitli g̃ọ̃r d: Diego monos camarco yuā Cualoc tonatiuh huel otlayohuac
viernes ylhuitzin Sancto San bernabe yuā monexti p̃ẹ San Diego S̃ṇ gregorio[2]
yey ora[3] qualo tonali [*f. 19*]

1612 3 decpaxivitli g̃ọ̃r D: Diego monos camarco
1613 4 Calli xiuitli g̃ọ̃r D: Diego monos camarco[4]
1614 5 dochtli xihuitli yaCuican g̃ọ̃r D: Gregorio nansianzeno tlaceCualoc huel tla-
poliuh
1615 6 Acaxivitli g̃ọ̃r D: Gregorio nansianzeno yquac tlallin [*sic*]

1616 7 decpaxivitli g̃ọ̃r D: Gregorio nanzianzeno tlaceCualoc
1617 8 Calli xivitli g̃ọ̃r D: Gre̥ọ̃ Nz̥ọ [*f. 19v*]
1618 9 dochtli xihuitli g̃ọ̃r D: Gre̥ọ naz̥ọ tlaceCualoc matlactica yn çe metztli yuā popoCac citlallin honcan peuhqui tlacalaquilli yeyey pesos[5]

1619 10 Acaxivitli g̃ọ̃r D: gre̥ọ nāz̥ọ tlatecihuiloc yuā quisaco ȳ eccacohuatli piloloc
tlitic[6] [*sic*]
1620 año 11 decpaxihuitli g̃ọ̃r D: Gre̥ọ̃ nāz̥ọ yquac acico nican atli san Pablo citlaltepec
yquac moteoCuitlayoti quauhtlachayali yhuā popoCac citlalin yuā miqui totatzin
amoSo quauhtla[7]

1621 12 Calli vitli [*sic*] g̃ọ̃r D: G̥r̥iọ̲ naz̥ọ Rey ypantera macoc[8]

1622 13 dochtli xihuitli g̃ọ̃r D: G̥r̥iọ̲ naz̥ọ tlacequaloc ypann ilhuitzin San fran̥c̥ọ yuā
teCuaylpi obispo D: alonso de la mota[9] [*f. 20*]

1623 1 acaxihuitli g̃ọ̃r D: G̥r̥iọ̲ naz̥ọ quisaco tlatlaçistli quihualhuicac tlacahuatzalli
quitlatihque huexotzinco[10] [*marginal note:* yc opa tlalpilli marques.]

1624 2 decpaxihuitli g̃ọ̃r d: G̥r̥iọ̲ naz̥ọ bisoRey Don lopeh ~~armen~~ de ~~pacheco~~ de

---

[1]This event actually occurred in 1621. A number of the region's annals have it wrong.

[2]Zapata (pp. 214–15) confirms that it was San Diego who appears and not Santiago (for the two
often nearly merge in Nahuatl texts), and gives the place as San Gregorio Metepec.

[3]In texts of this time *hora* is much more common in the meaning "at a certain time of day" than
as an indicator of duration. Yet in this text *hora* to indicate the hour is otherwise accompanied by
ipan, and once by the Spanish *a*. Thus I have chosen "for three hours" over "at 3 o'clock."

[4]In Zapata (pp. 218–19), 1613 was don Gregorio Nacianceno's first year as governor.

time water was brought here to Tlaxcala through the agency of señor Cristóbal de Santiago. Once again don Luis de Velasco became viceroy.

1609 13 House year. The governor was don Diego Muñoz Camargo. For the second time cabildo members were taken to Mexico City. Also in this year our ruler King Philip III died.[1]

1610 1 Rabbit year. The governor was don Diego Muñoz Camargo. At this time the wind and snow kept coming. All the trees fell and the animals suffered.

1611 2 Reed year. The governor was don Diego Muñoz Camargo. And there was a solar eclipse. It got very dark on Friday, the feast day of the holy San Bernabé. And Father San Diego appeared in San Gregorio.[2] The eclipse lasted for three hours.[3] [*f. 19*]

1612 3 Flint-knife year. The governor was don Diego Muñoz Camargo.

1613 4 House year. The governor was don Diego Muñoz Camargo.[4]

1614 5 Rabbit year. Don Gregorio Nacianceno was governor for the first time. It froze; there was great destruction.

1615 6 Reed year. The governor was don Gregorio Nacianceno. At this time there was an earthquake.

1616 7 Flint-knife year. The governor was don Gregorio Nacianceno. It froze.

1617 8 House year. The governor was don Gregorio Nacianceno. [*f. 19v*]

1618 9 Rabbit year. The governor was don Gregorio Nacianceno. It was freezing for ten days of one month. And there was a comet. At this point it began that tribute was 3 pesos for each [married couple or household].[5]

1619 10 Reed year. The governor was don Gregorio Nacianceno. It hailed and there were tornadoes. A black person was hanged.[6]

1620 11 Flint-knife year. The governor was don Gregorio Nacianceno. At this time water reached as far as here at San Pablo Citlaltepec. At this time the wooden latticework [in the church] was gilded. And there was a comet, and our father [a priest] died in the woods at Amozoc.[7]

1621 12 House year. The governor was don Gregorio Nacianceno. He was given the banner of the king [to parade about with].[8]

1622 13 Rabbit year. The governor was don Gregorio Nacianceno. It froze on the feast day of San Francisco, and bishop don Alonso de la Mota confirmed [children].[9] [*f. 20*]

1623 1 Reed year. The governor was don Gregorio Nacianceno. An epidemic of coughing broke out. A dried-up person brought it here. They burned him at Huexotzinco.[10] [*marginal note*: A second 52 years since the Marqués arrived.]

1624 2 Flint-knife year. The governor was don Gregorio Nacianceno. Viceroy don

---

[5]Zapata (pp. 226–27) has it that the amount was 3 pesos and 4 reales.

[6]According to Zapata (pp. 228–29), he was hanged for the death of a Spanish barber.

[7]See the entry for 1620 in the Puebla annals in this volume and the note there.

[8]Zapata (pp. 230–31) reports how the governor went about with the banner and scattered coins.

[9]See Mota 1945.

[10]See the annals of Puebla in this volume for 1622 and the note there.

almendalles yquac huala[1]

1625   3 Calli xihuitli g$^{or}_{:}$ D: Gre^o naz^o Donatiuh Cualoc huelayehuac [sic] ypann
         ilhuitzin Sanctho domas Sabado yuā momiquili obispo Donn alonso de la mota a
         5 de marzo a 10 hora

1626   4 dochtli xivitli g$^{or}_{:}$ d: G$^{rio}_{\equiv}$ naz^o moyanCuili quauhmantla aḤde Don Seph [sic]
         de cellis

1627   5 acaxivitli g$^{or}_{:}$ = d: Gre^o naz^o tlallolin ypā Jueues [f. 20v]

1628   6 decpaxihuitli g$^{or}_{:}$ D: G$^{rio}_{\equiv}$ naz^o chicahuac cocolis [sic] mochiuh

1629   7 CAlli xitli [sic] g$^{or}_{:}$ D: G$^{ri}_{\equiv}$ naz^o Yquac apachiuhque mexica y mochi calli
         huetzqui yuā moçenma ytlaltzin totlaçonantzin Rey MiChin moCuep nahualli
         quimamani mexica[2]

1630 años 8 dochtli xihuitli g$^{or}_{:}$ d: G$^{rio}_{\equiv}$ naz^o

1631   9 Acaxivitli g$^{or}_{:}$ d: gre^o naz$^o_{.}$ se albarecion el grorioso San miguel a Diego lasaro
         a 8 de mayo De 1631 años[3]

1632   10 decpaxivitli g$^{or}_{:}$ d: G^{rio} naz^o yquac yalohuac mexicatzinco mochiuh Cuep-
         otli[4] yuā cualo tonatiuh [f. 21]

1633   11 CAlli xihuitli g$^{or}_{:}$ d: G$^{rio}_{\equiv}$ naz^o tlallolin huel yohuatzinco

1634   12 Tochtli xihuitli g$^{or}_{:}$ D: gre^o naz^o yquac Mochiuh cocolistli huel chicahua mi-
         cohuac yuā xiti pohuete sentepecqui yc matlactli de mayo

1635   13 ACaxivitli g$^{or}_{:}$ D: Greg^o naz^o yquac hualya Rey don pedro marques[5]

1636   1 decpaxivitli g$^{or}_{:}$ D: Gre^o nz^o

1637   2 CAlli xivitli aḤde g$^{or}_{:}$ Denario [sic] D: Lurenso de pallençia yuā ycquac
         quiCauh ytequiuh Don Gre^o naz$^{o}_{\equiv}$ yc 3 te octobre[6] nimann icquac quicelli
         ytequih Don Diego hasinto [f. 21v]

---

[1]This is a confused entry. Viceroy don Lope Díez de Almendáriz, marqués de Cadereita, served
from 1635 to 1640. The arrival of such a viceroy is in fact mentioned in 1635. Scratched out is the
name "Pacheco," and in fact there were two viceroys with that surname in this era: don Rodrigo
Pacheco y Osorio (1624–1635) and don Diego López Pacheco, marqués de Villena (1640–1642).

[2]The entry offers several puzzles. It is as though almost unintelligible fragments of a longer
narrative are reproduced here, and in some cases possibly not correctly. I take the passage "moçenma ytlaltzin totlaçonantzin" to be equivalent to "the people of the land of our precious mother
[the area of Mexico City] scattered." "Moçenma" seems to derive from cemmana, most often
meaning to scatter, disperse. Here, against expectations, the land appears to be the subject, and
specifically, "the land of our precious mother," the latter term usually referring to the Virgin. It is
known from elsewhere that the people of Mexico City scattered through the surrounding region
during the worst of the floods. "The viceroy turned into a fish" seems an excessively whimsical
expression for this genre, but the construction as it stands is unambiguous. That the passage rests in
part on miscopying, however, remains likely. One suspects that an earlier version said something
like "the land of our great ruler the king." Nahualli can mean conjuror, sorcerer, etc., but also

Lope de Almendáriz came at this time.[1]

1625   3 House year. The governor was don Gregorio Nacianceno. There was a solar eclipse. It got very dark on Saturday, the feast day of Santo Tomás. And bishop don Alonso de la Mota died on March 5, at 10 o'clock.

1626   4 Rabbit year. The governor was don Gregorio Nacianceno. The alcalde for Huamantla, don Josef de Celis, was renewed.

1627   5 Reed year. The governor was don Gregorio Nacianceno. There was an earthquake on a Thursday. [*f. 20v*]

1628   6 Flint-knife year. The governor was don Gregorio Nacianceno. There was a serious epidemic.

1629   7 House year. The governor was don Gregorio Nacianceno. At this time the Mexica were flooded. All the houses fell. [The people of?] the land of our precious mother scattered. The viceroy turned into a fish [had to go about by water]. A sorcerer agitated the Mexica.[2]

1630   8 Rabbit year. The governor was don Gregorio Nacianceno.

1631   9 Reed year. The governor was don Gregorio Nacianceno. There was an apparition of the glorious San Miguel to Diego Lázaro on the 8th of May, 1631.[3]

1632   10 Flint-knife year. The governor was don Gregorio Nacianceno. At this time a party went to Mexicatzinco; a causeway was built.[4] And there was a solar eclipse. [*f. 21*]

1633   11 House year. The governor was don Gregorio Nacianceno. There was an earthquake very early in the morning.

1634   12 Rabbit year. The governor was don Gregorio Nacianceno. At this time there was an epidemic. A great many died. And on the 10th of May the bridge at Centepec collapsed.

1635   13 Reed year. The governor was don Gregorio Nacianceno. At this time the viceroy, don Pedro, Marqués, came.[5]

1636   1 Flint-knife year. The governor was don Gregorio Nacianceno.

1637   2 House year. The alcalde ordinario was don Lorenzo de Valencia. And at this time, on the 3rd of October, don Gregorio Nacianceno relinquished office.[6] Thereupon don Diego Jacinto accepted office. [*f. 21v*]

---

an animal alter ego and in general things of a secret nature. The word's proximity to *michin*, "fish," is suggestive. The last three clauses in this entry need to be taken with a grain of salt.

[3]Zapata (pp. 252–53) mentions the event, putting it in San Bernabé Icçotitlan in November.

[4]In Spanish usually Mexicaltzingo, on the shores of Lake Tetzcoco. Drainage works were in the process of being built.

[5]The writer has the first name of the viceroy wrong. Don Lope Díez de Almendáriz, marqués de Cadereita, served from 1635 to 1640. (See also n. 1 here.) Zapata too lacks the surnames and has the first name wrong, though in his case don Fernando; he too simply calls him marqués without specifying of what.

[6]Zapata (pp. 260–61) recounts a story in which this don Gregorio Nacianceno, the longtime indigenous governor of Tlaxcala, is accused of something. He is jailed first in Mexico City and then in Tlaxcala, and has his livestock establishment (estancia) and wheat confiscated. The implication may be that he acquired these wrongly using official influence. Zapata dates all this in 1636, having Nacianceno relinquish office and be replaced by don Diego Jacinto in August of that year.

1638   3 Tochtli xihuitl. g^{or} D: Diego Jasinto yhuā momiquili obispo Don gotieres
        pernardo De Quilos

1639   4 ACaxihuitli g^{or} D: Diego Jasinto yCuac Cepayauhhuitli Domingo ypan nahui
        ora peuhqui quiyahuitli Lones cemilhuitli cepayauh huel motolinique yolcame
        yc matlatli [*sic*] de henero

1640 año 5 decpaxihutli g^{or} D: antt^{o}nio de quepara yhQuac hualmohuiCac Señor obispo
        S̶r̶ ̶D̶ō Satepan hualla Rey ipan martes D: Juā De palabus[1]

1641   6 CAlli xivitli g^{or} D: antt^{o}nio de guebara no yquac amo quiCauhque ytequih:
        al̶deme yquac hualaque tlax^a Grerigos yc nohuiyan cura Juan de SanDobal San
        Juan huactinzo ohualtlamelauque[2]

1642   7 dochtli xihuitli g^{or} D: antt^{o}nio de quebara tlaceCualoc yuā hualya Rey D: Jo^a
        marques[3] [*f. 22*]

1643   8 ACaxihuitli g^{or} D: Antonio de quebara

1644   9 decpaxivitli g^{or} D: Antt^o de quebara yhuan calac cura topoyango D Nicolas
        ramos

1645   10 Calli xihuitli g^{or} D Diego Xinmenis yquac tlallolin yuā tonatiuh qualoc yuā
        tlacehualoc

1646   11 dochtli xihuitli g^{or} D: Diego ximenez – ypann ilhuitzin san marcos moteo-
        chiuh teocalli Cuetlaxcohuapa[4]

1647   12 ACaxihuitli g^{or} D p^o Luis Ludriques topoyanco al̶de D: Sebas$\underline{\text{n}}$ de dorres [*f.
        22v*]

1648   13 decpaxivitli g^{or} D fran^{co} della corona yhquac moteochiuh teopantli paroquia

1649   1 Calli xihuivitli g^{or} D fran^{co} de la corona yquac moteochiuh teocalli Cutlax-
        cohuapan [*sic*] yuā Rey momiquilli yuā Señor obispo mohuicac caxtillan D Ju^o
        de Palabos

1650 año 2 dochtli xihuitli g^{or} D: Diego Ximenes no yCuac huala Rey[5]

1651   3 Calli xihuitli g^{or} D: buenabentora tzapata[6] yCuac neçico pelon tomin[7] yuā
        Cuacloc [*sic*] tonatiuh [*f. 23*]

1652   4 decpaxihitli g^{or} D: feliphe ortis

1653   5 Calli xihuitli g^{or} D: feliphe ortis yhquac mochiuh cocolistli yuā quizaco

---

[1]In the Nahuatl there is an additional "don" inserted awkwardly after "Obispo," but I have
ignored it because it seems clear that the writer is trying to refer to the viceroy, whom in the end he
fails to name. The name of the bishop Palafox comes only at the end, where one would have
expected the viceroy's name. Zapata (pp. 266–67) clarifies the situation by reporting the arrival of
Palafox on July 16, and then on July 24, said to be a Tuesday in agreement with the present writer,
the arrival of the new viceroy, don Diego Pacheco, marqués de Villena and conde de Escalona. Our
writer may have been confused by the fact that in 1641 Palafox indeed became viceroy.

[2]Zapata (pp. 268–71) mentions both these events as well. The alcaldes served another term and
secular parishes were established. Zapata too emphasizes the speed and even stealth with which the
secular priests entered, and records fighting between them and the Franciscans.

1638   3 Rabbit year. The governor was don Diego Jacinto. And bishop don Gutierre Bernardo de Quiroz died.

1639   4 Reed year. The governor was don Diego Jacinto. At this time it snowed on Sunday; at 4 o'clock it began to rain. On Monday, it snowed all day. The animals really suffered. [This happened] on the 10th of January.

1640   5 Flint-knife year. The governor was don Antonio de Guevara. At this time the lord bishop don Juan de Palafox came. Afterwards, on a Tuesday, the viceroy came.[1]

1641   6 House year. The governor was don Antonio de Guevara. Also at this time the alcaldes did not give up their office. At this time secular priests arrived everywhere in Tlaxcala. The parish priest at San Juan Huactzinco was Juan de Sandoval. They came straight [to their new posts].[2]

1642   7 Rabbit year. The governor was don Antonio de Guevara. It froze, and a viceroy came, don Juan, Marqués.[3] [*f. 22*]

1643   8 Reed year. The governor was don Antonio de Guevara.

1644   9 Flint-knife year. The governor was don Antonio de Guevara. And don Nicolás de Ramos entered Topoyanco as parish priest.

1645   10 House year. The governor was don Diego Jiménez. At this time there was an earthquake and a solar eclipse, and it froze.

1646   11 Rabbit year. The governor was don Diego Jiménez. On the feast day of San Marcos the church at Cuitlaxcohuapan was consecrated.[4]

1647   12 Reed year. The governor was don Pedro Luis Rodríguez. The Topoyanco alcalde was don Sebastián de Torres. [*f. 22v*]

1648   13 Flint-knife year. The governor was don Francisco de la Corona. At this time the parish church was consecrated.

1649   1 House year. The governor was don Francisco de la Corona. At this time the church at Cuitlaxcohuapan was consecrated. And the viceroy died, and the lord bishop don Juan de Palafox went to Spain.

1650   2 Rabbit year. The governor was don Diego Jiménez. Also at this time a viceroy came.[5]

1651   3 House year. The governor was don Buenaventura Zapata.[6] At this time coins from Peru appeared,[7] and there was a solar eclipse. [*f. 23*]

1652   4 Flint-knife year. The governor was don Felipe Ortiz.

1653   5 House year. The governor was don Felipe Ortiz. At this time there was an

---

[3]The new viceroy was actually don García Sarmiento de Sotomayor, conde de Salvatierra. The writer is probably confusing him with don Juan Palafox, who served from 1641 to 1642. (See the entry for 1640.)

[4]This actually occurred in 1649. Note that the event is repeated in that year, correctly.

[5]Don Luis Enríquez de Guzmán, conde de Alba de Liste, viceroy of New Spain (1650–1653).

[6]This governor is the annalist Zapata, who in his own work (pp. 292–93) on this occasion styles himself don Juan Buenaventura Zapata de Mendoza.

[7]A number of people were arrested in this year for producing coins that were not pure silver. (Guijo 1952, vol. 1, pp. 185–86).

hobispo[1] yquac hualla bisoRey d: fran^co toque[2]

1654   6 dochtli xihuitli g^or. D: Jo^a de los santos no yCuac otlatotopocac ypan ChiCuey
        ora Jueues: A 26 de Febrero[3] — piloloque ychteque Jua fran^co Jua Miguel
        fran^co espinosa diego Alonso[4]

1655   7 Acaxivitl. g^or. D: Jo^a de los santos yquac quisaco sauatzintli [*f. 23v*]

1656   8. decpaxihuitli g^or. D Juā de los santos yhquac quisaco Señor obispo [inserted:
        D Diego Onsorio y lamas][5] yuā tlamauhtico tlacaychtequi ypan miercoles nochi
        ocalaqui teopan y tlatlaca yuā pipiltzitzintin

1657   9. Calli xihuivitli [*sic*] g^or. D: Jo^a de los santos ycCuac miqui alde mayor D:
        allonso amo nica miqui apitzatzco [*sic*] ypan sabado yuā miqui g^or. D: Jo^a de los
        santos yc 3 tonali de mayo no ypan xihuitli[6]

1658   i0. dochtli xihuitli g^or. D: Juan ni^colas cortes Santana[7] yquac quisaco cocolistli

1659   ii. ACAxivitli g^or. D Jo^a Nicolas Cordes yhQuac hocellica[8] palacio tequitli [*f.
        24*]

1660   i2. decpaxihuitli g^or. D: Ber^ue antt^onio de sallasal yquac hualla bisuRey D:
        ~~Sebas^an~~ Juan de leyBa de la cerda marq̄z de mancera[9] yuā sahuatli q̄saco

1661   i3. CAlli xivitli g^or. D: Ber^ue antto^o de sallasal yq̄c calac nicolas mendes Es-
        [~~cribano~~][10] yuā tlaceCualoc ypā S^n. mḡl

1662   1. dochtl. xihuitli g^or. D: Jo^a niS: [*sic*] cordes yQuac mayanaloc ce xicalli melio
        ypatiuh çe anega 3 p^s

1663   2. ACaxivitli g^or. D: NiColas mendes de lona yquac momiquili gora topoyanco
        D: Nicolas Ramos ypan ilhuitzin S^ra candelarria [*f. 24v*]

1664   3. decpaxihuitli g^or. D: NiColas mendes de lluna[11] ycuac hualla bisoRei D:

---

[1]In his entry for 1652 (pp. 294–95), Zapata says that the bishop came to Tlaxcala from Puebla
for the purpose of confirming children.

[2]Don Francisco Fernández de la Cueva, duque de Alburquerque, viceroy of New Spain (1653–
1660).

[3]No doubt connected with an eruption of Popocatepetl which other annals put in 1653.

[4]The four thieves are mentioned also in annals from Puebla, including the set in this volume,
which gives some more detail. Zapata (pp. 294–95) says that in 1652 three blacks who were the
slaves of one Luis García in San Luis Apizaco were hanged for having killed a Spanish mayor-
domo.

[5]For 1654, Zapata reports that the bishop came to Tlaxcala, and he gives the full name.

[6]Zapata (pp. 300–03) confirms this information. The alcalde mayor was the Spanish governor,
don Alonso de la Cueva.

[7]Zapata (pp. 302–03; see also note 176 there) does not include the name Santana. The meaning
may be that around the feast day of Santa Ana an epidemic broke out.

epidemic, and the bishop came out.[1] At this time the viceroy don Francisco, a duke, came.[2]

1654 6 Rabbit year. The governor was don Juan de los Santos. Also at this time there were repeated explosions at 8 o'clock on Thursday, February 26.[3] The thieves Juan Francisco, Juan Miguel, Francisco Espinosa and Diego Alonso were hanged.[4]

1655 7 Reed year. The governor was don Juan de los Santos. At this time the pox broke out. [*f. 23v*]

1656 8 Flint-knife year. The governor was don Juan de los Santos. At this time the lord bishop don Diego Osorio [de Escobar] y Llamas came out.[5] And a kidnapper came on a Wednesday and terrorized everyone. All the adults and children entered the church [to take refuge].

1657 9 House year. The governor was don Juan de los Santos. At this time the alcalde mayor don Alonso died. He did not die here, but at Apizaco, on a Saturday. And the governor don Juan de los Santos died on the 3rd day of May, also in this year.[6]

1658 10 Rabbit year. The governor was don Juan Nicolás Cortés de Santana.[7] At this time an epidemic broke out.

1659 11 Reed year. The governor was don Juan Nicolás Cortés. At this time the palace tribute duty [was accepted?].[8] [*f. 24*]

1660 12 Flint-knife year. The governor was don Bernabé Antonio de Salazar. At this time viceroy don Juan de Leiva y de la Cerda, marqués de Mancera, came.[9] And the pox broke out.

1661 13 House year. The governor was don Bernabé Antonio de Salazar. At this time Nicolás Méndez entered [as notary of the cabildo],[10] and it froze on the feast day of San Miguel.

1662 1 Rabbit year. The governor was don Juan Nicolás Cortés. At this time there was a famine. A gourd [of maize] cost half a real; a fanega 3 pesos.

1663 2 Reed year. The governor was don Nicolás Méndez de Luna. At this time the parish priest of Topoyanco, don Nicolás de Ramos, died, on Candlemas. [*f. 24v*]

1664 3 Flint-knife year. The governor was don Nicolás Méndez de Luna.[11] At this

---

[8]The form "hocellica" is opaque; if the intention was "hocelliloc," it would yield the meaning indicated above. Zapata (pp. 304–07) gives the background with his entry: "yhuā ytecopā mochiuh aḻḻde mayor yn omoteneuh D. p.º Billarohuel. ynic omochiuh Balacio. yn oxitica ce tlacoltica. ynic mochi tlacpacali. ça nima mochi yecauh yn ipa xihuitl." ("And it was by the order of the alcalde mayor aforementioned, don Pedro Villaroel, that the palace was constructed, one half of which had collapsed, the whole upper story. It was all completely finished in the [same] year.")

[9]Don Juan de Leiva y de la Cerda, marqués de Leiva, conde de Baños, viceroy of New Spain (1660–1664).

[10]The part in brackets has been scratched out in the original: one can barely make out the word "escribano" and then something else. Zapata (pp. 308–09) tells us that Nicolás Méndez was the son of a Portuguese father and an indigenous mother who entered the cabildo for the first time in 1661, against the will of some, as a regidor, but the next year he was indeed made notary of the cabildo.

[11]Zapata (pp. 344–46) gives don Juan Miguel Hernández as governor for 1664. Zapata as alcalde that year would seem to know. Yet he harbored a special enmity for Méndez de Luna.

Antonio Sebastian marq̄z de mancera[1]

1665   4. CAlli xihuitli g.ᵒʳ D: Nicolas mentes y xihui huetzi huey tlamahuisoli omochiuh ypān ilhuitzin san sebastian yohualtica ypā yei ora hualathui miercoles yn
otopo popocatzin nochi tletli yn oq̄xique niman ohuihuiyocac tlalticpactli yuā
omomiquili Dotlahtocahtzin Rey pelipeh terçero omochiuh Jora ypan agosto[2]

1666   5. tochtli xihui g.ᵒʳ D: Nicolas mendes de luna ypan tonali Jueves ylhuitzin san
Jua pauhtista oquinamiquico ylhuitzin Sanctissimo Sacramento ypan ce donali
hoquisqui

1667   6. ACaxihuitli g.ᵒʳ D: Nicolas mendes De Lona ypann ilhuitzin Santa orsola oto-
topocac ylhuiCatli ypan çe hora yhuā tlaco cuetlaxcohuapahuic [f. 25]

[1668]   7. decpaxivitli g.ᵒʳ D: nicolas mendes D. l.na
                          gno ll con f. 24[3]
1669   8. CAlli xihuitli g.ᵒʳ D: Juᵒ mḡl mᵗᵉ̱s de l.na[4] ypan martes ylhuitzin sᵗᵃ. ysauel
ocan omopehualtique dodatzintzin omahuaque oteyolCuitiya Dotatzin oquiluia
amo ticpi [sic] licensia oquito niteyolcuitis ca niteopixq̄ amo aquin nehcahualtis
huel oCuala cora D: anttᵒnio dorres topoyanco[5]

1670   9. dochtli xihui g.ᵒʳ D: Juᵃ mḡl hrz[6] ypann ilhuitzin totlaçohnātzin asubcio omo-
quatlatlaque[7] dotatzitzin: otequatlapā dodatzin sⁿ franᶜᵒ oquiquatlapanque cora
D: anttᵒnio de torres yuā Joᵃ descobal ayorate[8] yhuā motlali netzonxoes[9] ypan
corpus jueves Cuetlaxcohuapan

1671   10. acaxihuitli g.ᵒʳ D franᶜᵒ Luis ycatzinco yn Santisima Trinidad oquisaco
tlacajues otepohualCo namiq̄que yhuā telpopochtin ychpopochtin pipiltzitzin
fiscal[10] Lucas gregᵒ sanches masavatzin Jues D: Alonso de mesa =

---

[1]Don Antonio Sebastián de Toledo Molina y Salazar, marqués de Mancera, viceroy of New
Spain (1664–1673).

[2]An oath of allegiance to the new king.

[3]A closely related set of annals found in the AAMC has at this spot the words "cuaderno II con
folios 24", thus we can understand the meaning. What is not clear is if the writer of this set of
annals copied the phrase from another original without understanding what it meant, or if an inept
clerk in the Boturini library inserted the phrase here because he had seen it in another set of annals.
A note in a nineteenth-century hand inserted at the front of this set of annals indicates that it came
to the BNAH via the Boturini collection, and asserts that the annotation demonstrates "mucho
descuido." The comment's handwriting and ink in the original could indeed be interpreted as being
different from that of the rest of the document, and as having been inserted into a previously blank
space, but none of these elements are beyond doubt in my opinion.

[4]The governor was in fact don Nicolás Méndez de Luna (Zapata, pp. 414–15). The writer was
probably thinking of don Juan Miguel Hernández, whom he gives as governor for 1670.

[5]In the next entry, we learn that the aggressors here were visiting Franciscan friars.

time viceroy don Antonio Sebastián, marqués de Mancera, came.[1]

1665   4 House year. The governor was don Nicolás Méndez. A comet fell. A great prodigy occurred on the feast day of San Sebastián, at night. It was at 3 o'clock before dawn on Wednesday that Popocatzin [Popocatepetl] erupted. It was pure fire that came out, then the earth trembled. And our ruler King Philip III died. An oath was taken in August.[2]

1666   5 Rabbit year. The governor was don Nicolás Méndez de Luna. On a Thursday, the feast day of San Juan Bautista met the feast day of the most holy Sacrament. They came out on the same day.

1667   6 Reed year. The governor was don Nicolás Méndez de Luna. On the feast day of Santa Ursula, at half past 1 o'clock the heavens repeatedly made exploding sounds; it was toward Cuitlaxcohuapan. [*f. 25*]

[1668]   7 Flint-knife year. The governor was don Nicolás Méndez de Luna.

[Notebook II, with 24 folios][3]

1669   8 House year. The governor was don Juan Miguel Méndez de Luna.[4] On Tuesday, the feast day of Santa Isabel, our fathers began to quarrel. Our father was confessing people. They said to him, "You have no license [to confess people]." He said, "I will confess people, for I am a priest. No one will prevent me." The parish priest, don Antonio de Torres of Topoyanco, became very angry.[5]

1670   9 Rabbit year. The governor was don Juan Miguel Hernández.[6] On the feast day of our precious mother of the Assumption, our fathers broke each other's heads [had a big fight].[7] A Franciscan father did some head-breaking. They broke the head of the parish priest don Antonio de Torres along with Juan de Escobar, [assistant].[8] And a [. . .?] judge[9] was established on Thursday, Corpus [Christi day], in Cuitlaxcohuapan.

1671   10 Reed year. The governor was don Francisco Ruiz. On the feast day of the Santísima Trinidad a people-judge [census taker] came. He came to count people: married people, youths, maidens, and children. The fiscal[10] was Lucas Gregorio Sánchez Maçahuatzin. The judge was don Alonso de Mesa.

---

[6]Zapata (pp. 436–47 ff.) gives don Francisco Ruiz as the governor for 1670, though he was under arrest for a time, and possibly someone else held the governorship during that period.

[7]Given the rest of the paragraph, the writer probably intended "omoquatlapanque."

[8]In a closely related set of annals in the AAMC, this word appears as *ayudante*, "assistant."

[9]I cannot be sure of the meaning of what appears to read "netzcoxoes," except that it almost certainly refers to some sort of judge (*juez,* "xoes"). In two closely related sets of annals in the AAMC, this word seems to appear as "Wehen xoes" and "Nekon xoes" and remains untranslated by Ramírez; he clearly did not understand what he was seeing either. I note that in the original, the word "tlacajues" appearing in the next entry begins with an extremely ornate "tl" which almost gives the appearance of a W or N. It is my surmise that an original document once contained an almost illegible "tlacaxoes," which led to wildly varying iterations in the copies that stemmed from it. Zapata asserts that a judge came in this year to count the population (pp. 454–55). Elsewhere he has the forms "mexoes" and "ocxoes," maguey judge and pulque judge. A clump of magueyes was sometimes called a *metzontli,* so a possibility would be "metzonxoes," judge for stands of maguey.

[10]The reason for the mention of a church fiscal (apparently the one for Topoyanco) seems to be that that person helped in taking the census, as the fiscal is mentioned again in that same context in the entry for 1680, on that occasion the church being mentioned explicitly.

1672   11. decpaxihuitli g.ᵒʳ D: frnᶜᵒ Luis miercoles a 15 de junio bisperas corpus qui-
teteuique alɬde mayor D: Joᵃ de chabara yca tlallaquilli [*sic*] honca peuhq̃: ome
peso moxtlahua yuā nahui tomin ye ocalac BirRey motemacac[1] [*f. 25v*]

1673   12. Calli xihuitli g.ᵒʳ D: nicolas Mdes de Luna ypann ilhuitzin Sᵗᵃ Lucia miercoles a 13 de Diciembre omiqui bisoRey D: pᵒ doque de beragua[2] yuā miqui
BiReReyna depeyacac onca depossitado mocauh[3] yuā momiq̃ili obispo D: Diego
hosorio ypan sabado cuetlaxcohuapa tocdo yc mactlac yuā nahui octoBre

1674   13 dochtli xihuitli g.ᵒʳ D: Joᵃ miğl hrz yCuac quisaco huey atli ypann ilhuitzin
totlaçonantzin natibitate oteca yn atlɏᵃ sa yca huepalitli oquiquixtiaya ytlan atli[4]

1675   ACAxihuitli g.ᵒʳ D: Diego martin Faustino yCuac ylhuitz San Lurenço mixnamique macehualtzitzintin ynahuac alᶜᵃˡte mayor Don Leon de alza sa soltados
oquitlaqueuh oquipiaya[5] yua yhquac ohuateco yn christobal quisato topoyago
amo miqui [*faint marginal note*: yc yexpa tlalpili marq̃z]

1676   2 decpaxihuitli gᵒʳ D Diego de SanDiago sanno ipa xihuitli 1675 g.ᵒʳ D: Diego
m̄ Faustino omotocato cohuatepatli[6] opequi pinal nopaloca San lorenço quapias-
tla apapasco[7] ye nochi tlaxᵃteca tlalli possession omaquē omacoque

1677   3 Calli xihuitli g.ᵒʳ D Diego de SanDiago [*f. 26*]
1678   4 Dochtli xihuitli g.ᵒʳ D Diego Peres cuixcoatzin atle mochiuh

1679   5 çe acatli xihuitli g.ᵒʳ D pasCual Ramires
1680 años 6 Tecpaxihuitli g.ᵒʳ D franᶜᵒ Ruis ycatzinco santisma Trinidad oquisaco tlacaJues D Antoᵒ ortis de escalante otlacapouaco yca 2 yuā melio[8] namiq̃que
ytequih teopan Jueves yc 27 de março fiscal [*inserted in margin:* fiscal pᵒ
tzopan]

---

[1]Zapata tells us this story in detail, and the Spanish records complement what he has to say.
Over the protests of the indigenous cabildo, the Mexico City government had insisted on re-
counting the population. (See 1671.) The Spanish officials insisted that per capita payments would
actually be lowered, in that the old required contribution would be divided among a higher population. However, as the cabildo members seemed to expect, the government actually demanded the
old per capita contribution from each person on the new rolls, thus almost doubling the total
payment. Rioting ensued, and eventually a compromise was reached at 2 pesos 4 reales per household. The viceroy really did visit Tlaxcala later that year, and probably did give out significant gifts
to potential allies.

[2]Don Pedro Nuño Colón de Portugal, duque de Veragua, viceroy of New Spain in November
and December of 1673.

[3]It was actually the wife of the previous viceroy who died, while on her way back to Spain.
Zapata (pp. 530–31) puts the event in 1674.

1672   11 Flint-knife year. The governor was don Francisco Ruíz. On Wednesday the 15th of June, on the eve of Corpus [Christi day], they stoned the alcalde mayor don Juan de Echeverría because of the tribute. It began then that 2 pesos and 4 reales were paid [by each household]. At this time the viceroy entered [the city]; things [gifts] were given to people.[1] [*f. 25v*]

1673   12 House year. The governor was don Nicolás Méndez de Luna. On the feast day of Santa Lucía, Wednesday, December 13, the viceroy died, don Pedro, duque de Veragua.[2] And the vicereine died at Tepeaca, where she was left temporarily buried.[3] And bishop don Diego Osorio died on a Saturday, October 14. He lies buried in Cuitlaxcohuapan.

1674   13 Rabbit year. The governor was don Juan Miguel Hernández. At this time a big flood occurred on the feast day of the nativity of our precious Mother. Water filled everything. Only with boards did they get [the people?] out of the water.[4]

1675   [1] Reed year. The governor was don Diego Martín Faustino. At this time on the feast day of San Lorenzo, the indigenous people contended with the alcalde mayor, don León de Arsa. He just hired soldiers who were guarding him.[5] And at this time Cristóbal was carried away by the water. He got out at Topoyanco; he did not die. [*marginal note*: a third 52-year cycle since the Marqués]

1676   2 Flint-knife year. The governor was don Diego de Santiago. In the same year of 1675 [above], the governor being don Diego Martín Faustino, the common border was laid.[6] It began at the pine grove at Nopalocan [and went to?] where [the springs] are at San Lorenzo Quapiaztlan.[7] All the Tlaxcalans were given, and they took, possession of the land.

1677   3 House year. The governor was don Diego de Santiago. [*f. 26*]

1678   4 Rabbit year. The governor was don Diego Pérez Cuixcoatzin. Nothing happened.

1679   5 One Reed year [*sic*]. The governor was don Pascual Ramírez.

1680   6 Flint-knife year. The governor was don Francisco Ruiz. On the feast day of Santísima Trinidad a people-judge [census taker], don Antonio Ortiz de Escalante, came. He came to count people at the church on Thursday, March 27th so that 2½ reales[8] would be married people's contribution. The fiscal was Pedro Tzompan.

---

[4]The transcription and hence translation of this passage is uncertain; this must be the sense of it, however. A closely related set of annals in the AAMC reads "oteca in atl san ica huapallitl oquiquistiaya yn tla in atl." The last phrase may have meant "yn tlaca in atl," "the people from the water," but that error could have led to the confusion we apparently see here.

[5]These events are explained further in the entry for 1676.

[6]In 1675, Zapata says that the Spanish governor and the entire indigenous cabildo went to the field to consider the question of the border with Tepeaca and to mark the route of a new road which would serve as a dividing line.

[7]Nopalocan and San Lorenzo Quapiaztlan are both well known place names. In Trautmann 1980, there is no entry for *apapazco* as a toponym, but Molina tells us that *apapatztla* means springs of water, and the word here seems based on *apaztli*, water basin, bowl, tub.

[8]Since the contributions mentioned in the annals hover around 2 and 3 pesos, probably the meaning is 2 pesos and a half. Or the collection may have been at smaller intervals.

1681   7 Calli xihuitli yhuā yhquac oyaqui Don fran^{co} Ruis mexico tepantlatoqui omo-
chihuato[1] oquicahuilitehua ytequiuh Don pasCual Ramires yhuan huala bisoRei
Don thumas de la celDa marques de la lagon yc 6 de octobre de 1680 [*sic*]
años[2] = g.^{or} D pascual [*marginal note:* tlalolin pispera de San Ju^o ypan macuili
ora]

1682   8 dochtli xihuitli g.^{or} Don manuel de los Santos yquila[3] a 21 de Julio años de
1682 omochiuh conpento tlax^a monJas oquimochihuili S^r obispo D: manuel
pernantes de Santa crus + obispo de la puebla =

1683   9 çe acatli xihuitli g.^{or} D Martin Faustino a 5 de Julio a̅n̅os de 1683 hotlacati
ypiltzin bisuRei Don tomas maques [*sic*] de la lagona Sanno ypa xihuitl a 24 de
mayo hoyaque tlaxcalteca macehuali – espanoles oneliuhtaque ye ocalac a La
Velacruz [*f. 26v*] yCleses miyec omiqui cristiano[4] [*marginal note:* a 17 de mayo
ocalaque yncleses Beracrus 83 año]

1684   10 tecpaxihuitli g.^{or} Diego [*sic*] De Santiago
1685   11 cali xihuitli g.^{or} D Diego de Santiago ypan Domingo a 28 de octobre de 1685
años homoteochiuh yanCuican oquichiuh missa ypiltzin Don bernabe ytocatzin
Don manuel de los santos[5] clerico oquichiuh missa S^a maria acuitlapilco

1686   12 dochtl xihuitli g.^{or} D pasCual Ramires yhuā yaCuican tt^e omochiuh Antonio
de Lila[6]

1687   13 acaxihuitli g.^{or} D pasCual Ramires ypa miercoles yc 17 de Disiembre De
1687 años otepoh alcalte mayor D: fran^{co} antt^o y picaso desurero casa almoneda
sann icha fiscal Diego Sanches nican ocochico ceque

1688   1 tecpaxihuitli g.^{or} D fran^{co} rruys
1689   2 calli xihuitli g.^{or} D fran^{co} Ruis ypan Juebes yc 28 de Julio de 1689 años
homomomiquilli [*sic*] beneficiado[7] hocatca topoyango Don Antt^o torres[8] cuetlaxcohuaPan [*f. 27*] ypan ilhuitzin consepciontzin opopocac citlalin ypa xihuitli
de 1689 ycalaquiyā tonali popocaya [*marginal note:* momiquillito]

1690 años   3 dochtli xihuitli g.^{or} D pentora ximenes yāCuica oquichiuh tequitli tel-

---

[1]Zapata tells this story in more detail, indicating that although don Francisco, who was the son
of the previous governor of the same name, had the support of the altepetl, he was perhaps a bit too
young for the charge. He says don Francisco left for Mexico City in 1680. He does not say what
cause he went to argue, but given the paragraph's position immediately after the announcement of a
new census and a tax increase, I think we can deduce what people's complaints were.

[2]Don Tomás Antonio de la Cerda, conde de Paredes, marqués de La Laguna, viceroy of New
Spain (1680–1686).

[3]Zapata (pp. 590–91) gives this as the full name, explaining the cryptic word as it appears here.

[4]"Christians" here would have meant "Spaniards," as it usually did in its form *quixtiano*, but
perhaps in this case connected with religion, placing those referred to in opposition to the "infidel"
English. Zapata in describing these events refers to the pirates as "English Jews" (pp. 600–01).

1681   7 House year. And at this time don Francisco Ruiz went to Mexico City constituted as an advocate [for Tlaxcala's interests].[1] [While he was gone] he left his office to don Pascual Ramírez. And viceroy don Tomás de la Cerda, marqués de la Laguna, came on the 6th of October of the year of 1680 [*sic*].[2] The governor was don Pascual [Ramírez]. [*marginal note*: There was an earthquake on the eve of San Juan at 5 o'clock.]

1682   8 Rabbit year. The governor was don Manuel de los Santos y Aguila.[3] On July 21, 1682, a convent for nuns was established in Tlaxcala. The lord bishop of Puebla, don Manuel Fernández de Santa Cruz, built it.

1683   9 One Reed year [*sic*]. The governor was don Martín Faustino. On July 5, 1683 a child of viceroy don Tomás, marqués de la Laguna, was born. In this same year, on the 24th of May, Tlaxcalans departed [for Veracruz]. Indigenous and Spaniards went mixed up with each other. The English had already entered Veracruz, [*f. 26v*] and many Christians had died.[4] [*marginal note*: On May 17 in the year of '83 the English entered Veracruz.]

1684   10 Flint-knife year. The governor was [don] Diego de Santiago.

1685   11 House year. The governor was don Diego de Santiago. On Sunday, October 28, 1685, the child of don Bernabé, named don Manuel de los Santos,[5] was consecrated as a secular priest and celebrated mass for the first time. He said mass at Santa María Acuitlapilco.

1686   12 Rabbit year. The governor was don Pascual Ramírez. And Antonio de Lira was made [deputy] for the first time.[6]

1687   13 Reed year. The governor was don Pascual Ramírez. On Wednesday, December 17, 1687, the alcalde mayor don Francisco Antonio de Picaso, treasurer of the Casa de Moneda, counted people. Some [of his party] slept here at the home of the fiscal, Diego Sánchez.

1688   1 Flint-knife year. The governor was don Francisco Ruiz.

1689   2 House year. The governor was don Francisco Ruiz. On Thursday, the 28th of July of the year 1689, the former holder of the benefice[7] of Topoyanco, don Antonio de Torres,[8] died in Cuitlaxcohuapan. [*f. 27*] On the feast day of Concepción in the year of 1689 a comet appeared. It shone in the west. [*marginal note*: he went to die]

1690   3 Rabbit year. The governor was don Ventura Jiménez. He was a mere youth

---

[5]The primary name was "don Manuel de los Santos," and it is often seen in that form, but an additional "Salazar" became attached to it in an important way. Salazar was a lineage name with a long and distinguished history in Quiyahuiztlan; it was used by the priest's father before him and went all the way back to a governor of the mid-sixteenth century, (don) Hernando de Salazar. We sometimes see don Manuel de los Santos de Salazar, sometimes don Manuel de los Santos y Salazar. He was instrumental in preserving many sets of annals in the Tlaxcala region. See the introduction, fourth section, especially pp. 22–24.

[6]Zapata tells us (pp. 620–21) that Lira (full name Antonio Pérez de Lira) was a mestizo like Méndez de Luna. There he is alcalde for Ocotelolco, and "tt^e" here probably started as "allt^e."

[7]A *beneficiado* held permanent propriety rights to his post. In the English system, we would say that he held the living as opposed to merely acting as curate. See Schwaller 1987, p. 108.

[8]See entries for 1669–1670.

pochtontli[1] ohuala cora D Diego Miguel Cosorr motesoma pasqua nauitad[2]

1691   4 acaxihuitli g.^{or} D pentora xinmenes yhquac qualoc Donalli ypan Jueues yc
chicuanahui hora huel otlayohuac nochi onesque citlalime amo huel oyeheca
chicahua[. . .][3] bispera de San Bartolome a 23 de agosto † [*marginal note*: yhuan
omochiuh cora D Manuel de Salasal ohuala cura cosar]

1692   5 tecpaxihuitli g.^{or} D Miguel de çelli yhuan cepayau sabado ypan yei hora ho-
peuh quiyahuitli ylhuitzin hocatca Cantelaria ypan Domingo Lones martes
miercoles quisqui q̄yahuitli[4] miyec yocatli omiqui[5]

1693   6 calli xihui [*sic*] g.^{or} D pasqual Ramires yp[an] ylhuitzin Santa ynes yc 21 de
enero 1693 años y[pan] chicuei ora opoliuh aso yei ora onesqui mixtlayohua-
ticaya = mestli oqualoc

1694   7 tochtli xihuitli g.^{or} D pasqual Ramires ohuala tlacaJuez ytoca Do^n Josep
xinmeno de Salinas nicann omopouhque Santa ysabel tlaca santiago nican San
Luis nochi mopouhque fiscal Joseph Gregorio ypan sabado a 6 de nobiembre

1695   8 acatli xihuitli g.^{or} D pasqual Ramires a 13 de Setienbre otlacequaloc yhuan
opopocac citlalin yquisaya tonalli [*marginal note*: acaxihuitli] [*f. 27v*]

1696   9 tecpaxihuitli g.^{or} d Josephe Martin otlaçotic tlaoli matlactli peso çe carga[5]
ocatca yuā huala Bissurey Don Josep Salmiento Montesoma gonde[6] a dres de
nobienbre [*marginal note:* tecpaxihuitli]

1697   10 calli xihuitli g.^{or} D Bentora xinmenis yhuan oçepayauh yc 26 de enero
sabado opeuhqui q̄yahuitli nochi yehuac osepayauh yhuan otlallolin lones 9 ora
yehuac yuā oquilac[8] tonali a 25 feb^{ro} [*marginal note:* calli xihuitli]

1698   11 tochtli xihuitli g.^{or} D Miguel de celi oqualoc donali san tlaco a 10 de abril
[*marginal note:* tochtli xihuitli]

1699   12 acaxihuitli g.^{or} D pasqual ramires omomiquili obispo Don manuel bernandes
de Santa crus Domingo ypan naui ora a primero de febrero onpa tepexoxoman
alte mayor gonte de san roman vignos [*marginal note*: acaxihuitli]

---

[1]If "telpochtontli" were not in the singular, the sentence might be taken to mean that for the
first time male adolescents did tribute duty. The name Jiménez was illustrious in Ocotelolco ever
since the mid-sixteenth century, when Juan Jiménez was a holder of many offices.

[2]This phrase is squeezed into an already existing gap in a different ink; I would even argue that
it was in a different hand, a hand that also made an addition to the entry for 1689. The part of the
name reading "Cosorr" is especially difficult to read, and was apparently copied on different occasions over the next few years by the main author, but in his uncertainty he never spelled it the same
way twice. The person meant must have been don Miguel Osorio Moctezuma, a Spanish vecino of
Tlaxcala who claimed a distant relationship to the royal family of Moctezuma. In March of 1679 he
was at the Franciscan convent of Puebla, having begun his studies there when don Manuel Salazar
was still a novice. Nevertheless, he did not become a Franciscan, for he was clearly ordained as a
secular priest sometime after that. See John Carter Brown Library, Puebla de los Angeles Papers,
Informaciones de Novicios, vol. 5, ff. 165–71.

holding office for the first time.[1] The [new] parish priest, don Diego Miguel [Osorio] Moctezuma, came at Christmas time.[2]

1691   4 Reed year. The governor was don Ventura Jiménez. At this time there was a solar eclipse on Thursday at 9 o'clock. It got very dark. All the stars came out. The wind could not blow strong.[3] [It happened on] the eve of San Bartolomé, August 23. [*marginal note*: And don Manuel de Salazar was made a parish priest. The parish priest (Osorio) came.]

1692   5 Flint-knife year. The governor was don Miguel de Celis. And it snowed on Saturday; at 3 o'clock it began to rain. It was on Candlemas. On Sunday, Monday, Tuesday and Wednesday, rain came.[4] Many animals died.[5]

1693   6 House year. The governor was don Pascual Ramírez. On the feast day of Santa Inés, January 21, 1693 at 8 o'clock, [the moon] disappeared. In about three hours it appeared; it had been extremely dark. = There was a lunar eclipse.

1694   7 Rabbit year. The governor was don Pascual Ramírez. The people-judge [census taker] named don Josef Jimeno de Salinas came. Here were counted the people from Santa Isabel, Santiago and from here in San Luis. Everyone was counted. The fiscal was Josef Gregorio. [It happened] on Saturday, November 6.

1695   8 Reed year. The governor was don Pascual Ramírez. On September 13 it froze, and there was a comet in the east. [*marginal note:* Reed year] [*f. 27v*]

1696   9 Flint-knife year. The governor was don Josef Martín. Shelled maize became expensive; it was 10 pesos a load.[6] And viceroy don Josef Sarmiento Moctezuma, count,[7] came on the 3rd of November. [*marginal note*: Flint-knife year]

1697   10 House year. The governor was don Ventura Jiménez. And it snowed on January 26. On Saturday it began to rain. All night it snowed, and there was an earthquake on Monday at 9 o'clock at night. There was a solar eclipse[8] on February 25. [*marginal note*: House year]

1698   11 rabbit year. The governor was don Miguel de Celis. There was a solar eclipse, only half a one, on April 10. [*marginal note*: Rabbit year]

1699   12 Reed year. The governor was don Pascual Ramírez. Bishop don Manuel Fernández de Santa Cruz died at 4 o'clock, Sunday, February 1, at Tepexoxoman. The alcalde mayor was the Conde de San Román Vignos. [*marginal note*: Reed year]

---

[3]The last letter of *chicahuac* is missing, as the edge of the page is worn away. More importantly, there seems to be something wrong with this sentence. Perhaps the *amo* was inserted unintentionally or another word was left out after it. It would be more logical to assume that the "wind blew very strongly."

[4]The sentence could alternatively be understood to say that the rain came until Wednesday, when it stopped.

[5]The annals of Zapata peter out in the years before this and end with a brief entry for 1692, so that after this point names, offices, and salient events lack what has been a crucial control.

[6]One *carga* contained four fanegas (about a bushel and a half to the fanega).

[7]Don José Sarmiento de Valladares, conde de Moctezuma, viceroy of New Spain (1696–1701).

[8]I am convinced that "oquilac" rather than the expected *oqualoc* is an error that was produced in making derivative copies. The word is clearly meant to be *oqualoc* in the next entry, but there, too, could be read as "oquilac."

1700 13 tecpaxihuitli g.^{or} D pasqual ramires alcalte mayor gonte de San roman yhuan omomiquili totlatocatzin Rei a 5 de nobiembre[1] [*marginal note:* tecpaxihuitli]

1701 1 calli xihuitli g.^{or} D pasqual ramires ohuala tlacajues Don Luis yc 11 de febrero De 1701 ohuala alld^e ma^{yor} Don martin de Herrera ~~yhuan omo~~ [*marginal note*: calli xihuitli] [*f. 28*]

1702 2 tochtli xihuitli g.^{or} D p^o de San fran^{co} houala bissuRey D fran^{co} fernantes de le Cueua enriques doque de alburqueque[2] [*marginal note*: tochtli xihuitli]

1703 3 calli xihuitli g.^{or} D pedro de San fran^{co} omomiquili cora D migl de coso[r?]^o motesuma Sabado a 31 de março 1703 omotoca Domingo de ramos ypan macuili ora yhuan hoquimochihuili yanCuic missa yn Don pedro sanches yxhuitzin tecsitzin y Domigo [*sic*] a 14 de henero De 1703 años [*marginal note:* acaxihuitli[3] yaCuican omochiuh alld̶e̶ Don Diego felipe]

1704 4 tecpaxihuitli g.^{or} D manuel de los Santos[4] pasqual peres[5] alcalte topoyango [*marginal note:* tecpaxihuitli]

1705 5 CAlli xihuitli g^{or} D pasqual ramires ypan miercoles a 18 de Abril De 1705 años omocalaqui yn cora topoyango ytocatzin D Anbrosio fran^{co} Montoya ypiltzin D Josph bicario[6] [*marginal note:* calli xihuitli]

1706 6 tochtli xihuitli g^{or} D Pedro de San fran^{co} yhuan omomiquili san se xihui oquichiuh topoyango [*marginal note:* tochtli xihuitli]

1707 7 acatl xihuitli g^{or} D SalBador huel chicahua[c] teciuh oquiyauh oquincalxixini san loren[so] tlaca oquimayahuia teopantli Axocomanitlan yhua ocalaqui cura topoyango D Matheo martines ypan [~~Altares~~?] San cosme ylhuitzin San damian a 27 Setienbre [*marginal note*: acaxihuitli 1707 a^s] [*f. 28v*]

1708 8 tecpaxihuitli g^{or} D pasqual Ramires omomiquili cura topoyango ipa domigo [*sic*] a 4 de março de 1708 años oncan toctoc topoyãgo D Matheo martines yhuan otlalolin biernes de 16 de março quisa donalli[7] chicahuac oc cepa ipa sabado de gloria otlalolin tlaco oratica a 8 de abril [*marginal note:* 5 metztli oquichiuh]

1709 9 calli xihuitli g^{or} D feli~~phe Xinmenes~~ yhquac homomiquili ~~D pedro tecsis teopixcatzintli ocatca omomiquilito gohuatepequi ynahuac veracruz~~

17010 10 tochtli xihuitli g^{or} D liphe liphe [*sic*] Xinmenes yn omomiquili D pedro tecsis teopixcatzintli hocatca omomilito [*sic*] gohuatepequi ynahuac Xalapã ypan ilhuitzin San pelipe santiago a [1?][5?][8] de mayo de 1710 años onpa toctoc ohuala VisoRey Don Fran^{co} bernandes de la Cueva doque alborqueque

---

[1]The king actually died on November 1.

[2]Don Francisco Fernández de la Cueva, duque de Alburquerque, viceroy of New Spain 1702–1711.

[3]Here a House year and a Reed year have run into each other, the two counting as only one Christian calendar year and one year in the 13-year cycle.

[4]We know from Zapata's work that this was not the priest don Manuel de los Santos Salazar.

1700 13 Flint-knife year. The governor was don Pascual Ramírez. The alcalde mayor was the conde de San Román, and our ruler the king died on the 5th of November.[1] [*marginal note*: Flint-knife year]

1701 1 House year. The governor was don Pascual Ramírez. The people-judge, don Luis, came on February 11, 1701. The alcalde mayor don Martín de Herrera came. [*marginal note*: House year] [*f. 28*]

1702 2 Rabbit year. The governor was don Pedro de San Francisco. Viceroy don Francisco Fernández de la Cueva Enríquez, duque de Alburquerque, came.[2] [*marginal note*: Rabbit year]

1703 3 House year. The governor was don Pedro de San Francisco. The parish priest don Miguel de [Osorio] Moctezuma died on Saturday, March 31, 1703; he was buried on Palm Sunday at 5 o'clock. And don Pedro Sánchez, the grandchild of Tecciztzin, celebrated his first mass on Sunday, January 14, 1703. [*marginal note*: Reed year.[3] Don Diego Felipe became alcalde for the first time.]

1704 4 Flint-knife year. The governor was don Manuel de los Santos.[4] The Topoyanco alcalde was Pascual Pérez.[5] [*marginal note*: Flint-knife year]

1705 5 House year. The governor was don Pascual Ramírez. On Wednesday, April 18, 1705, a [new] parish priest entered Topoyanco, named don Ambrosio Francisco Montoya, child of don Josef [Vicario].[6] [*marginal note*: House year]

1706 6 Rabbit year. The governor was don Pedro de San Francisco; and he died. He served only one year. He was from Topoyanco. [*marginal note*: Rabbit year]

1707 7 Reed year. The governor was don Salvador [Ramírez]. It hailed and rained very hard. It made the houses of the San Lorenzo people collapse and knocked down the church at Axocomanitlan. And don Mateo Martínez entered as parish priest of Topoyanco on the feast day of San Cosme and San Damián, September 27. [*marginal note:* Reed year, 1707] [*f. 28v*]

1708 8 Flint-knife year. The governor was don Pascual Ramírez. The parish priest of Topoyanco, don Mateo Martínez, died on Sunday, March 4, 1708. He lies buried at Topoyanco. And there was a strong earthquake on Friday, March 16, toward the east.[7] Again on Holy Saturday, April 8, there was an earthquake that lasted half an hour. [*marginal note:* He served five months.]

1709 9 House year. The governor was don Felipe Jiménez. At this time ~~don Pedro Sánchez Tecciz, who was a priest,~~ died. ~~He died at Coatepec, near Veracruz.~~

1710 10 Rabbit year. The governor was don Felipe Jiménez. At this time don Pedro [Sánchez] Tecciz, who was a priest, died. He died at Coatepec, near Jalapa, on the feast day of San Felipe and Santiago, May [1?][5?],[8] 1710; he lies buried there. And Viceroy don Francisco Fernández de la Cueva, duque de Alburquerque, came.

---

[5]Normally the holder of this office bore the don.

[6]I take "Vicario" as a family name; if it means vicar, the vicar could have had a son before he was ordained, or the new priest could have been the illegitimate son of the vicar.

[7]It seems that "quisa tonalli" is for "yquisayan tonalli."

[8]Today this saint's day is celebrated on May 3.

17011   acaxihuitli g^{or} D feliphe ximenes ypann ilhuitzin tlaçonantzin agosto sabado ocatca domingo ypan matlactli onçe ora yohuac hotlallolin ohuehuesque teopantin san Lorenso axocomanitla yaCuictlalpan santiago michaqui nativitas[1] veuesque torretin cuetlaxcohuapan

17012   12 tecpaxihuitli g^{or} D Salbador Ramires atle omochiuh

17013   13 calli xihuitli g^{or} D Salbador Ramires atle omochiuh

17014   1 tochtli xihuitli g^{or} D Salbador RAmires atle omochiuh [*f. 29*]

17015   2 Acaxihuitli g^{or} D feliphe ximenes yhquac ocalac yn cura topoyanco Dō Juan Matias gaueson ypan ome tonalli octobre yhuā omomiq̄li cura ocatca Sancta Crus D manouel de salasal a 19 de agosto yuan omiqui D pedro de san fran^{co} gouerna[dor] ocatca[2]

17016   3 decpaxihuitli g^{or} D p^{o} paretes atliuesian chane yhuan ocalaqui Bisorei a 16 de Junio D Bartasal de suniga[3]

17017   4 calli xihui g^{or} D SalBador ramires de metzontlan

17018   5 tochtli xihui g^{or} D SalBador rami [*sic*] de metzontlan

17019   6 acaxihuitli g^{or} D SalBador ramires de metzontlan

17020   7 decpaxihuitli g^{or}

---

[1]Trautmann 1980 lists Santiago Michac in the partido of Nativitas.
[2]There is some confusion here. The same man was earlier described as dying in office in 1706.

1711   [11] Reed year. The governor was don Felipe Jiménez. On the feast day of our precious mother in August—it was on Saturday or Sunday—at 11 o'clock at night there was an earthquake. The churches at San Lorenzo Axocomanitlan, Yancuictlalpan, and Santiago Michac in Nativitas[1] fell down. Towers fell in Cuitlaxcohuapan.

1712   12 Flint-knife year. The governor was don Salvador Ramírez. Nothing happened.

1713   13 House year. The governor was don Salvador Ramírez. Nothing happened.

1714   1 Rabbit year. The governor was don Salvador Ramírez. Nothing happened. [*f. 29*]

1715   2 Reed year. The governor was don Felipe Jiménez. At this time don Juan Matías Cabezón entered Topoyanco as parish priest on the 2nd day of October. And the former parish priest of Santa Cruz, don Manuel de Salazar, died on August 19; and the former governor don Pedro de San Francisco died.[2]

1716   3 Flint-knife year. The governor was don Pedro de Paredes of Atlihuetzan. And viceroy don Baltasar de Zúñiga entered on the 16th of June.[3]

1717   4 House year. The governor was don Salvador Ramírez from Metzontlan.

1718   5 Rabbit year. The governor was don Salvador Ramírez from Metzontlan.

1719   6 Reed year. The governor was don Salvador Ramírez from Metzontlan.

1720   7 Flint-knife year. The governor was [. . .]

---

[3]Don Baltasar de Zúñiga y Guzmán Sotomayor y Mendoza, duque de Arión, viceroy of New Spain (1716–1722).

Glossary

ALCALDE. A first-instance judge attached to a local municipal government. Sometimes *alcalde ordinario*.

ALCALDE MAYOR. Spanish magistrate and administrator of a large district, here Puebla or Tlaxcala.

ALGUACIL. Constable. *Alguacil mayor*, chief constable. *Alguacil menor*, lower or lesser constable.

ALTEPETL. Nahuatl word for any state, but especially a local ethnic state. It applies to Tlaxcala as a whole, but also to its four large subdivisions. In indigenous Puebla it likewise applies to both the whole indigenous group and its three constituent parts.

AUDIENCIA. High court of New Spain, in Mexico City. Full name Royal Audiencia.

CABALLERO. Gentleman, horseman, here knight of a military order.

CABECERA. Head town, capital of a district, used by the Spaniards of indigenous settlements. Here the word refers to one of the four constituent subdivisions (altepetl) of Tlaxcala as a whole.

CABILDO. A municipal council, or a session of such a council, or a body such as a cathedral chapter, or at times a broader assembly to discuss some matter of public interest.

CALVARIO. Calvary, referring to things ranging from a wayside cross to a small chapel, but here indicating a collection of chapels erected by the Franciscans in the upper reaches of the barrio of San Francisco.

CHICHIMEC. Blanket term applied by both the Nahuas and the Spaniards to the indigenous peoples of the north of Mexico.

CHINO. An ethnic term originally for people of Philippine origin, then used for certain mixtures; in the Puebla text it is used to refer to indigenous-African mixtures.

COFRADÍA. Confraternity, lay sodality.

COLEGIO. College, in the sense of an establishment where religious reside together and also usually carry on some sort of training and education of the young.

CONDE. Count, title of nobility borne by several viceroys.

CONGREGATION. Translates *congregación*, a Spanish attempt to concentrate the people of an indigenous district in a central place.

CONVENT. 1. an establishment of nuns. 2. The cloister and living quarters of a group of male religious.

CORREGIDOR. Spanish magistrate and administrator of a large district, virtually the same as alcalde mayor.

CUITLAXCOHUAPAN. Nahuatl name for Puebla. Also Cuetlaxcohuapan.

DOCTRINA. Spanish for Christian doctrine and indoctrination. Also used to denote an indigenous parish.

DUQUE. Duke, a title borne by some viceroys.

ENCOMIENDA. Grant, usually to a Spaniard, of an indigenous sociopolitical unit under its own constituted authority to provide the Spaniard with labor and/or tribute, depending on the time, place, and conditions.

FANEGA. A Spanish dry measure often said to be equivalent to a bushel and a half.

FISCAL. 1. Chief steward of a church, here always indigenous. 2. High Spanish official, prosecuting attorney and legal representative of the crown.

GACHUPÍN. Derogatory name for a peninsular Spaniard, one born in Spain.

GOVERNOR. Here translates *gobernador*, the highest official of an indigenous altepetl in the Spanish-style municipal government. Also at times the title of the main Spanish magistrate of Tlaxcala, often called alcalde mayor.

GUARDIAN. Here, prior of a Franciscan establishment.

HOSPITAL. In addition to caring for the sick like a modern hospital, a hospital in the sense used in the annals served the poor more generally. Operated by a group of religious, it contained a church serving the community and living quarters for the religious as well as dormitories for patients.

JUDGE-GOVERNOR. Same as governor.

LICENCIADO. Title of the holder of an academic degree above bachelor and below doctor, usually in secular or canon law.

MAESTRE DE CAMPO. Field-master, marshal, high military rank.

MARQUÉS. Marquess, lord of a border region, title of nobility borne by several viceroys. When used without modification in the texts it refers to the conqueror Cortés.

MATLALCUEYE. "One with blue-green skirts," name of the mountain in the Tlaxcalan region now called Malinche.

MESTIZO. A person of mixed Spanish and indigenous descent.

MISSION. In the Puebla annals, a campaign of religious revitalization carried out by the members of a religious order or orders; *not* a permanent establishment on the periphery for the conversion of pagans and instruction of new converts.

MONASTERY. Translation of Spanish *monasterio*, which was used in New Spain for what are strictly speaking friaries, the establishments of mendicant friars.

OBRAJE. Works, shop, mill, an operation on an industrial or almost industrial scale for the production of any of various kinds of items for sale, most often specifically textiles.

OBRERO. Here, commissioner for building projects.

OIDOR. Civil judge on the Royal Audiencia.

PEOPLE-JUDGE. Translation of *tlacajuez*, a person delegated to carry out a census.

PLAZUELA. A small plaza, public square.

POPOCATEPETL. "Smoking mountain," the name of a great volcano west of Puebla and east of Mexico City. Called Popocatzin and tepetl Popocatzin in the texts.

PROCESIÓN DE GLORIA. A religious procession of the kind generally performed on Holy Saturday, the day before Easter.

REAL. Coin or value amounting to one-eighth of a peso.

REGIDOR. Councilman in municipal government. *Regidor mayor*, chief councilman.

TEPIXQUI (pl. TEPIXQUE). Nahuatl for "one who is in charge of people," a lower official of the indigenous municipal government or church organization.

THEATINE. A name often applied to the Jesuits.

VARA. Measurement, the Spanish yard, a little less than an English yard.

VICEROY. Highest royal official in New Spain, resident in Mexico City.

Bibliography

Abbreviations used in the notes:

AAMC   J. J. Ramírez, "Anales antiguos de México y sus contornos," in the BNAH

BNAH   Biblioteca Nacional de Antropología e Historia, Mexico City

TA   Lockhart, Berdan, and Anderson, *The Tlaxcalan Actas*

Zapata   Don Juan Buenaventura de Zapata y Mendoza, *Historia cronológica de la Noble Ciudad de Tlaxcala*

Zerón Zapata   Don Miguel Zerón Zapata, *La Puebla de los Angeles en el siglo XVII: crónica de la Puebla*

Aguirre Beltrán, Gonzalo. 1972 [1946]. *La población negra de México: un estudio etnohistórico.* México: Fondo de Cultura Económica.

Altman, Ida. 2000. *Transatlantic Ties in the Spanish Empire: Brihuega, Spain and Puebla, Mexico, 1560–1620.* Stanford, Calif.: Stanford University Press.

_____. Forthcoming. *The War for Mexico's West: Indians and Spaniards in New Galicia, 1524–1550.* University of New Mexico Press.

Aveni, Anthony F. 1980. *Skywatchers of Ancient Mexico.* Austin: University of Texas Press.

Bennett, Herman. 2003. *Africans in Colonial Mexico: Absolutism, Christianity, and Afro-Creole Consciousness, 1570–1640.* Bloomington: Indiana University Press.

Barlow, Robert, ed. and trans. 1948. *Anales de Tlatelolco: Unos anales históricos de la nación mexicana y códice de Tlatelolco.* México: José Porrúa.

Boone, Elizabeth Hill. 2000. *Stories in Red and Black: Pictorial Histories of the Aztecs and Mixtecs.* Austin: University of Texas Press.

Boone, Elizabeth Hill, and Walter Mignolo, eds. 1994. *Writing Without Words: Alternative Literacies in Mesoamerica and the Andes.* Durham: Duke University Press.

Byland, Bruce. 1993. "Introduction and Commentary." In *The Codex Borgia: A Full-Color Restoration of the Ancient Mexican Manuscript*, repainted by Gisele Díaz and Alan Rodgers. New York: Dover Publications.

Cañeque, Alejandro. 2004. *The King's Living Image: The Culture and Politics of Viceregal Power in Colonial Mexico.* New York: Routledge.

Cardoso, Gerald. 1983. *Negro Slavery in the Sugar Plantations of Veracruz and Pernambuco, 1550–1680: A Comparative Study.* Washington, D. C.: University Press of America.

Carochi, Horacio, S. J. 2001. *Grammar of the Mexican Language, with an Explanation of its Adverbs (1645).* Bilingual edition by James Lockhart. UCLA Latin American Center Nahuatl Studies Series, 7. Stanford, Calif.: Stanford University Press and UCLA Latin American Center Publications.

Carrasco, Davíd and Scott Sessions, eds. 2007. *Cave, City, Eagle's Nest: An Interpretive Journey through the Mapa de Cuauhtinchan No. 2.* Albuquerque: University of New Mexico Press.

Carrión, Antonio. 1970 [1897]. *Historia de la ciudad de Puebla de los Angeles*. Puebla: Editorial José M. Cajica.

Castillo Palma, Norma Angélica, and Susan Kellogg. 2005. "Conflict and Cohabitation between Afro-Mexicans and Nahuas in Central Mexico." In *Beyond Black and Red: African-Native Relations in Colonial Latin America*, ed. by Matthew Restall.

Celestino Solís, Eustaquio, and Luis Reyes García, eds. and trans. *Anales de Tecamachalco, 1398–1590*. México: Fondo de Cultura Económica.

Chance, John K. 2000. "The Noble House in Colonial Puebla, Mexico: Descent, Inheritance, and the Nahua Tradition." *American Anthropologist*, 102: 485–502.

Chimalpahin Quauhtlehuanitzin, don Domingo de San Antón Muñón. 1997. *Codex Chimalpahin: Society and Politics in Mexico Tenochtitlan, Tlatelolco, Texcoco, Culhuacan and Other Nahua Altepetl in Central Mexico*. 2 vols. Ed. and trans. by Arthur J. O. Anderson and Susan Schroeder. Norman: University of Oklahoma Press.

_____. (given here as Chimalpáhin, Domingo). 1998. *Las ocho relaciones y el memorial de Culhuacan*. Ed. and trans. by Rafael Tena. México: Cien de México.

_____. 2001. *El Diario*. Ed. and trans. by Rafael Tena. México: Cien de México.

_____. 2006. *Annals of His Time*. Ed. and trans. by James Lockhart, Susan Schroeder, and Doris Namala. Stanford, Calif.: Stanford University Press.

Cline, S. L., ed. and trans. 1993. *The Book of Tributes: Early Sixteenth-Century Nahuatl Censuses from Morelos*. UCLA Latin American Center Nahuatl Studies Series, 4. Los Angeles: UCLA Latin American Center Publications.

Cohen, Martin. 2001 [1973]. *The Martyr Luis de Carvajal: A Secret Jew in Sixteenth-Century Mexico*. Albuquerque: University of New Mexico Press.

Contreras Cruz, Carlos, Francisco Téllez Guerrero, and Claudia Patricia Pardo Hernández. 1999. "Parroquias y calidad étnica en la Puebla de los Angeles en 1777." In *De Veracruz a Puebla: Un itinerario histórico entre la colonia y el porfiriato*, ed. by Carlos Contreras Cruz and Claudia Patricia Pardo Hernández. México: Instituto Mora.

Cook, Noble David. 1998. *Born to Die: Disease and New World Conquest, 1492–1650*. New York: Cambridge University Press.

Dibble, Charles, ed. and trans. 1963. *Historia de la nación mexicana: Códice de 1576*. Madrid: Ediciones José Porrúa Turanzas.

García, Genaro. 1991 [1918]. *Don Juan de Palafox y Mendoza, obispo de Puebla y Osma, visitador y virrey de la Nueva España*. Puebla: Gobierno del Estado de Puebla.

Gerhard, Peter. 1981. "Un censo de la diócesis de Puebla en 1681." *Historia Mexicana*, 120: 530–60.

_____. 1993 [1972]. *A Guide to the Historical Geography of New Spain*. Norman: University of Oklahoma Press.

Gibson, Charles. 1950. "The Identity of Diego Muñoz Camargo." *Hispanic American Historical Review*, 31: 195–208.

_____. 1964. *The Aztecs Under Spanish Rule*. Stanford, Calif.: Stanford University Press.

_____. 1967 [1952]. *Tlaxcala in the Sixteenth Century*. Stanford, Calif.: Stanford University Press.

Gibson, Charles, and John Glass. 1975. "A Census of Middle American Prose Manuscripts in the Native Historical Tradition." In *Handbook of Middle American Indians*,

Vol. 15. Austin: University of Texas Press.

Gillespie, Susan. 1989. *The Aztec Kings: the Construction of Rulership in Mexica History*. Tucson: University of Arizona Press.

Gómez García, Lidia, Celia Salazar Exaire, and María Elena Stefanón López, eds. 2000. *Anales del barrio de San Juan del Río: crónica indígena de la ciudad de Puebla, siglo XVII*. Puebla: Instituto de Ciencias Sociales y Humanidades.

Guha, Sumit. 2004. "Speaking Historically: The Changing Voices of Historical Narration in Western India, 1400–1900." *American Historical Review*, 109: 1084–1103.

Guijo, Gregorio Martín de. 1952. *Diario, 1648–1664*. 2 vols. México: Editorial Porrúa.

Gutiérrez, Verónica. 2008. "Spanish-Indigenous Collaboration in Colonial Puebla de los Angeles: el Barrio de Santiago Cholultecapan." Paper presented at the annual meeting of the American Society for Ethnohistory, Eugene, Oregon.

Haring, Clarence. 1966 [1910]. *The Buccaneers in the West Indies in the XVII Century*. Hamden, Conn.: Archon Books.

Hassig, Ross. 2001. *Time, History and Belief in Aztec and Colonial Mexico*. Austin: University of Texas Press.

Hernández Yahuitl, María Aurelia. 1999. "Las ceremonias funerarias en la Ciudad de los Angeles dedicadas a las mujeres de la corte." In *La presencia femenina en la Puebla novohispana, siglos XVI y XVII*. Puebla: Honorable Ayuntamiento del Municipio de Puebla.

Hirschberg, Julia. 1979. "An Alternative to Encomienda: Puebla's *Indios de Servicio*, 1531–1545." *Journal of Latin American Studies*, 11: 241–64.

Hoekstra, Rik. 1993. *Two Worlds Merging: The Transformation of Society in the Valley of Puebla, 1570–1640*. Amsterdam: CEDLA.

Karttunen, Frances. 1992 [1983]. *An Analytical Dictionary of Nahuatl*. Norman: University of Oklahoma Press.

Karttunen, Frances, and James Lockhart. 1976. *Nahuatl in the Middle Years: Language Contact Phenomena in Texts of the Colonial Period*. University of California Publications in Linguistics, 85. Berkeley and Los Angeles: University of California Press.

Kirchhoff, Paul, Lina Odena Güemes, and Luis Reyes García, eds. and trans. 1976. *Historia Tolteca Chichimeca*. México: Instituto Nacional de Antropología e Historia.

Krug, Frances. n. d. "The Nahuatl Annals of the Tlaxcala-Puebla Region." Unfinished doctoral dissertation, Department of History, UCLA.

Krug, Frances, and Camilla Townsend. 2007. "The Tlaxcala-Puebla Family of Annals." In *Sources and Methods for the Study of Postconquest Mesoamerican Ethnohistory*, ed. by James Lockhart, Lisa Sousa, and Stephanie Wood.

Lane, Kris. 1998. *Pillaging the Empire: Piracy in the Americas, 1500–1750*. Armonk, N.Y.: M. E. Sharpe.

Launey, Michel. 1979. *Introduction à la langue et à la littérature aztèques*. Vol. 1: *Grammaire*. Paris: L'Harmattan.

Leibson, Dana. 1994. "Primers for Memory: Cartographic Histories and Nahua Identity." In *Writing Without Words: Alternative Literacies in Mesoamerica and the Andes*, ed. by Elizabeth H. Boone and Walter Mignolo.

Leicht, Hugo. 1967 [1934]. *Las calles de Puebla: estudio histórico*. Puebla: Comisión de

Promoción Cultural del Gobierno del Estado de Puebla.

León-Portilla, Miguel. 1992. "Have We Really Translated the Mesoamerican 'Ancient Word'?" In *On the Translation of Native American Literatures*, ed. by Brian Swann.

Liebman, Seymour. 1970. *The Jews in New Spain: Faith, Flame, and the Inquisition*. Coral Gables, Fl.: University of Miami Press.

Lockhart, James. 1991. *Nahuas and Spaniards: Postconquest Central Mexican History and Philology*. UCLA Latin American Center Nahuatl Studies Series, 3. Stanford, Calif.: Stanford University Press and UCLA Latin American Center Publications.

———. 1992. *The Nahuas After the Conquest*. Stanford, Calif.: Stanford University Press.

———. 1999. *Of Things of the Indies: Essays Old and New in Early Latin American History*. Stanford, Calif.: Stanford University Press.

———. 2001. *Nahuatl as Written: Lessons in Older Written Nahuatl, with Copious Examples and Texts*. UCLA Latin American Center Nahuatl Studies Series, 6. Stanford, Calif.: Stanford University Press and UCLA Latin American Center Publications.

Lockhart, James, ed. and trans. 1993. *We People Here: Nahuatl Accounts of the Conquest of Mexico*. UCLA Center for Medieval and Renaissance Studies. *Reportorium Columbianum*, 1 (gen. ed. Geoffrey Symcox). Berkeley: University of California Press.

Lockhart, James, Frances Berdan, and Arthur J. O. Anderson. 1986. *The Tlaxcalan Actas: A Compendium of the Records of the Cabildo of Tlaxcala (1545–1627)*. Salt Lake City: University of Utah Press.

Lockhart, James, Lisa Sousa, and Stephanie Wood, eds. 2007. *Sources and Methods for the Study of Postconquest Mesoamerican Ethnohistory*. Electronic publication: http://whp.uoregon.edu/Lockhart/index.html.

López de Villaseñor, Pedro. 1961 [1781]. *Cartilla vieja de la nobilísima ciudad de Puebla*. México: Imprenta Universitaria.

López Gonzaga, Leticia. 1999. "La presencia femenina en el comercio de la Puebla de los Angeles." In *La presencia femenina en la Puebla novohispana, siglos XVI y XVII*. Puebla: Honorable Ayuntamiento del Municipio de Puebla.

Loyde Cruz, Inocentes. 1999. "Propietarias poblanas en los siglos XVI y XVII." In *La presencia femenina en la Puebla novohispana, siglos XVI y XVII*. Puebla: Honorable Ayuntamiento del Municipio de Puebla.

Malvido, Elsa. 1973. "Factores de despoblación y de reposición de la población de Cholula (1641–1810)." *Historia Mexicana*, 23: 52–110.

Marcus, Joyce. 1992. *Mesoamerican Writing Systems: Propaganda, Myth and History in Four Ancient Civilizations*. Princeton, N. J.: Princeton University Press.

Marín Tamayo, Fausto. 1989. *Puebla de los Angeles: orígenes, gobierno y división racial*. Puebla: Universidad Autónoma de Puebla.

Marley, David. 1993. *Sack of Veracruz: The Great Pirate Raid of 1683*. Windsor, Ontario: The Netherlandic Press.

Martínez Baracz, Andrea. 2008. *Un gobierno de indios: Tlaxcala, 1519–1750*. México: Fondo de Cultura Económica.

Molina, fray Alonso de. 1970 [1571]. *Vocabulario en lengua castellana y mexicana y mexicana y castellana*. México: Ediciones Porrúa.

Morales, Francisco, O. F. M. 1973. *Ethnic and Social Background of the Franciscan*

Friars in Seventeenth-Century Mexico. Washington, D. C.: Academy of American Franciscan History.

Mota y Escobar, don fray Alonso de la. 1945 [ca.1625]. *Memoriales del Obispo de Tlaxcala*. México: Talleres Gráficos de la Editorial Stylo.

Mûsili, Elias al-. 2003. *An Arab's Journey to Colonial Spanish America: The Travels of Elias al-Mûsili in the Seventeenth Century*. Ed. and trans. by Caesar Farah. Syracuse, N.Y.: Syracuse University Press.

Namala, Doris. 2002. "Chimalpahin in His Time: An Analysis of the Writings of a Nahua Annalist of Seventeenth-Century Mexico Concerning His Own Lifetime." Doctoral dissertation, UCLA.

Nicholson, H. B. 1971. "Pre-Hispanic Central Mexican Historiography." In *Investigaciones contemporáneas sobre historia de México*. México: Universidad Nacional Autónoma de México.

Núñez y Domínguez, José de Jesús. 1945. *Don Antonio de Benavides, el incógnito "tapado."* México: Ediciones Xochitl.

Oudijk, Michel, and Matthew Restall. 2007. "Mesoamerican Conquistadors in the Sixteenth Century." In *Indian Conquistadors: Indigenous Allies in the Conquest of Mesoamerica*, ed. by Laura Matthew and Michel Oudijk. Norman: University of Oklahoma Press.

Palmer, Colin. 1976. *Slaves of the White God: Blacks in Mexico, 1570–1650*. Cambridge, Mass.: Harvard University Press.

Peña Espinoza, Jesús Joel. 1997. "Los jesuitas: camino a los altares, regocijos para Puebla." In *Presencia de la Compañía de Jesús en la Puebla de los Angeles*, ed. by María Aurelia Hernández Yahuitl and Xavier Cacho Vázquez. Puebla: Honorable Ayuntamiento del Municipio de Puebla.

Pizzigoni, Caterina, ed. and trans. 2007. *Testaments of Toluca*. UCLA Latin American Center Nahuatl Studies Series, 8. Stanford, Calif.: Stanford University Press and UCLA Latin American Center Publications.

Prem, Hanns J. 1988. *Milpa y hacienda: tenencia de la tierra indígena y española en la cuenca del Alto Atoyac, Puebla, México, 1520–1650*. México: Centro de Investigaciones y Estudios Superiores en Antropología Social.

Restall, Matthew, ed. 2005. *Beyond Black and Red: African-Native Relations in Colonial Latin America*. Albuquerque: University of New Mexico.

_____. 2009. *The Black Middle: Africans, Mayas and Spaniards in Colonial Yucatan*. Stanford, Calif.: Stanford University Press.

Reuter, Timothy, ed. and trans. 1992. *The Annals of Fulda. Ninth-Century Histories,* vol. 2. Manchester, England: Manchester University Press.

Reyes García, Luis. 1977. *Cuauhtinchan del siglo XII al XVI: formación y desarrollo histórico de un señorío prehispánico*. Weisbaden, Germany: Franz Steiner Verlag.

Reyes García, Luis, ed. and trans. 2001. *¿Como te confundes? ¿Acaso no somos conquistados? Anales de Juan Bautista*. México: Centro de Investigaciones y Estudios Superiores en Antropología Social.

Riley, James D. 2007. "Priests and the Provincial Order in Tlaxcala, 1650–1792." In *Religion in New Spain*, ed. by Susan Schroeder and Stafford Poole.

Riva Palacio, Vicente, and Manuel Payno. 1870. "El tapado." In *El libro rojo, 1520–1867*. México: Díaz de León.

Roberts, Alexander, and Arthur Cleveland Coxe, eds. 1994 [1885]. *Ante-Nicene Fathers: The Writings of the Fathers down to A. D. 325. Volume 4: Tertullian*. Peabody, Mass.: Hendrickson Publishers.

Schäfer, Ernesto. 1947. *El Consejo Real y Supremo de las Indias. Vol. 2: la labor del Consejo de Indias en la administración colonial*. Seville: Escuela de Estudios Hispano-Americanos.

Schroeder, Susan. 1991. *Chimalpahin and the Kingdoms of Chalco*. Tucson: University of Arizona Press.

Schroeder, Susan, and Stafford Poole, C. M., eds. 2007. *Religion in New Spain*. Albuquerque: University of New Mexico Press.

Schwaller, John F. 1987. *The Church and Clergy in Sixteenth-Century Mexico*. Albuquerque: University of New Mexico Press.

Sierra Silva, Pablo Miguel. 2008. "Conflict and Coexistence: The Afro-Indigenous Obraje in Puebla de los Angeles." Paper presented at the annual meeting of the American Society for Ethnohistory, Eugene, Oregon.

Sigal, Pete. 2005. "The Cuiloni, the Patlache, and the Abominable Sin: Homosexualities in Early Colonial Nahua Society." *Hispanic American Historical Review,* 85: 555–94.

Sousa, Lisa, Stafford Poole, C. M., and James Lockhart, eds. and trans. 1998. *The Story of Guadalupe: Luis Laso de la Vega's* Huei tlamahuiçoltica *of 1649*. UCLA Latin American Center Nahuatl Studies Series, 5. Stanford, Calif.: Stanford University Press and UCLA Latin American Center Publications.

Swann, Brian, ed. 1992. *On the Translation of Native American Literatures*. Washington, D. C.: Smithsonian Institution Press.

Toussaint, Manuel. 1954. *La catedral y las iglesias de Puebla*. México: Editorial Porrúa.

Townsend, Camilla. 2006. *Malintzin's Choices: An Indian Woman in the Conquest of Mexico*. Albuquerque: University of New Mexico Press.

_____. 2006a. "'What in the World Have You Done to Me, My Lover?' Sex, Servitude and Politics among the Pre-conquest Nahuas as Seen in the *Cantares Mexicanos*." *The Americas*, 62: 349–89.

_____. 2009. "Glimpsing Native American Historiography: The Cellular Principle in Sixteenth-Century Nahuatl Annals." *Ethnohistory*, 56: 4.

_____. 2010. "Don Juan Buenaventura Zapata y Mendoza and the Notion of a Nahua Identity." In *The Conquest All Over Again: Nahuas and Zapotecs Thinking, Writing, and Painting Spanish Colonialism*, ed. by Susan Schroeder. Sussex, Australia: Sussex Academic Press.

Trautmann, Wolfgang. 1980. "Catálogo histórico-critico de los nombres de lugar relativos a Tlaxcala." Puebla: Fundación Alemana para la Investigación Científica.

_____. 1981. *Las transformaciones en el paisaje cultural de Tlaxcala durante la época colonial*. Weisbaden, Germany: Franz Steiner Verlag.

Utrera, fray Cipriano de, O. M. C. 1950. "El Tapado de México." In *El tapado de México y el de Santo Domingo*, ed. by José de Jesús Núñez y Domínguez. Trujillo, República Dominicana: Tip. Franciscana.

Villa Flores, Javier. 2008. "Wandering Swindlers: Imposture, Style and the Inquisition's Pedagogy of Fear in Colonial Mexico." *Colonial Latin American Review*, 17: 251–72.

Vinson, Ben. 2001. *Bearing Arms for His Majesty: The Free-Colored Militia in Colonial Mexico*. Stanford, Calif.: Stanford University Press.

Vinson, Ben, and Matthew Restall, eds. 2009. *Black Mexico: Race and Society from Colonial to Modern Times*. Albuquerque: University of New Mexico Press.

von Germeten, Nicole. 2006. *Black Blood Brothers: Confraternities and Social Mobility for Afro-Mexicans*. Gainesville: University Press of Florida.

White, Hayden. 1987. *The Content of the Form: Narrative Discourse and Historical Representation*. Baltimore, Maryland: Johns Hopkins University Press.

Wood, Stephanie. 2003. *Transcending Conquest: Nahua Views of Spanish Colonial Mexico*. Norman: University of Oklahoma Press.

Zerón Zapata, don Miguel. 1945 [ca. 1700]. *La Puebla de los Angeles en el siglo XVII: crónica de la Puebla*. México: Editorial Patria.

Zapata y Mendoza, don Juan Buenaventura. 1995. *Historia cronológica de la Noble Ciudad de Tlaxcala*. Ed. and trans. by Luis Reyes García and Andrea Martínez Baracs. México: Universidad Autónoma de Tlaxcala and Centro de Investigaciones y Estudios Superiores en Antropología Social.

Index